MW00579918

TAMING THE OCTOPUS

THE LONG BATTLE FOR ~ THE SOUL OF ~ THE CORPORATION

TAMING THE OCTOPUS

Kyle Edward Williams

W. W. NORTON & COMPANY
Independent Publishers Since 1923

Frontispiece: Created for *Puck* magazine in 1904, Udo Keppler's cartoon of the grasping Standard Oil octopus would come to represent the excesses of American big business. *Udo J. Keppler, "Next!," September 7, 1904. Library of Congress, Prints & Photographs Online Catalog, LC-USZCN4-122.*

Printed in the United States of America
First Edition

For information about special discounts for bulk purchases, please contact W. W. Norton Special Sales at specialsales@wwnorton.com or 800-233-4830

Manufacturing by Lakeside Book Company
Book design by Brooke Koven
Production manager: Louise Mattarelliano

ISBN 978-0-393-86723-7

W. W. Norton & Company, Inc.
500 Fifth Avenue, New York, N.Y. 10110
www.wwnorton.com

W. W. Norton & Company Ltd.
15 Carlisle Street, London W1D 3BS

1 2 3 4 5 6 7 8 9 0

For Sally, Abraham, and Dominic, and in memory of Dad.
Caritas omnia sperat.

A corporation has no natural existence and therefore has no natural or inalienable rights such as natural persons have. The difference is broad and well marked between the natural man and the artificial person. God made man, and men make governments, while the government creates the corporations.

—TOM BROWN
Southern Mercury, 1890[1]

If anything is certain to destroy our free society, to undermine its very foundations, it would be a widespread acceptance by management of social responsibilities in some sense other than to make as much money as possible. This is a fundamentally subversive doctrine.

—MILTON FRIEDMAN
Academic seminar, 1958[2]

Stakeholder capitalism is not about politics. It is not a social or ideological agenda. It is not "woke." *It is capitalism* . . .

—LARRY FINK
BlackRock Letter to CEOs, 2022[3]

CONTENTS

INTRODUCTION

What Is the Corporation Good For?

Its sucker-lined tentacles reach across vast expanses of an eastern United States darkened by ominous rain clouds, the tentacles winding and tightening around the Capitol Building in Washington, DC, a state legislative house, cargo ships, and the gasping figures of industrial bosses. Its reach stretches beyond the ocean—to parts unknown. Ensnaring oil derricks, refineries, and railroads, the red-eyed octopus bears a name across its head, figured as a colossal storage tank: Standard Oil. Readers who picked up the weekly humor magazine *Puck* in early September of 1904, perhaps stealing a brief respite after a long shift on a production line, came across this striking lithograph in the centerfold.

The magazine satirized and skewered corruption wherever it could be found—and there was no greater symbol of the abuse of economic power than Standard Oil, the monopolistic giant that had dominated the petroleum industry for decades and was poised to move into the newly discovered oilfields of the Southwest. *Puck* was the largest magazine of its kind, and, each week, more than 90,000 subscribers and many thousands of others who borrowed copies from friends and neighbors or bought it at newsstands waited eagerly to see who the progressive cartoonists would target next. One newspaper editor at the time observed that "there was no corner in the land" in which the magazine did not exert its influence.[1] The same could be said of the octopus.

This wasn't the first time that the octopus was invoked to describe a corrupt and powerful corporation. The novelist and muckraking journalist Frank Norris used the imagery to great effect in his 1901 novel *The Octopus: A Story of California*, which told of the battle between farmers in the San Joaquin Valley and a powerful railroad that took possession of their lands and ruined their fortunes.[2] A few decades earlier, Joseph Potts, a petroleum industrialist, said that the Standard Oil trust's purchase of his competitors pushed them "shivering with dislike into the embrace of this commercial octopus."[3] Calling John D. Rockefeller's monopoly an octopus wasn't just an insult. The image conveyed what everyone already knew, that the company had its hands in everything: in railroads, pipelines, refining, consumer marketing, not to mention the boardrooms of transportation companies, the halls of state legislatures, and the offices of newspapers.

In Scandinavian folklore, colossal octopus-like beasts known as Kraken come up from the ocean depths to overtake ships.[4] English sailors sometimes called them bloodsuckers. Spineless and feral, it was an animal whose nineteenth-century depictions made it out to be extremely clever, intelligent, and capable of obscuring itself with billowy ink.

Americans have long been conflicted, confused, and often anxious about the entity known as the corporation. Frequently infatuated with the power and size of big business, Americans have also been deeply fearful and suspicious of it. The founding fathers associated corporations with the abuses of the British Crown, which is one reason they gave neither Congress nor the executive the power to incorporate, leaving this duty to the states. James Madison expressed a peculiarly American attitude about corporations most succinctly when he wrote to a friend in 1827 that they may "be useful, but they are at best a necessary evil only."[5]

It is difficult to overstate the degree to which the rise of large corporations provoked a crisis in American life. Beginning first with the railroad and communications industries in the 1870s and then encompassing industries from cigarettes to cars, these concentrations of capital and employment, thriving on vertical integration and technological innovations, shook up everything that Americans had known about the economy. New industrial corporations remade capitalism, and the ramifications of the US Supreme Court's 1886 *Santa Clara County* decision, which extended constitutional protections for corporate "persons," became more widely known at the turn of the century. Corporate personhood itself evoked the freakish.[6] The *New York Times* quipped, "a corporation has neither a body that can be kicked nor a soul that can be sent to perdition."[7] Economist John R. Commons would later imagine unkickable bodies and undamnable souls. "While the corporation has no soul," he wrote, "yet it has a mysterious will somewhere that acts like a soul."[8]

The year after *Puck* ran its famous cartoon, the federal government opened an investigation into Standard Oil because of the trust's monopolistic practices that provoked a conflict known as the Kansas Oil War.[9] Doubtless with an octopus in mind, one governor in 1905 implored his fellow progressives to take the "monster"—the Standard Oil trust—by the neck and "compel it to be decent."[10]

In different guises over the past century and more, the corporate monster has been an object of fascination and populist repulsion. And it still haunts our political culture. When journalist Matt Taibbi took stock of the financial crisis of 2007–2008 in the pages of *Rolling Stone*, he called Goldman Sachs a "great vampire squid wrapped around the face of humanity."[11]

In recent years, however, business leaders have come to believe that what James Madison thought was a "necessary evil" is actually the last great institution capable of making the world a better place. For Silicon Valley entrepreneurs no less than Fortune 500 CEOs, a shift has occurred: the bottom line is out, and changing the world is in. Call it conscious capitalism. Or shared value. Or corporate social responsibility. Many consumers, regulators, and activists expect big-business executives to act like good, responsible citizens and steer their firms accordingly—maybe more now than ever before. And many leading executives are more than willing to heed the call.

That has meant taking public stands on controversial issues. At Starbucks, JPMorgan Chase, Amazon, and other major companies, executives have expressed opposition to the overturning of *Roe v. Wade* by implementing policies that cover travel expenses for employees seeking abortions. "I understand the anxiety and concern that many of you and your families may be feeling at this moment," PayPal's CEO Dan Schulman wrote to workers. "I want to be clear: caring for our employees is our highest priority." In the days after the 2020 election, a group of about thirty chief executives from Walmart, Goldman Sachs, Johnson & Johnson, and other firms organized a response to Donald Trump's efforts to overturn the election results.[12] Nike, meanwhile, has celebrated its programs for young women's empowerment in the developing world and supported Colin Kaepernick's protest against police violence. Executives at Whole Foods (bought by Amazon in 2017) tout their firm's support for a "virtuous circle entwining the food chain, human beings and Mother Earth." And more and more Wall Street banks are taking environmental, social, and governance (ESG) standards and rankings into account for their investment strategies, which has trickled down to business valuations and, increasingly, managerial strategy.

According to a recent survey, 92 percent of executives agree that corporate leaders should take a stand on social issues.[13] And although activists tend to be suspicious of corporate America, many on the political Left have cautiously welcomed this business support for progressive causes. Companies are "obligated to use their voice and influence when core principles of democracy are threatened," wrote Sherrilyn Ifill, then president of the NAACP Legal Defense Fund.[14]

But for every liberal or progressive who sees corporate social commitments as steps toward a better world, there are perhaps just as many conservatives who think the CEOs have taken flight from reason and forgotten who butters their bread. When a supposedly radicalized management mandates training against racism for its employees, for example, it is implementing a program of "soft totalitarianism." And by exchanging business sense for social change, corporations are undermining free enterprise. "Corporate power has increasingly been utilized to impose an ideological agenda on the American people," said Florida governor Ron DeSantis.[15] "Woke capital," to use a phrase coined by *New York Times* columnist Ross Douthat, has taken over corporate America.[16] The problem, as conservatives see it, is that market actors are not acting like the profit-seeking agents they should be. They are letting other motivations—the expectations of the cultural elite or the desire for popular approval or even social control—make them negligent of their actual duties, and all of this to the peril of our economy.

At the surface, we see efforts to make corporations align with one side's values, whether progressive or conservative, but a deeper understanding of this corporate culture war reveals underlying assumptions that each side makes about the corporation. It is further confused by the rhetoric of many executives and management gurus. Critics of corporate power often decry superficial public relations or outright cynicism in corporations that parrot the rhetoric of social responsibility. Corporate leaders make merely cosmetic changes or vague future promises, critics conclude, about working conditions, environmental responsibility, and product safety. When it comes to the way big business actually does business, fleeting expectations and Aquarian rhetoric have outpaced prospects for real change. "Don't be evil" isn't just an abandoned slogan of Google. It is a diversion from difficult questions about power, responsibility, and democratic expectations. Only by understanding what a corporation is and what it is good for can we begin to make our way out of this conflict—or at least to know where genuine disagreements lie.

The corporation is no longer novel or freakish to us in the way that it was to the generations that first called it the octopus, but populist anxieties about corporate threats to democracy and to the American people stubbornly persist. The history of corporate social responsibility is a story of the struggle on the part of activists, executives, regulators, and others to make this institution accountable—to domesticate the very thing that many doubted was even capable of being domesticated.

But accountable to whom or to what?

That is the question driving this book, which examines the history of corporate power and social responsibility from the bottom up—and the top down. Because how we think about the purpose of business is inseparable from how we have decided to govern our economic institutions, this book investigates the origins and meaning of academic theories, legal constructs, and political concepts that have shaped the history of the corporation in the modern United States. It weaves these ideas into the stories of businesspeople, employees, consumers, and activists who have waged battles over business decisions, managerial strategies, and public policy—and who have sometimes fought for roads not taken.

At the center of this story is the large, publicly traded corporation—and not primarily smaller businesses or closely held firms—because this institution has done more to fashion American life than has any other kind of business. For this is also a story about the modern form of the corporation, a legal person who has been created again and again by state legislatures since the early years of the American republic. Two hundred years ago or so, those legislatures made sure to judge whether it was necessary for a new corporation to be created, for what purpose, and for how long. This deliberation mattered because the corporation was granted special privileges that allowed it to amass capital and to be covered in legal protections that no one else enjoyed. By the end of the nineteenth century, the legal process for making a new corporation had become routine—more like opening a checking account than something esoteric like asking the government to create a new legal person. It's still the case that no corporation exists without a state making it so, meaning large, publicly traded corporations are still concessions of the power of government. But we have almost entirely forgotten this history. When seen in a new light, the strangeness of this seemingly familiar institution is made clearer—and suggests rethinking what we thought we knew about the corporation's relationship to democracy and to the common good. In order to understand how this peculiar legal form became an unstoppable dynamo of business power, its tentacles wrapped around the globe many times over, we have to go back a hundred years or so—to a time we now know as the Progressive Era.

ONE

The New Princes of Industry

Would Theodore Roosevelt rise to the occasion? He was mistakenly known at the time, and still is remembered today, as "Trust-Busting TR," Rough Rider turned scourge of the monopolists, but the real story is more complicated.[1] As president, he set about steering corporate power through a series of gentlemen's agreements.[2] Not content with nudging or influencing corporations from the outside, he wanted the federal government to reach inside firms and set the standard for what corporations should do—and what responsibilities they should have. "We do not wish to destroy corporations," Roosevelt said in 1902, "but we do wish to make them subserve the public good."[3] Far from a trust buster, TR was a "trust musterer" who wanted to enroll big business into a progressive partnership with the executive branch.[4]

In 1907, a wrenching financial panic caused the New York Stock Exchange to teeter on the edge of collapse.[5] Although far more centered on the lending houses of Wall Street, the panic seemed to be an ominous sign that the post–Civil War era that had been punctuated by damaging financial crises—in 1873, 1893, 1896, and now 1907—stubbornly refused to come to an end. Roosevelt responded to the 1907 crisis in part by pushing for legislation that would rein in large corporations. Written by members of a progressive lobbying organization called the National Civic Federation (NCF), the bill would have established a formal process of federal licensing, charters, and transparency.[6] "Is it not time that we go further and bring these great corporations under control?" asked progressive economist Jeremiah Jenks at one of the group's major conferences.[7] Much like laws that regulated food such as the Pure Food and Drug Act of 1906, which prohibited interstate transport of adulterated or mislabeled food, such policies would benefit industry, Roosevelt insisted, by providing national standards. Effectively, Roosevelt argued for the regulation of business for the benefit of business.[8]

The following year, Republican US Rep. William Hepburn introduced the new bill in Congress. The original drafts, written by Jenks, former mayor of New York City Seth Low, and other NCF members, envisioned a voluntary system in which corporations might register with the federal government. Participating firms would regularly submit financial statements and internal information and provide access to books, records (including contracts and agreements), and accounts. There was a progressive form of a quid pro quo that underwrote this idea: compliance with supervision by the Bureau of Corporations provided the guarantee that the Department of Justice would not pursue antitrust action against a compliant corporation.[9] As Roosevelt's allies further revised the proposed legislation, they gave the executive branch incredible power over the new corporate order. By establishing constant administrative oversight by means of close consultation and cooperation with corporate managers, this legislation would have transformed them into "well-paid public servants rather than old-style capitalists."[10]

It's a remarkable fact that the Hepburn bill was the first and only legislation endorsed by a president that was premised on the theory that corporations are not private institutions—and that the internal governance of the corporation should reflect that.

TR gave voice to the impulse—strong among populists, radicals, and many progressives—that democratic interests ought to govern the economy and, especially, corporate institutions. The proposal would have brought the corporate system under the power of popular politics, granting the president "power to regulate and control all corporation business of the country," the *New York Times* pointed out.[11] As such, the bill earned the near universal opposition of business groups, both large and small, and never made it out of committee. It expresses, however, one important way Americans tried to square corporate power with democratic expectations: by treating corporations as if they were governmental institutions possessing rights and responsibilities subject to political supervision.

The rise of corporate capitalism at the beginning of the twentieth century fueled the fires of a thousand social movements. Whether feminist or labor unionist, populist or socialist or progressive, all of them tried to reckon with a far-from-bloodless revolution that left almost nothing in American society and politics untouched. People at the time called it the "trust question," a term evoking doubts about the trustworthiness of new social institutions—while at the same time invoking the financial trusts, which were only the most visible and scandalous of the new economic behemoths. But no single phrase could plausibly represent the size and scope of this menacing tumult. The *Puck* cartoon of the Standard Oil octopus evoked not only the grotesque and the wily but also the vital dynamism, the sheer energetic potential, of these new institutions.

In the early twentieth century, Americans began to exchange a long-held anxiety about corporate power for an ambivalent, if unsteady, admiration. It's not that the anxiety entirely disappeared; rather, the advantages of corporate capitalism left few untouched:

middle-class professionals, the rising ranks of consumers, unionized workers, Wall Street financiers, imperialist political leaders—even those radical farmers from the South and Midwest whose cash crops made it to world markets only by way of railroads. As the GNP grew from $17.4 billion to $103.1 billion between 1899 and 1929 (mostly due to the rapid growth of vertically integrated firms, such as American Tobacco or Standard Oil before it was broken up by the US Supreme Court in 1911), most social groups came around to the idea that there was something useful, if still at times dangerous, about the corporation.[12]

And for those who suspected that they had something to gain from allowing the corporate form of business to be dynamic and more or less free from political control, a rising group of business executives proposed that a new style of leadership, as yet untried, and not structural change could reconcile the corporation with democratic expectations.

Gerard Swope was one such business leader. Gerard was born into a lower-middle-class immigrant family in St. Louis, Missouri: his father, Isaac (so taciturn that his friends sometimes called him "Silent Swope"), started a small business making watches, and his mother, Ida, took care of the children.[13] Gerard Swope was educated at the Massachusetts Institute of Technology then got a job in Chicago with the Western Electric Company, a manufacturing firm that would soon be bought up by AT&T. It was there in Chicago that Swope rose through the ranks of the engineering department in the late 1890s during a time when he was living at Jane Addams's Hull House, a so-called settlement house that sought to serve the urban working class. He taught evening classes to workers and became acquainted with a range of social reformers such as Julia Lathrop (soon to be head of the Children's Bureau of the Department of Labor) and Florence Kelley (dominating influence behind the Consumers' League of New York City).[14] Swope made a hasty ascent to the top. He became a vice president and director at Western Electric, and, after World War I, president of the international arm of the General Electric Company (GE), and, in 1922, president of the company itself. By that time, GE was making light bulbs, electrical transformers and sockets, radios, and other products of the early electric age.

Swope was appointed president of GE at the same time that his colleague, Owen D. Young, was made the new chairman. This new leadership pair boosted GE's market share, but their most innovative contributions came in the area of industrial relations.[15] Their main tool? Workers councils—otherwise known as company unions—aimed at facilitating reconciliation between labor and management within the firm itself. The pair initiated a revolution in GE's industrial relations by pioneering what some scholars have called welfare capitalism: higher wages, profit sharing, insurance, various educational and social benefits, and pensions.[16]

Even such critics as Ida Tarbell and Lincoln Steffens—progressives who had made a name for themselves decades earlier as muckrakers who focused on abuses by big business through their exposés of Standard Oil and municipal governments—now celebrated this movement of enlightened business leadership. Tarbell, who published a biography of Young in 1932, declared him a "new type of industrial leader." It was universally agreed, Tarbell asserted, that there was no such thing as private business any longer. "Industry is learning that as power increases so does responsibility."[17]

In speeches and pamphlets throughout the 1920s and early 1930s, the GE duo explained their philosophy to colleagues and the public. In the pulpit of New York City's Park Avenue Baptist Church in 1929, where the liberal Protestant minister Harry Emerson Fosdick preached most Sunday mornings, Young explained his philosophy of managing General Electric:

> There are three groups of people who have an interest. . . . One is the group of fifty-odd-thousand people who have put their capital in the General Electric Company, nameless stockhold-

> ers. Another is a group of well toward 100,000 people who are putting their labor and their lives into the business of the General Electric Company. The third group is composed of the customers and the general public.[18]

At an address before a meeting of social scientists in 1932, Young said, "The old notion that the heads of business are the paid attorneys of stockholders, to exploit labor and the public in the stockholders' interest is gone—I hope forever."[19]

Young outlined a theory of business leadership that he called *trusteeship*. It was a bold defense of executive responsibility: the manager was not in any significant sense an agent for shareholders—at least insofar as that title might infer that he had an obligation to do everything that shareholders wanted. Ownership had become divorced from responsibility, as he put it. For Young, this meant the manager was one whose responsibility was to accept a vocation as a kind of tribune or protector of the interests of the people—or the nation, or the communities of the nation—writ large. "One no longer feels the obligation to take from labor for the benefit of capital, nor to take from the public for the benefit of both," he explained, "but rather to administer wisely and fairly in the interest of all."[20]

The legality of such claims wasn't exactly settled. Didn't business leaders have fiduciary duties to shareholders? In a consequential 1919 court case, shareholders had sued Ford Motor Company over $60 million in profits that had been retained in company accounts. Two shareholders, John and Horace Dodge (who also owned a competing car company), claimed that the money rightly belonged to shareholders and was due to them periodically as dividends.[21] The Michigan Supreme Court ruled partially in the brothers' favor and required the company to dispense about $20 million in dividends. In the decades after the ruling (and indeed, to the present day), the justices' reasoning has been widely cited as a legal bulwark against managerial autonomy. "A business corporation is organized and carried on primarily for the profit of the stockholders," the court's decision in *Dodge v. Ford Motor Company* declared. "The powers of the directors are to be employed for that end." According to the ruling, a company can't take its resources and use them for some other purpose besides profit. But, importantly, the decision also invoked the principle of *business judgment*, which gave wide latitude to managers to figure out for themselves the best way to pursue profit.[22] Executives, in other words, are the ones with the expertise to make judgments about what's profitable or not.

In the decades after World War I, it became common for business leaders to speak of a certain social responsibility to different groups. Swope celebrated a threefold understanding of social trusteeship: a trusteeship on behalf of the public, workers, and shareholders. "A business is an institution for service," he said in 1926 to a gathering of business-press editors and publishers.[23] This model of business leadership paired the notion of *noblesse oblige* (the virtue associated with the old WASP elite and, before them, the British elite who, so it was idealized, used their privilege judiciously and prudently for the benefit of all) with a new sociological appreciation for the role of organizations in mass society. Even a conservative such as Herbert Hoover advocated what he called the "American system," or, more prosaically, the "Cooperative Committee and Conference System." Business firms had social responsibilities and, in Hoover's America, the business manager was the final decision-maker.[24] "The directors and managers of large concerns, themselves employees of these great groups of individual stockholders or policy holders," he wrote in *American Individualism* in 1922, "reflect a spirit of community responsibility."[25]

Such socially enlightened business leadership, it seemed to many, was the way of the future. No more socialist radicalism or anarchy, which had in previous years led to outbreaks of violence, bombings, and assassinations, such as the Ludlow Massacre of 1914 in which National Guard troops and private guards killed twenty-one people (including some children and women) who were striking against Colorado Fuel and Iron Company or the bombing of the home of a Tulsa oil executive's house in 1917 (blamed, probably falsely, on the International Workers of the World).[26] No more ruinous competition, which had led to those panics and depressions in 1873, 1893, 1896, and 1907. Such turmoil could be a thing of the past, if only business leadership could be exercised in the right way.

In 1928, Herbert Hoover declared in his radio-broadcast speech accepting the Republican presidential nomination that a new age of abundance was at hand. "We in America today are nearer to the final triumph over poverty than ever before in the history of any land," he said from his hometown of Stanford, California. "The poorhouse is vanishing from among us." Although he was bitterly punished by his Democratic opponent a few years later for that statement, Hoover expressed little more than the conventional wisdom of the day. As the economist John Kenneth Galbraith put it, 1928 was "the last year in which Americans were buoyant, uninhibited, and utterly happy." It seemed as if the violent cycle of economic booms and busts had been planed down. The much-lauded efficiencies of the new managerial order seemed to speak for themselves. That is, until the orderliness of what John Dewey called the "corporate age" started to crumble—and get shaken up like the pieces of an overturned chessboard.[27]

WHAT IS AN OLD STORY to us was a stupefying event to those who lived through the Wall Street crash of September and October 1929. "What failures loomed, none could say," *Time* magazine commented that fall. "Would the nightmare, to many tragically cruel, never end?" It wasn't at all clear at first what the crash portended or that it would turn out to be the first act to an extended

Great Depression that stretched well into the next decade. In three years, the Dow index lost nearly 90 percent of its value. Then as now, Wall Street represented only a slice of the US economy, but, by almost any measure, the rest of American business was going off the rails, too. The country's steel mills operated at 12 percent of their capacity. Industrial manufacturing shrunk by half. The unemployment rate rose to 24.9 percent, and real GDP declined 26 percent. From an emptied-out reservoir in the middle of New York's Central Park to public land at the Port of Seattle, homeless encampments began to spring up as early as the fall of 1931. One former lumberjack named Jesse Jackson became known as the mayor of Seattle's Hooverville—what he later called the "abode of the forgotten man."[28]

Through all of this, President Hoover implored Americans to soldier on and warned them, as he did the day before the election, not to be "led astray by false gods arrayed in the rainbow colors of promises." His hesitation at building up key relief programs contributed, in part, to Franklin D. Roosevelt's landslide victory on November 8, 1932. The New York patrician promised to lift up the "forgotten man at the bottom of the economic pyramid." Just how he planned to do that was not certain—not even to himself, at least not in those heady days of the early campaign. FDR possessed a notoriously adaptive mind and pragmatic disposition.[29] And even though he campaigned on a more active role for the federal government in the nation's economy, unfolding events would soon give more definite shape to his policies.

It was far from guaranteed, for one, that a reconsideration of corporate capitalism—or the social responsibilities of management—would be a defining feature of the new administration. But such a reckoning was forced upon the administration by a man that few had heard of before—at least not until he became a household name in the early months of 1933.

That man was Ferdinand Pecora. A Sicilian immigrant, he

came to the United States in the 1880s as a child and grew up in the Chelsea neighborhood of Manhattan. In 1896, he saw the Populist Party dynamo William Jennings Bryan speak at Madison Square Garden when Bryan was on the campaign trail. "Mr. Bryan had the finest voice that I have ever heard," he later recalled. "He held that big throng just enchanted, partly by the wizardry of his voice I think as well as by the content of his speech."[30]

After putting in time as a prosecutor in New York, Pecora earned a reputation as a brilliant cross-examiner. His penchant for chasing corruption was enough for the political organization Tammany Hall to push him out of the running for district attorney in 1929. He went after the "bucket shops" (gambling houses that took bets on the movements of stocks and commodity prices) and showed how they were tied to bigger banking concerns. He worked (and waited) in private practice until, one day, Peter Norbeck, a Republican US senator from South Dakota and chairman of the Banking and Currency Committee, called him up on a Sunday in January 1933 asking him to take over as the lead counsel to finish a final report of an investigation into how the widespread practice of short selling (a way of profiting when the value of an asset falls) on Wall Street might have contributed to the 1929 crash. The job was for six weeks. And it paid $59 per week. Pecora said yes.[31]

After taking the lead counsel position, he hired a handful of working-class lawyers and assistants, many of whom were also first-generation immigrants, and set up shop in shabby offices in midtown Manhattan. There he realized that the Senate resolution authorizing the committee to undertake an investigation "into stock exchange practices," as the language put it, and not just into short selling was exceedingly broad. Pecora steered the investigation away from the exceptional cases and shined a light on the deceptions and misdeeds that were lurking behind the most respectable institutions in American business—names such as Morgan Bank and National City Bank. Pecora wanted to take on the corporate executives and their allies in finance.

After his inauguration in March of 1933, FDR decided that even though Pecora's ambitions were risky (or probably because they were risky), he wanted to protect him. With a slate of Democratic candidates riding a wave of economic desperation and sweeping Congress, Duncan Fletcher, a longtime US senator from Florida, took charge of Norbeck's committee and reappointed Pecora as lead counsel.[32] Roosevelt next convinced Fletcher and Pecora to go after J. P. Morgan, Jr., of J. P. Morgan & Company. It was just the sort of fight that Pecora had been preparing for—maybe for his entire professional life. The cigar-chomping Pecora was more than a shrewd investigator; he was a brilliant showman who understood from the start that in order for the congressional hearings to be useful, they had to grab the attention of the public. Somewhere there would be a farmer who had defaulted on his mortgage and who would be reading transcripts of the hearings printed in the newspaper. Somewhere else, an anxious storekeeper would worry over his account books while he listened to a radio report about Pecora's fight.

For weeks, this clash between Pecora and the House of Morgan captured the American imagination. There was no more effective generator of public outrage than to turn Morgan, a picture of refined wealth and propriety, into an icon of Wall Street's malfeasance. With his attack on Morgan, Pecora made himself the scourge of what *Time* dubbed the "banksters."[33]

When Pecora on behalf of the Banking and Currency Committee sent Morgan a twenty-three-question letter, Morgan refused to answer seven of the questions. When Pecora asked for financial records, Morgan likewise demurred. When Pecora requested a meeting, Morgan asked that they convene at his own stately office in what was known simply as the "house on the corner," a four-story limestone building with nine enormous windows that looked onto the intersection of Wall and Broad Streets. It was his seat of dominance, an icon of his family's name, and even though there was no sign to be found outside, everyone knew it was the home of J. P. Morgan & Company. Pecora insisted that the meeting take place instead at his rented office in midtown. "I felt it might be a good thing to do something which might convey to Mr. Morgan the impression that he was not going to meet Ferdinand Pecora the individual," recalled the lead counsel, "but that he was to meet a representative of the United States Government." Even still, Morgan referred to him privately as a "dirty little wop" and a "second-rate criminal lawyer."[34]

The Pecora hearings, the initial part of which had begun in late May of 1933 and stretched to the end of June that year, were a national event. For the hearings, Fletcher moved the committee to the large and august Senate Caucus Room, a rectangular space flanked by columns with Corinthian capitals: it had three grand windows, an ornately decorated ceiling of gilded classical designs, and it could seat hundreds. It was enough space for all the photographers, journalists, lights, amplifiers, and spectators, but it was still packed.

There was an odd disjunction in the caucus room. On the one hand, having spent weeks interviewing Morgan and his associates and poring over financial records, Pecora was loosed upon his witnesses, often walking through detailed steps of transactions and business decisions that left senators in the dark and often guessing at what Pecora was trying to accomplish. On the other hand, the public was eager to learn more, newspapers often printed transcripts from the previous day, and the room itself was abuzz with laughter, applause, and disruptive commotion, leading Chairman Fletcher to complain to the spectators at one point, "Some of you do not seem to care anything about the noise you are making."

The frenetic hearing resonated with a nation's pent-up anger over the abuse of economic power. The most sensational headlines to come out of the Pecora investigation had to do with income taxes. Or, rather, the lack of income taxes. The partners of J. P. Morgan & Company collectively paid only $48,000 in 1930 and nothing at all in the next two years. Though not illegal, it was a bad look for the most powerful name in American finance during an unprecedented economic crisis.

Other revelations were more substantive. The bank had floated $6 billion in new securities over the previous fourteen years. More than fifty of the country's largest corporations each held daily deposits of over $1 million there. J. P. Morgan & Company's vast financial holdings added up to 126 directorships and trusteeships in nearly ninety firms—all of which totaled about $20 billion in capital. And only the most lucrative firms and socially connected individuals could do their business with J. P. Morgan & Company. The private bank made it a practice to distribute newly floated securities at discounted rates to well-connected individuals such as Secretary of the Navy (and New England blue blood) Charles Francis Adams; the chairman of the Democratic National Committee; a US Supreme Court justice; New York Stock Exchange president E. H. H. Simons; and the American aviator Charles Lindbergh. The constant drip of findings over two weeks painted a portrait of concentrated economic power and elite self-dealing that further stoked the fires of populist sentiment. And although J. P. Morgan, Jr., and other financiers were stars of the ignominious show, the real quarry was the attorneys, accountants, and account books that could explain the financial products and legal forms that were the secret building blocks of the new American economy. One listener to this extended scuffle between Washington and Wall Street was a young lawyer and ambitious intellectual named Adolf Berle, Jr.—and he wanted to change everything about the rules that governed both the big corporations and the banking houses.

Berle was obsessed with the secret building blocks that were churned up by Pecora and described in the daily newspapers and the hearing transcripts. Berle joined FDR's so-called Brain Trust in early 1932 and quickly became a vital advisor and speech writer for the candidate.[35] The most definitive statement of the campaign came with FDR's Commonwealth Club address, given in San Francisco in September 1932 and written mostly by Adolf Berle and his wife, Beatrice Bishop Berle.[36] The speech laid out a case for a new kind of liberalism. The future was a corporate future, one in which the wealth of the country might one day be controlled by a dozen corporations or by one hundred people. The way forward was not to break up the corporations; to construct such a massive antitrust program was to attempt the impossible. "The task of government in its relation to business is," FDR said, "to assist the development of an economic declaration of rights, an economic constitutional order." He called business a public trust that was held together by a social contract and by the bonds of responsibility that goes with power.[37]

The Harvard-trained attorney told his wife, Beatrice, that his deepest ambition in life was to be the "American Karl Marx," a real social prophet.[38] Like Marx, Berle had a rutilant desire to understand the structures of power that lie hidden beneath the surface of everyday life. During the years that straddled the 1929 crash, he studied the building blocks of corporate institutions and financial instruments and imagined how they could be arranged and rearranged.[39] With a $7,000 grant from the Social Science Research Council, he and his old military bunkmate, an accountant named Gardiner Means, went to work at Kent Hall, on the eastern edge of the Columbia University campus, on what became *The Modern Corporation and Private Property*.[40]

The book was, among other things, an obituary for the old market economy. Monopoly and oligopoly were no longer exceptions, Berle and Means argued. They had become the modus operandi of the new corporate system.[41] In an array of tables and charts, Means showed that the 200 largest corporations in the United States, as of January 1930, controlled nearly one-half of all nonbanking corporate wealth and about a quarter of the national wealth.[42] And this was no accident of the crash of 1929; concentration was a trend throughout the 1920s as a result of mergers, acquisitions, and higher rates of growth among the largest firms.

At the same time, stock ownership had become widely dispersed. It was typical that in large firms, the majority of shares were spread thinly, leaving a substantial minority of shares held by one person, institution, or small group.[43] The dispersion of ownership correlated with corporate size, too. With an increasing amount of private savings going into securities markets (at the time, about half), a large portion of wealth for the first time consisted of interest in businesses over which no one individual owned a majority part.[44] The language of Adam Smith and the nineteenth-century political economists had "ceased to be accurate," these new liberals wrote, "and therefore tend[s] to mislead in describing modern enterprise as carried on by the great corporations."[45]

Berle and Means overstated the degree to which the nineteenth century was governed by supply and demand, the invisible hand, and the natural law of the markets—but all of that could be forgiven for the insightful analysis that they made about the separation of corporate ownership from control. This was the thesis that there had emerged a "control" element within most major corporations that made the real business decisions, and it was separate from the ownership faction—and shareholders were always imagined, erroneously, as the owners of corporations. The new corporate regime had reshuffled the power, responsibilities, and motivations of the old capitalism of the nineteenth century—the one dominated by small-business owners, shopkeepers and factors, financiers and partnerships.[46]

This was the danger: Increasingly, management delegated to itself unchecked power, making itself into the "new princes" and "economic autocrats" of industry. A specter of absolutism loomed over the new concentrations of capital.[47] But, as Berle pointed out in a subsequent article called "High Finance: Master or Servant," the "control point" was not the sole possession of management. Through more informal mechanisms, people outside the firm could gain control—and sometimes for their own benefit and to the detriment of management, workers, and other shareholders.[48] On Wall Street, where the financial class looked out for itself and enforced an "almost unbreakable ideological unity" among the major banking institutions, high finance could be the master, protecting itself with costly legal and financial instruments and arcane knowledge.[49] Whether it belonged to management or investors, control belonged to insiders.

It appeared to Berle and Means that the bedrock of a capitalist system—private property ownership—was eroding before their eyes. "The 'owner' of industrial wealth is left with a mere symbol of ownership," they wrote.[50] Depending on how you felt about capitalism, of course, this wasn't necessarily a bad thing. It suggested the possibility that the individualistic pursuit of profit had reached a twilight and that cooperation, not self-interest, could serve as the new ethic for a new spirit of capitalism—or post-capitalism.[51]

The more immediate question that Berle and Means posed—which set the terms for how generations of policy makers and intellectuals would think about corporate power—was whether the control element could be directed toward more democratic ends. "The next few years will probably determine whether the elements of power or control now tied to finance," they wrote in 1933, "remain in the hands of the financial group or whether they pass, measurably, into the hands of the community."[52] While Berle advocated reform of the financial system through a state-supervised system of disclosures, he also demonstrated an interest in other tools such as a national incorporation system, a national planning policy, and a public financing administration. But it was the first, the reform of Wall Street, that would be his lasting legacy. "Although we didn't know it then," Berle later said, "we were pounding out the principles on which the Securities and Exchange Legislation enforced today is based."[53]

In late March of 1933, Roosevelt delivered a message to Congress calling for federal supervision of investment securities.

Interstate commerce prevented states from effectively regulating this sector of the economy, and business self-regulation was no longer an option. But Roosevelt and his aides wanted to avoid a situation in which the government would be in the position of giving a stamp of approval to an investment. A federal guarantee on securities would never work. "There is, however, an obligation upon us to insist that every issue of new securities to be sold in interstate commerce shall be accompanied by full publicity and information," he said, "and that no essentially important element attending the issue shall be concealed from the buying public." This was a fundamental progressive belief that public disclosure of business behavior would shame industrial leaders into acting ethically. The rallying cry of this agenda was a spin on the old rule of *caveat emptor*: "Let the *seller* beware."[54]

DURING THE WEEKS THAT J. P. Morgan, Jr., and his colleagues were in the nation's capital for the Pecora hearings, they resided at the Carlton Hotel, a Beaux-Arts style eight-story building a stone's throw from the White House and two miles from the Senate Office Building. The retinue of attorneys, secretaries, stenographers, and partners took up a floor of suites and rooms that cost a cool $2,000 per day.[55] Sharing a much more modest room just one floor below were two young lawyers, James M. Landis and Benjamin V. Cohen, who had been recruited by FDR's inner circle. They had arrived by train back in April from Boston and New York on much different business. The Harvard-trained legal pair had hammered out the basics of a new securities law along with another Roosevelt insider named Thomas Corcoran. In the mornings, Landis and Cohen would eye Morgan and his entourage as they stepped into the elevator and rode together down to the hotel lobby. "We had a room on the seventh floor and the whole eighth floor was taken up by J. P. Morgan," Landis remembered. "Of course he didn't know us. He didn't know that we were termites boring into his kingdom."[56]

Their time in Washington was short. Landis had to return to Cambridge to teach law classes and resorted subsequently to taking the train to the nation's capital for long hours of weekend work with Cohen and Corcoran.[57] But this was more than just a weekend project. Nicknamed the "little hot-dogs," the three were protégés of Felix Frankfurter—a Harvard Law School professor, FDR confidante, and future US Supreme Court justice—who found themselves drawn into the policy making and politics of the new administration. They were all in different ways involved in the long process of writing and passing the Securities Act of 1933, the Securities Exchange Act of 1934, and the Public Utility Holding Company Act of 1935; in addition, Landis would serve on the board of the newly created Securities and Exchange Commission.[58]

Cohen, Corcoran, and Landis wanted to require transparency and disclosures in order to protect investors, but they also wanted to avoid placing significant burdens on companies and investors. They built on the blue sky laws that had passed through the legislatures of many states in the 1920s and the British Companies Act of 1929, all of which focused on regulating via business disclosures. Capital still needed to flow, and nothing would threaten the political viability of reform like proposing some legislation that might throttle it.

FDR did not need to further stir up the public's outrage as the Pecora hearings had done. The drumbeat of labor radicalism was the background noise for everything the New Deal sought to accomplish. Between 1933 and 1937, American labor unions recruited about 5 million new members, with the total of union members reaching nearly 7 million by decade's end.[59] The impetus for corporate reform had emerged from the fires of popular politics, but it was being shepherded into the confines of expertise and consensus among a well-heeled and powerful elite. Roosevelt's policy makers sought to involve responsible professionals who might be affected by the law—not just business leaders and managers, but also accountants, brokers, and bankers.

The Securities Act, which New Deal insiders finally hammered out in early 1933, changed the way corporations and banks related to the public. That started with disclosures—a mountain of disclosures. The amount of information that corporations were required to file with the federal government upon issuing new securities was unprecedented: detailed balance sheets, profit-and-loss statements, salaries and perquisites of the company's officers and directors, the commissions of the underwriters, the names and contact information of the lawyers who were consulted on the issue, and a variety of other items of information.[60] The bill also imposed civil liabilities on corporations, directors, officers, accountants, and others who filed the registration information if it was found to be deceitful or fraudulent. The administration of the act was in the hands of the Federal Trade Commission, which created a six-member board in charge of collecting, publishing, and analyzing this new trove of corporate data.

The new act had shortcomings. For one thing, it covered only the issuance of new securities, leaving more than a billion already in circulation untouched.[61] Critics such as Adolf Berle, Jr., and his friend, the soon-to-be US Supreme Court justice, William O. Douglas, urged the creation of more robust regulatory institutions. "There is nothing in the Act which would control the speculative craze of the American public, or which would eliminate wholly unsound capital structures," Douglas wrote along with the legal scholar George Bates in the pages of the *Yale Law Journal*. He urged administrative control over the market.[62]

The act was passed in 1933 on the assumption that Congress would amend it with improvements the next year. In the meantime, however, opposition grew both to the 1933 act and to further legislation that was being planned for the following year. Bankers blamed the Securities Act for a slowdown in the capital markets and, increasingly, claimed that uncertainty over regulation was impeding an economic recovery.[63] "The Stock Exchange Bill is receiving a terrific beating," Landis wrote to Frankfurter in early 1934. "All the corporate wealth of this country has gone into the attack and carried it all the way up to the White House."[64]

Landis and company, under mounting pressure from Wall Street and particularly the New York Stock Exchange chairman Richard Whitney, hesitated to amend the 1933 act. They feared that their opponents would gut their reform efforts. Berle worked behind the scenes, urging greater aggressiveness on his fellow New Dealers.[65] "If anything is going to be done to that Act," he wrote to Landis, "I would rather we did it than have someone else do it—which is likely."[66] As he told Roosevelt's committee on revision, the securities merchants had discredited themselves.[67] But members of the New York Stock Exchange dealt one card they still had in hand: a capital strike. As the volume of stock declined, the average value of new securities collapsed toward the end of 1933—to a thirteen-year low.[68] The "unbreakable ideological unity" of Wall Street was tough to crack. "Presumably they will get over this," Berle wrote.[69]

New Dealers followed up with the Securities Exchange Act of 1934, which focused more narrowly on cleansing the exchange of what they called speculation. By forcing federal supervision of the stock exchange and a limited control over the exchange's rules, the act brought the demand for disclosure and publicity to bear on the business of stock trading. The 1934 act required the registration of all listed securities (not just newly issued ones) with a new administrative body called the Securities and Exchange Commission (SEC). While outright restrictions on insider trading would not come until much later, the new law generally sought to limit the power of insiders to capitalize on their information in the market. It brought more specialized professional standards to the exchange by separating the work of brokers from that of dealers and from that of underwriters. And it imposed for the first time a limitation on the use of credit to trade or sell stocks and corporate bonds.[70]

Less radical supporters of the Securities Exchange Act simply hoped that it would bring legitimacy back to the markets. "It is my belief that the investing public will find the markets to be firmer in their foundations because of the safeguards and because of the increased marginal requirements and the elimination of shoestring speculators," said Joseph P. Kennedy, a conservative New Dealer. President Roosevelt's nomination of Kennedy as the first SEC chairman shocked Landis and Cohen. They worried that Kennedy, who had political and financial connections to the banking elite of Boston and New York, would fail to maintain the brave if pragmatic project of Wall Street reform that they had helped to launch.[71] Kennedy made it clear to Wall Street from the outset that "their game would not be ruined."[72] His first address, broadcast nationally, was reassuring: "We regard ourselves, as the President has said, as partners in a cooperative enterprise. We do not start off with the belief that every enterprise is crooked and that those behind it are crooks."[73] Even when Landis took over the chairmanship of the SEC about a year later, the message to Wall Street remained largely unchanged: his speeches and articles, no less than his administration, focused on "supervised self-regulation."[74]

The SEC represented a new form of regulation in the political economy of the United States, one that had only been hinted at by earlier institutions such as the Federal Reserve Board or the Federal Trade Commission. The drafters of the legislation believed that the problems they were trying to solve could not be grasped by a slow-to-react Congress.[75] Accordingly, they constructed an administrative institution that would evolve over time by creating its own rules, recommending further legislation, and strategically choosing how to carry out its mandate.[76]

Landis called it the *administrative process*. The conditions of industrialization and mass democracy had, so he and his allies said, made obsolete the lumbering structures of the legislative, judicial, and executive branches. Institutions such as the SEC, Landis argued in a book-length apologia, were not extensions of the executive branch.[77] They were in some sense combinations of all three branches.[78] Regulatory agencies were necessary because the court system's case-by-case method was "slow and costly." Worse, the court system's common-law conception of the judiciary as mere umpire between opposing parties failed in cases when a modern corporation, endowed with special powers by government grant, and operating at a scale larger than many state governments—and soon enough perhaps larger than the federal government—would be unlikely to face litigants that have "equal economic power." The SEC, in short, could initiate action independently. It would make rules and execute judgments.[79]

Administrative law was, then, a kind of experiment in how to rationalize and regulate corporate capitalism. The expert would play a role, in Landis's mind, not just in parsing the technical problems that arose from the often opaque world of financial services. By working in the "quiet of a conference room," away from the "turmoil of a legislative chamber or committee room," with specialized credentials to solve specialized problems, the expert could ensure that "calmness of atmosphere in which wise administration flourishes."[80] Disinterested expertise would make the administrative process work.[81]

In the long Depression that followed the Crash of 1929, policy makers such as Landis stood squarely against the laissez-faire ideology that markets could self-correct, let alone allocate the costs and benefits of mass production and distribution fairly. They, too, had little faith in the initiative of business leaders to exercise the kind of social trusteeship that people such as Gerard Swope and Herbert Hoover envisioned. Perhaps most consequentially, they had also lost faith in the political institutions of representative government, exchanging the congressional chamber for the conference room, the heat of mass movements for the cool rationality of experts.[82]

The new headquarters of the SEC, a shabby office building just off the National Mall, a hand-me-down from the Interstate Commerce Commission, would nevertheless stand for years, as *Fortune* magazine put it, as a shrine to the "outraged feelings of the voters of 1932."[83] From those shabby offices (and, soon, its regional ones scattered around the country), the SEC trained its expert eyes on the flow of capital and the machinery of the stock market. But still, corporate power with other, gripping tentacles lurked outside its view—and outside its congressional mandate.

"CONFIDENTIALLY, we are now working on a federal incorporation law which I hope will be presented to Congress in the next Session," Adolf Berle wrote to William O. Douglas in late 1933. "You can count on me to pull an oar on federal incorporation," Douglas responded.[84] In the early days of Franklin D. Roosevelt's presidency, the two were the most vocal supporters of a progressive federal incorporation law—not unlike that proposed by Theodore Roosevelt less than thirty years before. FDR had asked Berle specifically to work on a federal incorporation proposal, and Berle's personal papers from this time reflect his legal genius searching for a new way to redesign the large corporation.[85] For his job as advisor to the National Recovery Administration, Berle's colleague Gardiner Means also put together a proposal, detailing its history, constitutionality, and policy advantages. The state-based system, as he put it, created corporations "without thought of responsibility." A federal system, Means reckoned, would allow lawmakers to structure the internal governance of interstate corporations to provide for supervision and democratic control of corporations, thus steering them toward more socially responsible ends.

A federal solution to the chartering of corporations was proposed from some sector of the Democratic Party every year of the 1930s beginning in 1933. When a committee consisting of industry and federal representatives, including Landis and Berle, made its formal report to Roosevelt on the stock exchange bill in January 1934, the sequel legislation to the previous year's Securities Act, they recommended federal incorporation for corporations engaged in interstate commerce, not just further regulation of the stock market. A federal system replacing and updating the patchwork of state laws (by then dominated by the state of Delaware, which had won the race to the bottom of lax corporation laws) was, the report concluded, the "most effective way to deal with certain evils," including the manipulation of stock prices and insider dealing.[86] The topic came up repeatedly during congressional hearings on the Securities Exchange Act of 1934 and was considered by many to be the logical complement to the narrow, finance-focused securities acts.[87]

Even though many administration allies believed that the federal government should get involved in chartering corporations—and even though FDR himself was supportive of the idea—there was stiff, and sometimes petulant, opposition from both business leaders and rival New Dealers. Thomas Corcoran waved off the proposal at a Senate hearing in late February, calling it a "dilatory plea" to put action off and a "red herring." It would be far too complicated to pass.[88] Frankfurter urged Roosevelt to hold off.[89] And he voiced his skepticism to Douglas about such "large schemes of which you speak for curbing corporate abuse" and dismissed Douglas's concerns as naïve:[90]

> [I]n your letters to me you are fiercely outspoken about the wickedness of Wall Street and gently suggest that I'm a sap in not knowing how wicked they are, and the only thing to it is to boil them in oil. But yet the fact is that it is you who've had damned little experience in these matters, who've had next to nothing to do with the actual mechanism of committees and courts.[91]

The plan for federal incorporation legislation was shelved in 1934 because of the "mass of details to be considered," reported the *New York Times*.[92] It was floated again in 1935 as a possible replacement for the National Recovery Administration after the latter was declared unconstitutional, and US senators William Borah, a progressive Republican from Idaho, and Joseph O'Mahoney, a Democrat from Wyoming, beat the drums for several years.[93] "It is the culmination of a struggle which has been going on in the United States since most of us now living were born," O'Mahoney told a radio audience in 1936 (referencing the fight for federal incorporation during the presidency of Theodore Roosevelt), "to prevent a comparatively few persons of great ability and skill, but little conscience, to manipulate the corporation laws of a few states to the disadvantage of the entire nation."[94] By 1938, however, whatever enthusiasm for the federal incorporation plan that existed in the administration was lost. Even Douglas, by then SEC chairman, had measured the political winds and abandoned the project.[95] As later chapters in this book show, the idea of federal incorporation, though, was never entirely forgotten.

When it came to regulating corporations, the New Deal was a half-finished project that brought financial markets under the purview of administrative law but left the internal governance of large corporations largely untouched. The unintended consequence was that the New Deal (as it actually existed, not as many hoped it would be) established at the federal level a property regime for corporations, grounding the moral and political legitimacy of large corporations in the proprietary claims of shareholders.[96] This federal policy of treating corporations as if they were the property of shareholders—and requiring the officers and directors to fulfill a fiduciary duty to those who hold stock—would leave a long and important legacy in the history of capitalism. And, quite outside the intention of liberals, the New Deal left open the door to developments later in the century that would make shareholder value the primary measure of management.

The early decades of the twentieth century developed three

competing understandings of how to solve the corporate crisis and define what a corporation is. Theodore Roosevelt, along with many populists, progressives, and radicals who predated his administration (each in their own, often quite divergent manners), wanted direct political supervision of monopolies and a new system of nationalist government that would hold unscrupulous hoarders of productive property accountable to responsible representatives of the public. Progressive-minded business leaders such as GE's Gerard Swope wanted the responsible representatives to come not from popular elections but from the experience and expertise of those who had created or had risen to the top of large, successful corporations. Such social trusteeship enabled executives to use the great power of management for the good of the public. But the New Deal constructed a new system of financial accountability. It not only cordoned off the problem of corporate power from the winds of popular politics but also treated corporations as mere pieces of property, owned by and for the financial benefit of shareholders.

TWO

The Single and Most Serious Danger

There was no other decade in American history when the business executive had more power than in the 1950s. Corporations grew to unprecedented size—there had never been a comparable institution—and industry twisted into concentrated knots. New mergers made the corporation still bigger, testing the corporation's—and the public's—limits. Although, as the pollster Elmo Roper concluded, Americans were still suspicious of the private sector, the vast majority of the country agreed that big business was a good and necessary thing.[1]

Roosevelt's call for an arsenal of democracy fit to destroy fascism abroad had transformed industrial manufacturing at home into a concentrated and organized partner of the national state. The production accomplishments of American business during World War II proved once and for all that the large corporation was no longer an enemy of American democracy; it was the most powerful ally in promoting liberalism around the globe.[2] The war, in short, gave business leaders the chance to leave behind the ideological battles of the 1930s and the cloud of animosity and distrust—stirred up by radical political movements, the Pecora hearings, and labor union militancy—that had hung over big business since the Crash of 1929.[3] In the 1940s, business used advertisements, radio programs, and other PR ephemera to cast for-profit industry as the sole institution capable of conjuring the miracle of wartime production that saved democracy and, indeed, Western civilization.[4] "The defense production job is the greatest news story of our generation. All the citizenry is watching," said conservative money-giver and Sun Oil titan J. Howard Pew in 1941. "With a vigorous public relations program, competitive enterprise can dramatize its strength more successfully today than its enemies have ever been able to dramatize its occasional temporary mistakes."[5]

Other changes were afoot. Wall Street, that chief rival to managerial control, was no longer the kingmaker it once was. The House of Morgan was a ghost of its former self, a diminutive bank of marginal significance. Lower Manhattan had quieted down and grown more cautious. Industry also grew increasingly secure in the vast subsidies that began flowing from a military-industrial complex ramping up in the early Cold War, as well as by the relative peace achieved with most major unions through the so-called Treaty of Detroit, the deal that General Motors first, and then Ford and Chrysler, struck with Walter Reuther's United Auto Workers.[6] And anticommunism along with the new Keynesian consensus that growth can and should be managed by large institutions had pushed dissent to the furthest margins. An unprecedented (and to this day unequaled) economic boom, after twenty years of terrifying crisis, made potential recruits to the anticorporate cause scarce. It was a good time to be a man in a gray flannel suit.

The system of financial governance laid out in the New Deal securities laws of the early 1930s—and regulated by the Securities and Exchange Commission—receded in social and economic significance in the 1950s. Managed funds and large institutional investors were becoming bigger players on Wall Street. They were averse to risky ventures. They sought steady, predictable income from well-established industries, above all those that fed the expanding population's appetite for consumer goods and both military and civilian construction. The system of corporate democracy, by which stock market prices and shareholder votes crowned executives and directors and influenced the business decisions of a company, was in a state of decay. The annual shareholders' meeting, in the words of Adolf Berle, Jr., was little more than "a kind of ancient, meaningless ritual like some of the ceremonies that go on with the mace in the House of Lords."[7]

Although there was in the air a general consensus that the big corporation, in Peter Drucker's words, was America's "representative social institution," there were still bubbling under the surface blistering anxieties about corporate capitalism and, on the margins, growing opposition to the power of professional management.[8] A range of political and economic groups—from nascent libertarians and antitrusters to civil rights activists and corporate raiders—appealed to the language and techniques of the market as they sought to make postwar corporate order more accountable and democratic.

JAMES PECK WAS one of only five shareholders present at the annual meeting of Greyhound Bus Lines in 1948.[9] He and Bayard Rustin, both of whom were organizers of the Congress of Racial Equality, bought shares of the company the year before. They were radical pacifists who participated in the first Journey of Reconciliation, one of the earliest Freedom Rides, in which black and white activists rode on interstate buses in open disregard for transportation companies' segregation policies (which flouted the US Supreme Court's decision in the 1946 case *Morgan v. Virginia* banning racial discrimination in travel across states). Greyhound wasn't the only bus company operating in the South; neither was it the most dominant. But it was publicly traded. That made it vulnerable to shareholder activism in a way that private companies and networks of independent firms were not. When Peck rose to give a statement at the 1948 shareholders' meeting in Wilmington, Delaware, calling on the corporation to "abolish immediately the illegal practice of segregated seating," he was playing the part of the citizen-shareholder, reprising its role to fit the needs of the nascent civil rights movement.[10]

The Securities and Exchange Commission (SEC) had developed new rules just a few years earlier that allowed shareholders to propose their own candidates for director under the supervision of regulators. Rule 14a-8, sometimes called the foundation of corporate democracy, also gave shareholders access to the proxy statement, a document that every publicly traded corporation was required to send out to all those who owned stock informing them of resolutions, candidates, and other matters coming up at the annual meeting. As one SEC chairman involved in drafting these regulations put it, "entrenched and irresponsible control is as odious in corporate life as it is in political life." The purpose of SEC regulations was to give shareholders a more effective and ordinary means to participate in business policies and to hold directors and top-level managers more accountable. But SEC policy makers did not have social activists in mind when they made the rules; they thought of corporate accountability as a financial matter that could be safeguarded by protecting the fiduciary obligations of executives.[11]

Even though the new rules provided wide latitude to shareholders, Peck had a chilly reception at the Greyhound meeting. The corporation secretary refused to allow the activists to propose a resolution, though he did permit Peck and Louis Redding, a local NAACP official, to speak briefly.[12] They explained the need for the company to post notices for Greyhound employees informing them of the recent US Supreme Court case outlawing racial segregation in interstate travel.[13] Although Greyhound had not established a company-wide policy of enforcing segregation on its buses, some employees had tried to have both Peck and Rustin arrested the previous year, they said.[14] After speaking, Peck and Redding were followed by other shareholders who called them Reds and encouraged the company to let things be "as they always have been."[15]

Two years later—in 1950—Peck and Rustin submitted a proposal eight months in advance of the meeting, in compliance with SEC rules. Again, they were met with resistance from Greyhound, and the activists appealed to the federal government. By March 1950, the SEC approved as a proper subject of a shareholder proposal the following statement: "A Recommendation that Management consider the advisability of abolishing the segregated seating system in the South."[16] The company protested that the proposal was too late by that time and refused to put the resolution on the agenda or to distribute the proxy statement to shareholders. Peck and Rustin picketed on the sidewalk outside the building where the meeting was held in downtown Wilmington, distributing anti–Jim Crow leaflets and carrying signs that read "Greyhound Corporation Unfair to Negroes" and "Greyhound Follows the Dixiecrat Party Line."[17] Again, they were met with accusations from those who attended that they were communists. The only response they were able to get from the company was that black people in the South preferred segregation.[18]

As this dispute unfolded, the company's vice president, Robert Driscoll, said such matters of policy were for management to decide, not stockholders. Never mind that the resolution was framed as a recommendation, not a binding directive. But the pair decided to propose the resolution again in 1951, many months ahead of time, under the assumption that they were on sure legal footing since the SEC had already approved the resolution the previous year.[19]

That's when the rug was pulled out from under Peck and Rustin. As Peck explained in a 1951 article for the NAACP publication *The Crisis*, an SEC official named Harry Heller concluded that the proposal should not be included in the meeting because it addressed "essentially a general political, social or economic problem" for "propaganda purposes."[20] The resolution, in fact, addressed a particular company policy regarding the interstate transportation business. But the SEC decided against Peck and Rustin anyway.[21] Heller later explained, somewhat incredibly, the perspective of the SEC in a law review article: "The Commission determined that the primary motive of the stockholder was the advancement of a cause with which the stockholder had a close association, rather than the solution of a problem pertinent solely to the corporation itself."[22]

It was a frustrating setback, but Peck, a patient and veteran activist, kept pushing. With financial assistance from the Congress of Racial Equality (CORE), Peck filed suit against Greyhound in the Southern District of New York in April 1951. He sought an injunction to prevent the company from printing its proxy solicitations without the proposal.[23] Peck claimed that the SEC's reversal happened as a result of pressure from Greyhound.[24] The judge, however, was not impressed. He denied the motion to place an injunction on the company, telling Peck to appeal the decision with the SEC itself.[25]

Greyhound proceeded with the 1951 meeting without Peck and Rustin's complaints. The two planned to return the next year even if, as Peck said at the time, their chances were slim. "Even if we succeed in this step, it will not mean that our proposal will be accepted," he wrote. "At the 1948 stockholders' meeting, the man designated by the corporation as official proxy holder held proxies for over 6 million of the corporation's 9 million shares of common stock."[26] In short, management was all but guaranteed a win. What was the point of all this, then? Publicity. "Our campaign has succeeded in getting the all-important racial issue repeatedly before the public, and that is worthwhile."[27]

The promise to return to the Greyhound meeting was impeded, however, by the SEC. In January 1952, the commission issued new rules that severely restricted the criteria for legitimate proxy solicitations from stockholders. Now the commission determined that any proposals were illegitimate that promoted "general economic, political, racial, religious, social, or similar causes."[28]

Those rules stifling shareholders and empowering management would stay on the books until the 1970s, effectively removing the question of civil rights as a legitimate topic of shareholder consideration. The SEC's "alleged purpose is to protect the rights of stockholders," Peck wrote. "In effect, it works hand-in-glove with the big corporations."[29] It was not the only time that management would benefit from the steady hand of SEC rule-makers.

For an insurgent set of investors who came onto the business scene in the 1950s, the new corporate system reeked of complacency. These investors were innovators in surprising strategies of hostile takeovers, financial leveraging, and sophisticated forms of conglomeration. They took on the business establishment in high-profile clashes and headline-grabbing acquisitions. At times, such innovations in investment strategy directly lent themselves to an ideological assault on management.

Like most entrepreneurs, Louis Wolfson was driven initially not by greed or ideology but by the pragmatic convention of trying to make a business—any business—successful. Wolfson grew up in Jacksonville, Florida, and he maintained a lifelong tan to prove it. A natural athlete who boxed in his teenage years, Wolfson went to the University of Georgia in 1930 on a football scholarship. But he left Athens two years later after a season-ending shoulder injury. He went back to Jacksonville to his father's junk and scrap-metal yard, which was hit hard by the Great Depression. With this experience in the family business, Wolfson was schooled in the humblest form of arbitrage: not so much turning trash into treasure but finding value where no one else was looking.

Later branded by the *Saturday Evening Post* as "Florida's fabulous junkman," Wolfson's big break came in 1946. He bought up two shipbuilding companies on the cheap during the wave of war industry selloffs.[30] Over the next few years, he sold the assets and closed down the shipyards at great profit. Next he bought an interest in a film studio for $400,000 and later sold it for $1.2 million. In 1949, Wolfson set his sights on Capitol Transit, a congressionally chartered holding company that controlled the transit system of Washington, DC. Wolfson didn't care particularly about public transportation. He was alert, however, to Capitol Transit's unusual hoard of more than $6 million in cash reserves. Wolfson bought a controlling interest for a little over $2 million and proceeded to liquidate the company's accounts through higher dividends.[31] He rounded off the decade with a proxy fight for a Manhattan-based construction company, chalking up a majority of directorships and eventually taking the title of chief executive.[32]

At every chance he took, Wolfson bemoaned the loss of the "pioneering spirit which helped build this nation." Instead of energetic business leaders possessing the vital initiative and individualism to adapt to changing conditions and produce a vigorous economy, the managerial class had drifted off into listlessness and conformity. It was a somewhat conventional critique of big business, to be sure, but coming from the mouth of a self-styled outsider such as Wolfson, it possessed an authenticity that most critics of corporate bureaucracy noticeably lacked. Big business was overrun with "robot executives," he said, and had become devoted to rigid methods and obsessed with appearances. "These are the men—and I am sure they are well known to you—who are reluctant to attempt anything not well established by precedent," Wolfson told a group of executives. "They fear to venture into new paths or to encourage fresh ideas."[33]

Wolfson made himself an expert in doing what few were willing and able to do in the 1950s: prowl American industry for firms that were sitting on a lot of cash and were managed by a sedate board of directors and executive leadership. If management didn't have firm control of the voting stock, Wolfson pounced. While Wolfson developed a reputation as a kind of anticorporate outlaw, he was far from the only one pioneering this form of business strategy. There were fights over companies ranging from New York Central Railroad to 20th Century Fox. Perhaps the most infamous was the one that gave Wolfson the national spotlight for a brief moment in the mid-1950s. That was his battle for control of Montgomery Ward.

The retail company had been controlled by Sewell Avery, a cautious and conservative businessman who had been chairman since the early 1930s. By the time Louis Wolfson started looking through the financials, Montgomery Ward was sitting on a nest egg of nearly $300 million and hadn't opened a new store in more than a decade, leading some on Wall Street jokingly to refer to the company as the "Ward's Bank and Trust Company."[34]

The company, however, was flagging behind a much more energetic and profitable Sears, Roebuck and Company. Wolfson's plan, which he laid out in July 1954 to a group of investors on a yacht anchored in New York City's Hudson River, was to buy up stock quietly through shell companies and intermediaries.[35] But when a mistaken disclosure listed Wolfson as the purchaser of 10,000 shares, the financial press was alerted to the attempt to take control of Montgomery Ward. The share price jumped $20. Instead of backing down, Wolfson held a press conference at the Biltmore Hotel where he laid out his case against Avery, whose leadership he said was "a glaring and notorious example of private enterprise in reverse gear." In a frenetic campaign that looked like a presidential run, Wolfson traveled the country speaking about the virtues of shareholder democracy and giving his pitch to Ward shareholders. He even released a sixteen-page pamphlet called "A Rescue Plan for Your Investment and Your Rights," which explained how Ward's management was complacent and how the business was falling behind Sears.[36]

The company went to the unusual step of singling out Wolfson in its annual report for 1955, detailing his controversial and questionable record as a businessman. "The most serious problem facing your company as the new year begins is the highly publicized campaign of Louis E. Wolfson of Jacksonville, Florida to gain control of the corporation," management wrote. "We are convinced that the security of investment which you now have would be destroyed if he were placed in control."[37]

Wolfson's takeover attempt produced mixed results. Ward's counter-campaign was able to hold Wolfson back and gave up only three of the nine directorships (one of which he took himself), but the company, unlike Greyhound's response to Peck and Rustin, implemented many of the demands Wolfson had made, such as opening more catalog-sales offices and spending millions more on advertising.[38]

Despite the great expense of his campaign for Montgomery Ward, Wolfson quickly recouped what he had spent on the abortive proxy fight.[39] He soon turned to other ventures, including attempts to take over George Romney's American Motor Corporation as well as the successful financing of film and stage productions. Wolfson's penchant for high-stakes moves was not primarily ideological, it should be noted. As a gambling man who, according to one exposé of midcentury Las Vegas, lost more than $400,000 in a single night and would while away his final decades in the world of horse racing, Wolfson may have had some addictive tendencies.[40] But in subsequent years, he made himself into a kind of prophet issuing jeremiads against the management of big business. "We need to replace robot executives with constructive individualism. We must adjust the needs of the business organization for orderly procedures with society's need for individual initiative," he said. "American enterprise must permit the individual to make his fullest possible contribution, rather than relegate him to the role of a well-oiled automaton. By doing so, we can recapture the pioneering spirit that made America."[41]

Although Wolfson cast himself as a spokesman for self-starterism and a champion of inventors, entrepreneurs, and researchers, the kind of creativity he actually practiced was financial. He asserted control over publicly traded business firms by means of proxy contests and the purchasing of shares. And in this regard, he was not alone. One study found a steady increase of shareholder insurgency in the first half of the twentieth century.[42] Proxy contests ticked up in the late 1940s and early 1950s before plateauing at around twenty-five per year, an average that persisted for decades.[43] Waging a proxy fight was one way of gaining control of a corporation. By amassing a bloc of shareholders committed to voting against management, organizers could replace a sufficient number of directors to force changes at the managerial level. In a related and sometimes complementary method, speculators purchased a requisite number of shares to gain a controlling portion of outstanding securities. Such open-market bids for control were fairly common in the early 1900s and in the 1920s, before precipitously declining in the Great Depression years. Cash tender offers returned in the postwar era, reaching as many as eight per year in the late 1950s before shooting up to as many as thirty per year by the end of the next decade.

The rise of an activist Wall Street reverberated in American public life in a variety of ways. The press learned that the corporate raiders made for good copy and churned out multipage profiles and sensational headlines covering their feats. The story of Louis Wolfson, for one, was recounted in the national newspapers, magazines, and a popular paperback titled *Fight For Control* written by a journalist and PR man named David Karr, which recounted the deeds of corporate raiders in the 1950s. An encomium to the proxy fight, the book cheered on the victory of shareholders over big business.[44]

Washington turned its attention to the stock market situation in 1955 beginning with an investigation from the Senate Banking Committee. In the heat of the fight over Montgomery Ward, Sewell Avery wrote a letter to the committee asking for a prompt inquiry into Wolfson, his interests, and his motivations.[45] Avery characterized Wolfson as an upstart of dubious character whose short business record was ethically fraught at best. The Senate's investigation, which stretched from March to July of 1955, included testimony from Wolfson, representatives of Montgomery Ward (the aging Avery fell into ill health shortly after the proxy contest concluded and soon stepped down), and numerous industry leaders and experts.

Intent on maintaining its regulatory mandate, the Securities and Exchange Commission reacted swiftly to such stirrings from the Senate by proposing in May 1955 rule changes pertaining to proxy fights and formally adopting them in April 1956.[46] The rules, which required new financial disclosures from directors, nominees, and those financing or conducting proxy solicitations, made it much more difficult for would-be "proxyteers" to wage their battles in secret or utilize the element of surprise by buying up shares under assumed names or with shell corporations. More significant, the rules required that all public materials and promotions used in proxy fights such as speeches and advertisements be filed with the SEC and subject to disclosure regulations, thus limiting the ability of corporate raiders to wage the kind of high-energy publicity campaigns that Wolfson had excelled at. The SEC, using its administrative tools to react quickly to changing circumstances, stood like a floodwall against the new activism of Wall Street.[47]

The use of shareholder votes and proxy battles was a new, novel, and flashy way to fight against the managerial establishment, but there were other, more traditional methods at hand. And the old antitrust movement still fired the American imagination, this time powered by a new fuel: anticommunism.

ESTES KEFAUVER WAS one of the most ambitious politicians of the 1950s. He had the drive and political acumen of a presidential contender, but his greatest liability, arguably, was a matter of timing. For one thing, he was an old-school populist—the type who, if he'd been born a few decades earlier, would probably have cast a ballot for that firebrand William Jennings Bryan in 1896. But Kefauver lived during a moment that had little use for anything hinting at an ambitious overhaul of American politics and, especially, the system of big business. More apt was his rival Adlai Stevenson's program for a "New America," which welcomed the rising "age of abundance" for its supposed ability to improve quality of living, race relations, and poverty rates.[48] It was a program of reformism fit for the American Century, a stepping-stone to the "growth liberalism" that would characterize John F. Kennedy's presidency and the Democratic Party of the 1960s.[49] Kefauver in many ways stood outside that movement within the party.

As it so often does, this brazen, even costly, drive to excel came from an experience of loss; that is, the loss of an older brother in a swimming accident that haunted Kefauver from boyhood. He was traumatized by the regret of not being at his brother's side to help—having swum ahead—when the swift river currents took his brother under. At the crucial age of adolescence, Kefauver began to take up the burden—consciously or not—of fulfilling the hopeful but dashed expectations of his family for his older brother.[50]

Forty years later, at the height of his political power, it is difficult not to suspect the toll that this weight exacted: a presidential candidate awakened on the 1956 campaign trail by an aide holding out a water glass filled almost to the top with Scotch whisky. "Senator, it's time to get up." He drained the glass before going out into the Florida sun to shake hands and give speeches, his kerosene breath not entirely concealed by the constant chewing of Sen-Sen breath fresheners. "He was the first politician I'd ever seen up close," recalled the veteran journalist Russell Baker, "when the terrible, destructive heat of ambition was on him so intensely that he seemed to be killing himself."[51]

Kefauver directed the heat of his ambition toward two powerful systems in American society. His interrogations of mafia bosses broadcast to a national audience in 1950 was a hit with the first generation of Americans to own their own televisions. In 1957, the senator went after big business with the same fervor, such that one right-wing columnist mockingly called the hearings "the greatest TV show of them all."[52] Critics called him a populist demagogue, but, although he had a flair for showmanship (and for chasing headlines), he was sincere in his belief that the power of corporate managers was threatening to undermine democratic capitalism and, crucially, US leadership in the Cold War. (This skepticism of big business was something Kefauver came by honestly: his father had been a supporter of "The Great Commoner," William Jennings Bryan, and his first political memories were of campaigning for Woodrow Wilson when he was a boy.)

Kefauver's penchant for making himself unpopular with his Democratic colleagues hampered his ambition. Lyndon Baines Johnson, the Senate majority leader in 1956, kept him off the Foreign Relations Committee, giving the prestigious spot to the much more junior, though obviously rising star, John F. Kennedy. When Kefauver finally gained control of the Subcommittee on Antitrust and Monopoly, he made it his own, greatly expanding the size of the staff to forty-one—then the largest committee on Capitol Hill. And he stacked it with friends and advisors who had experience at the Federal Trade Commission, the Antitrust Division of the Justice Department, and the New Deal–era Temporary National Economic Committee.[53] It was from this influential perch that Kefauver would exercise the form of power at which he excelled: bringing powerful people in front of the cameras and microphones to question them in detail about the organizations they controlled—all in the name of democracy.

From 1957 until Kefauver's death in 1963, the committee investigated how corporations set prices. There was a growing concern that some industries had become insulated from and not sufficiently reactive to markets, which suggested that big business exercised a form of unaccountable (or less accountable) power under corporate capitalism. John M. Blair, an antitrust economist who became Kefauver's right-hand man in the investigation of administered prices, had written about it in his 1938 book *Seeds of Destruction: A Study in the Functional Weaknesses of Capitalism.* "We are living in an administered price system," Blair wrote, "in which a large proportion of prices are determined not by the freedom of action between supply and demand but by administrative control usually exercised by large corporations."[54] Kefauver's hearings eventually forced the Democratic Party to address the issue in its party platform in 1960. In a campaign speech touting the committee's work, Kefauver translated this indictment into plain American English: "It is a battle to preserve free enterprise. When competition is killed by a few monopolistic giants, free enterprise strangles and the small and medium-sized businessman and the small farmer strangle with it."[55]

Kefauver drew on an older tradition of antimonopoly that held business power in suspicion for its tendency—always to be vigilantly watched—to undermine republican virtues. It was a political tradition that was more of a natural fit for the nineteenth century than the twentieth. And, indeed, suspicion of big business was dominant in the early republic and, again, in the Gilded Age. But by the postwar era, worries over business power had come to seem obsolete, even un-American. Perhaps it's for this reason that Kefauver liked to trot out in speeches an apocryphal prophecy from Abraham Lincoln, which did the convenience of grounding his anticorporate aspersions in the most American of American leaders: "Corporations have been enthroned and an era of corruption in high places will follow," Lincoln supposedly said in a dubious quotation that began circulating during the era of the Agrarian Populists, "and the money power of the country will endeavor to prolong its reign by working upon the prejudices of the people until all wealth is aggregated in a few hands and the Republic is destroyed."[56] The apocryphal Lincoln supplied a phrase for the title of Kefauver's last book, which was published after his death and summarized the key findings of his committee, *In a Few Hands: Monopoly Power in America*.[57]

In the opening hearing for the Senate investigation into administered prices in July 1957, Kefauver indicted the executive branch's enforcement of antitrust laws. It was the so-called rule of reason that erroneously admitted that "size and power, no matter how great, do not constitute a violation of the Sherman Act," he said. But all of that was water over the dam. "The reality is that within a broad area of the economy," he said, "prices are set, not automatically by the unseen hand of competition, as are the prices of wheat and hogs, but by the conscious and deliberate action of corporation managers who have the power to set prices."[58] But, after years of conducting hearings, he was forced to concede that "monopoly is seldom, if ever, a blatant affair" and that "it lies behind the lines, unobtrusive and unseen," he wrote. "Sheer familiarity with the level of prices for a commodity, and the fact that there is no spectacular increase, blunts our sense to the presence of monopoly."[59]

In successive industries, from prescription drugs and automobiles to steel and bakeries, the committee traced the unobtrusive and largely unseen lines of monopoly power that were threaded throughout the economy. Kefauver's committee was good at drumming up controversy and generating headlines about, for example, the pharmaceutical industry, which hid known side effects from doctors and kept drug prices high, or automobile manufacturers, which neglected to make vehicles safer while ensuring new models would become obsolete as quickly as possible.[60] His staff presented the most incendiary revelations just in time for newspaper deadlines and developed close working relationships with reporters. Kefauver and committee staffers appeared on television programs such as *Meet the Press* and on a weekly radio program from Kefauver's office.

By exposing the misdeeds of big business, which could

only be accomplished with exhaustive investigations and with muckraking-style press releases and leaks, the managers could be held to account. That's what Kefauver meant when he called big business expanding into more and more industries the "single and most serious danger today."[61] The management of corporations had become untethered from the oversight of markets. No longer did managers take prices, reacting as humble servants to the desires of consumers. Now they administered prices. This was, as Kefauver was always eager to point out, a threat to America's ability to represent itself credibly as the leader of a democratic economic system. But in lieu of Kefauver's wish for an ambitious antitrust program of decentralization and enforced competition, his solution—publicity and federal oversight—was always ad hoc and ultimately reactive. And, importantly, it depended on the force of his personality to sustain and wield the power of a Senate committee. It was not to last.

By the time Wilma Soss appeared at Senator Kefauver's administered-prices hearings in 1959, she was already a well-known fixture at annual shareholders' meetings across the country, where she regularly showed up to question, for example, the management of General Motors about consumer safety or AT&T about its stingy dividends. That April, Soss testified at length about executive compensation plans, including bonuses and stock options, that enriched management at the expense of shareholders, consumers, and workers. She needed little prodding from Kefauver, who only occasionally interjected with commentary on how her testimony demonstrated the need for the latest regulatory bill under consideration.[62] Soss was fluent in the language of corporate democracy, a discourse that cast concerned shareholders as the true custodians of business in contrast to "un-American" executives. "I have been at meetings," Soss said, "where I thought I was in Russia."[63]

Such brash rhetoric was but one tool in Soss's bag of communication methods. A successful public relations consultant from San Francisco, Soss had made a name for herself in 1949 when she attended the annual meeting of US Steel clad in a late-nineteenth-century style two-piece outfit with an enormous purple plumed hat. "This costume represents management's thinking on stockholder relations," she told the press.[64] It wasn't the last costume she would wear to a highly publicized meeting. Years later, in 1960, she dressed as a janitor complete with a mop and pail for the Columbia Broadcasting System's meeting, at which she called for the network, then embroiled in a years-long quiz show scandal, to clean up its act.[65] When costumes no longer got the attention she sought, Soss took to interrupting meetings and getting herself thrown out—sometimes literally carried out by security.[66] Dubbed by her critics "Queen of the Gadflies" and "the Dorothy Parker of stockholders' meetings," she was an inveterate attender from the 1940s until her death in the 1980s.

But if Soss was a performer—and that she definitely was, perhaps to a fault—she was deadly serious about her mission to transform stockholder relations: not only to make management more accountable to the interests and (importantly) the judgment of those who owned shares but also to revolutionize the way shareholders themselves related to the corporation. She was particularly interested in recruiting women to become more involved. After seeing how dismissive management had been of her participation at annual meetings and realizing that more than half of US Steel's shareholders were women, Soss founded the Federation of Women Shareholders in American Business in 1947. "Hundreds of women called my office to offer their support," she told the *New Yorker*: "I suddenly realized that women investors constituted a group that had never been organized."[67] She called on US Steel to appoint a woman to the board of directors. "It's a shameful fact that women own companies but can't get top jobs in them," she said.

Not merely ahead of her time on gender roles, Soss was driven by Cold War concerns. She identified women as a social group that needed to be made a part of big business, lest they fall for the "siren song of statism." Casting the movement of common stockholders as the last line of defense against socialism, she called for a "people's enterprise system" in which "the corporate vote is cherished and deemed a civilian duty equal to that of casting the political ballot."[68]

Soss did not start the popular movement for shareholders; in fact, she arrived on the scene just as it was reaching a crescendo. The main personality behind midcentury corporate democracy was Lewis D. Gilbert, who, along with his brother John J. Gilbert, attended more than 100 annual meetings every year for fifty years.[69]

This was how the Gilberts explained the stakes of the 1950s: corporate democracy versus unchecked power. And the way that they defined corporate democracy was in terms of shareholder control—not just control over the election of directors or occasional votes on resolutions but increasingly direct control over the business decisions and strategies of major corporations. Theirs was not a movement for shareholder value, narrowly defined in the abstractions of financialization. They advocated for regional meetings in convenient locations in order to encourage popular attendance and other reforms, such as allowing floor resolutions and improving financial transparency.[70] Even their demands for higher dividends, for example, were justified in terms of keeping management accountable to shareholders—imagined by Wilma Soss and Lewis Gilbert as both citizens and owners of the corporation. And although this was a marginal movement, the Gilberts' tenacity kept their demands in the spotlight as they tussled with chairmen and executives year in and year out. Soon their annual report sold more than 8,000 copies per year, purchased primarily by common shareholders, a relatively small but highly prized demographic representing 10 percent of households in the United States.[71]

Most of these shareholders knew little or nothing about these demands, but some did rise to join the fray. Lewis Gilbert, for example, got inspired to attend his first meetings during the early Great Depression as revelations of financial misconduct seized America's consciousness—the misconduct soon spotlighted by the Pecora hearings. Possessing Consolidated Gas Company of New York stock—a gift from his parents—Gilbert one day passed by homeless encampments to attend the company's annual meeting—to "do something that would help."[72] Not knowing the rules of the business meeting, Gilbert rose up to speak and was interrupted by a motion to adjourn. Such indifference to shareholders, he recalled later, was what prodded him to "fight this silent dictatorship over other people's money."[73] His first big dustup came at the 1937 meeting of the Bethlehem Steel Company at which he proposed that Charles M. Schwab, longtime company head and chairman, receive a drastically smaller salary. The annoyingly young Gilbert, then only twenty-nine years old, was threatened with physical violence by the company president.[74] No matter. He returned the next year to demand that Schwab not take compensation at all.[75]

With family wealth (which was one reason he could spend his entire spring jumping on one plane after another to attend shareholders' meetings), Lewis Gilbert and his brother founded Corporate Democracy, Inc., which produced an annual report from 1939 to 1979 covering the meetings, resolutions, and governance issues of hundreds of publicly traded corporations. At hundreds of stockholder meetings over the decades, Gilbert had confrontations similar to the one he had with Bethlehem Steel, usually with similar results and consistent attention from the business press. Dubbed early on as a "corporate gadfly," the epithet stuck. Gilbert, for his part, considered himself a sincere defender of democracy. "I have always believed we cannot have good political government unless we have good corporate government," he wrote. "Trying to reform political life without first cleaning up corporation management is simply putting the cart before the horse."[76]

THE RAIDERS AND ACTIVISTS garnered big newspaper headlines for their attacks on management, but a fringe of academic economists and legal theorists were quietly developing a far more devastating critique of executives—and big-business liberalism. A young lawyer named Henry Manne, though often forgotten today, would become its most consequential proponent.

The descendant of Romanian Jews, Manne was one of two boys born in New Orleans to a family that found its livelihood in shopkeeping. As Henry's grandfather had done in Missouri, Henry's father opened a dry-goods store in Memphis a few years after Henry's birth, and it was there in the 1930s and 1940s that Henry gained firsthand experience with business. "My whole life's philosophy can be traced back to those early beginnings," he remembered.[77] After World War II, Manne attended nearby Vanderbilt University where he came under the influence of an economics professor who urged him to continue his studies in law at the University of Chicago.[78] There Manne shed his interest in labor law for a less conventional libertarianism.[79]

The beachhead of a new, heterodox view of the corporation was the law school and the economics department at the University of Chicago. And the main leader of this movement, at least at first, was a professor named Aaron Director. A "steel-minded devotee of free markets," as Manne remembered him, Director belonged to a libertarian circle of scholars that included Friedrich Hayek, Milton Friedman, George Stigler, and W. Allen Wallis.[80] With money from the right-wing William Volker Fund, the libertarian stalwart Henry Simons brought Director to Chicago in

1946.[81] Simons understood that Director was the key to keeping alive and promoting what he called "traditional liberal" ideas in American politics.[82]

Director excelled at that task. He was one of the early members of the Mont Pelerin Society, an organization that promoted neoliberal thought and which Hayek founded in 1947.[83] With his brother-in-law Milton Friedman, Director participated in public events promoting right-wing economic ideas.[84] Director never finished his dissertation or wrote a major monograph, but in many ways he helped to establish a field called "law and economics" through his institutional labors—he established the field's titular journal, for example, and mentored budding law students such as Robert Bork and Richard Posner, both of whom would go on to become leading legal theorists and jurists.[85] But, in the long run, perhaps his most important student was Manne.

Under the wing of Director, Manne was introduced both to the ideological landscape of the postwar conservative movement and, more important, the method of using economic theory to understand the law and legal institutions—and almost everything else. "It was clear to me very early that economics was important in most of the courses I was taking in law school," Manne said.[86] Director famously argued, for example, that market competition naturally "destroys *all* types of monopoly" and that the government alone was capable of creating the kind of concentrated economic power one sees in a genuine monopoly. One could hardly imagine an assertion that ran more counter to the progressive and New Deal liberalism that had dominated American economic and political thought for five decades. Director gave little proof of such claims, but what he lacked in evidence, he made up for in rhetorical bluster.[87]

Director's approach to legal education was idiosyncratic and almost completely unheard of in law schools at the time. "With the exception of perhaps six to eight people at the University of

Chicago and four or five more scattered around the country," Manne said, "there was literally no remnant of libertarian philosophy in academic economics in America."[88] After graduating, the ambitious Manne tried his hand at a conventional academic career. He never shed the ideas that he learned from Director, and he remained preoccupied with Director's mission: to make an economically libertarian method of legal education mainstream.[89]

The young Henry Manne watched with frustration as the SEC proposed and adopted new rules that protected management elites from hostile corporate takeovers in the mid-1950s—takeovers that Manne believed were the surest signs of an active and healthy market. An outsider himself trained by outsiders to his profession, perhaps it was natural for Manne to identify with the rebel Louis Wolfson.[90] Director was the immediate source for such iconoclasm, but Manne found other, more remote mentors as well. After graduating from the University of Chicago and while attending Yale Law School, Manne spent his free time reading the Austrians Ludwig von Mises and Friedrich Hayek, neither of whom found much of a reception in the United States—at least not until Hayek won the so-called Nobel Prize in Economics (formally, the Sveriges Riksbank Prize in Economic Sciences in Memory of Alfred Nobel) in the 1970s. (That prize, by the way, was concocted by economists who invented their own Nobel in a bid to give the discipline greater legitimacy—almost seventy years after the Swedish chemist Alfred Nobel's posthumous foundation began awarding laureates in literature, peace, physics, and so on.)

Ludwig von Mises offered, for example, a theory of what he called "praxeology" to explain how human decision-making functions in an individualistic and economically rational manner. A social collective "has no existence and reality outside of the individual members' actions," he explained.[91] This was a thoroughly contractual and atomistic worldview that looked askance at institutions of common life: society, the state, or corporations. Where liberal orthodoxy prized collective action for the prosperity, justice, and rationality it had achieved, von Mises understood society only in terms of the fictitious "solitary individual, acting on his own behalf only and independent of fellow men."[92]

As for Friedrich Hayek, his 1945 article "The Use of Knowledge in Society" laid the conceptual foundations for the idea that markets produce "spontaneous order." As in his best-selling book, *The Road to Serfdom*, Hayek pitted planning against markets, marking out the latter as the most efficient mechanism for coordinating human action. Hayek imagined every discrete market transaction not just as an exchange of commodities but also as a mechanism for communicating information.[93] "It is more than a metaphor to describe the price system as a kind of machinery for registering change," he wrote, "or a system of telecommunications which enables individual producers to watch merely the movement of a few pointers, as an engineer might watch the hands of a few dials, in order to adjust their activities to changes of which they may never know more than is reflected in the price movement."[94] Markets, in short, are efficient because they are epistemological networks that run through the whole of society and channel what would otherwise be the chaos of specialization into a general kind of order.

Manne understood that the dark chink in the armor of midcentury corporate liberalism was its failure to explain the meaning of social responsibility or to develop enforceable standards for the managerial performance of social duties. Without the market as a guide or without law as a predictable rule, the evaluation of managers had no objectivity. The only objective measure available was shareholder value—an idea he had become thoroughly convinced of decades before almost anyone else would. "It is a certainty that no company's stock ever appreciated in value because of a charitable contribution made by that company," he wrote.[95] Let the price system govern—let markets and individual market actors pursue profit—this was the rallying cry that Manne heard in his formative years of legal and economic education and to which he added his voice as a junior professor.

Even as Manne and his fellow libertarians made the case that business leaders were not adequately exacting in their pursuit of profits, the anxiety bubbling under the surface of American political culture expressed almost exactly the opposite—that big business had become *too* rational, conformist, and focused on the bottom line. The reading public developed an appetite for sociological studies of the corporation and psychological examinations of the managerial personality such as *The Lonely Crowd*, *White Collar*, and *The Organization Man*, all academic studies turned popular paperbacks. These books probed the decline of American individualism in the rise of bureaucratic business. And films such as *The Man in the Gray Flannel Suit* (first a book, then a 1956 movie starring Gregory Peck) and *Executive Suite* (also based on a novel) told stories in which anxious characters found themselves caught between the petty avarice and ambition of management and their own personal misgivings about the pursuit of a successful career. The annual shareholders' meeting often served as the backdrop for underdog stories about the small-time stockholder standing up to the big boss. Such was the case in *The Solid Gold Cadillac*, a 1956 comedy about a marginal investor in a billion-dollar corporation who leads a stockholder revolt and replaces the board of directors.[96] (The main character was based on Wilma Soss.)

In each case, the message was remarkably consistent: corporations alienated workers and pushed around small businessmen, investors, and consumers—all the while amassing huge profits. Americans, still ready to accept and even celebrate corporate capitalism amid the postwar boom, nevertheless remained deeply ambivalent about the concentration of economic power. And, as secure as the man in the gray flannel suit was in his economic and political position in those years, he was never free from care—not entirely. The anxious line of reasoning that lurked in the minds of business leaders was that this everyday ambivalence might somehow be transformed into something more organized and more threatening. The question was what to do about it.

THREE

Building the City of God

In a confidential memo to executives, directors, and managers, the DuPont chemical company sounded the alarm that American popular culture was coming after big business in the 1950s. Tracing various characteristics of the opposition's unremitting assault (and name-dropping some critics familiar from the previous chapter), "The Attack on Bigness" memo enumerated the aspersions cast on industrial capitalism in the postwar era. Corporations were a Goliath pushing around small businesses and consumers, all the while amassing profits and using the Republican Party as a chosen tool in politics. The nameless, faceless bureaucracy of the corporation was undermining the individualistic character of the American people. Or so it was claimed.

"Day after day, in press and forum, in television, imaginative literature and in scholarly treatise," the memo read, "are nurtured the myths of gargantuan, irresponsible, anti-social concentrations of power; of ruthless, profit-hungry managements; and of large business smashing small, denying to Americans the right to 'freedom of opportunity.'" The internal memo counseled executives and plant managers that they should not ignore the damaging effects of pop culture. To do so would expose DuPont to significant risks, even perhaps the "ultimate dissolution of the company" and the end of free enterprise along with it.

DuPont became an industrial juggernaut by manufacturing gunpowder and then dynamite. By the time Harold Brayman, a former newspaper columnist, became the company's public relations chief and circulated this memo, the company had expanded into the production of everything from polyester and nylon to Lycra and body armor—with 90,000 employees and $1.8 billion in yearly revenue.[1] Brayman recommended a conventional solution: shore up public opinion favorable to big business. As he had put it in a public lecture to executives, "the businessman is normally reluctant to talk out loud, he frequently shuns the spotlight, and is content with plugging his wares, not himself."[2] As a result, the consumer products of the era were well known—even celebrated as signs of affluence and American success—while the businessman remained "obscured from view." Executives and managers must take a more active role, he counseled, in explaining to the public how the success of private business was for the good of society. It was a fairly timid if vague set of recommendations, amounting to little more than what was conventional PR wisdom by the mid-1950s—and an underwhelming prescription for what might be a potentially terminal diagnosis. Missing, too, was any sense that corporations had done something to contribute to this supposed crisis.

Whereas Brayman and his colleagues sounded a defensive, even McCarthyist note about a popular political culture secretly and deliberately turned against private business by an ungrateful, possibly radical, group of artists, intellectuals, and producers, others within the business community were open to interpreting popular anxiety about corporate power in more realistic terms. Consider the words of Thomas Watson, Jr., the renowned president of IBM. "Bigness itself is a relatively new phenomenon in our society," he explained in a series of public lectures sponsored by the consulting group McKinsey. "Even if nothing else had changed, the vast concentrations of power in our society would demand that businessmen reconsider their responsibilities for the broader public welfare."[3] Watson, whose firm at the time employed nearly 150,000 people and had more than $1 billion in yearly revenue, offered a daring diagnosis of the dramatic transformations of the capitalist system over the past several decades.[4] He spoke of the rise of the *new capitalism*—an economic system less driven by competition and led by corporations that were freed from the imperatives of cutthroat profit-seeking.

But the difference between the DuPont memo and Watson's lectures was not simply a difference in tone or in diagnosis. The memo circulated by Brayman was more focused on preserving the special interests of business—more akin to defenses that right-wing business leaders led against the New Deal. Watson's lectures, by contrast, appealed to executives as representatives of all of the major interests of society—workers, consumers, community members, and suppliers *in addition to* stockholders and even the corporation itself.

Watson joined other liberals, among whom were many academics and intellectuals, in promoting this movement in its earliest years. The language of *business statesmanship* was popular during those years—and that's the term primarily used in this chapter. But whatever language they used, the key problem that Watson and his allies puzzled over was how to properly balance the imperatives of private interests and the public good within the corporate system.

The irony was that this debate also generated new doubts about the relationship between business power and American democracy. To what degree did the Cold War economy actually constitute a new capitalism? Surely competition still existed—or, more troublingly, if it in fact no longer existed, how could this system be considered democratic? And, perhaps most significant, who got to decide what it meant to be responsible? In other words, if not shareholders, who managed the managers?

ADOLF BERLE, JR., was one liberal who had become somewhat embarrassed by his alarmist attitude about the abuse of corporate power decades earlier.[5] By the 1950s, he had gone from stints in the Roosevelt and Truman administrations to positions at liberal thank tanks and back to his perch as a professor at Columbia University Law School. The ultimate corporate liberal, he was an eager, vocal supporter of business leaders who wanted to think beyond the profit motive.

But, to his credit, if he had become somewhat self-satisfied with the accomplishments of the New Deal generation, few disagreed with him. In those years, public intellectuals such as economist John Kenneth Galbraith argued that managerial experts had solved most of the major economic conflicts, and sociologist Daniel Bell asserted that the political ideologies that had driven global politics for more than 100 years were now obsolete. Even left-wing critics of New Deal liberalism such as C. Wright Mills came to believe that the corporate system—for all of its faults and injustices—was fundamentally immovable. Most Americans now worked for, bought from, and lived their lives under the shadow of big business.[6] Celebrate it or complain about it, corporate capitalism was a fact of life.[7] Once a question just a half-generation earlier, for both supporters and critics the modern corporation was now a given.

When Adolf Berle looked around at the mid-twentieth-century world of business, he saw many of the same signs that troubled him so deeply decades earlier in the years when he was writing *The Modern Corporation and Private Property*. For one thing, industrial concentration wasn't going away. It appeared, rather, that competition was in further decline. Economist Maurice Adelman showed in a widely cited study the presence of pervasive oligopoly, including the fact that 135 firms owned 45 percent of industrial assets and the 200 largest employers represented less than 1 percent of all business firms.[8]

Corporate consolidations have usually come in waves, and the most recent one had not been that long ago. An unusually dire Federal Trade Commission (FTC) report found evidence of a merger wave in the late 1940s driven by anticompetitive conspiracy. Large firms sought to consolidate wartime gains and expand their market positions by acquiring small businesses.[9] For example, as part of its postwar expansion strategy, the defense contractor and aircraft manufacturer Northrop purchased a small company called Salsbury Motors that specialized in making scooters.[10] On a much larger scale, the powerful Mellon family's Pittsburgh Coal Company merged in 1945 with the Rockefeller family's Consolidation Coal Company to become the largest bituminous coal producer in American history.[11] Such stories played out across the country in those years, with 1,800 firms disappearing into consolidation between 1940 and 1947.[12] "If nothing is done to check the growth in concentration," the FTC warned in 1948, "either the giant corporations will ultimately take over the country, or the government will be impelled to step in and impose some form of direct regulation."[13]

Perhaps the surest sign that corporate concentration was on the American mind was the enormous popularity of *Fortune* magazine's "500 list," first published in 1955. Enumerating the top companies' revenues, assets, and profits, it was an annual celebration of a peculiarly American feeling of the sublime—the corporate sublime.[14] "The jobs we want done require bigness—big thinking, big organization, daring experimentation," the public relations leader Earl Newsom wrote. "Americans, more than any other people on earth, like bigness."[15]

As competition between firms waned, consumer markets also grew more anemic. Economist Gardiner Means, one-time collaborator with Adolf Berle, had conceived of the idea of administered prices.[16] No longer did the largest firms rely on the market mechanism—the vast network of interactions between buyers and sellers—to set prices; instead, a relatively small number of managers within highly concentrated industries set prices for a predetermined period of time. Means originally used the concept of administered prices to explain how inflexible prices and production prolonged the Great Depression. "When the General Motors management," Means explained, "sets its wholesale price for a particular model and holds that price for 6 months or a year the price is an administered price."[17] But after World War II, the idea served the purposes of intellectuals and policy makers to criticize unfair prices and the market insularity of big business.[18] At his committee hearings on antitrust issues, Senator Estes Kefauver, for example, gave sustained attention to the problem of administered prices.

And then there were the financial markets. In the late 1940s, big corporations were awash in cash. Profits soared. Executives did not deflate ballooning corporate profits with a surge in dividends or massive cuts to consumer prices. They plowed "retained earnings" back into their companies, financing the construction of new industrial plants and research and development. This was a relatively new phenomenon in the history of American business. As recently as 1940, retained earnings had eclipsed long-term debt on the balance sheets of most corporations, and, by 1947, retained earnings shot past capital procured by securities markets—both common and preferred stock—and would remain the largest financial source for the rest of the twentieth century.[19] During the immediate postwar period, American business had depended on retained earnings to furnish about 70 percent of new capital necessary for working capital, new equipment, and other needs.[20]

This revolution in corporate finance had far-reaching implications, the most significant being that it further consolidated managerial control over the corporation. No longer did executives have to be as reliant on long-term debt investments or the issuance of new securities. The tire manufacturer B. F. Goodrich, for example, planned a $200 million expansion, building new plants and acquiring other companies, largely financed by retained earnings.[21] The rising significance of retained earnings did not, of course, render those sources of capital obsolete—they still played a powerful role in the fortunes of big business. But huge pools of retained earnings (the kind that Louis Wolfson was trying to sniff out) provided executives with much greater leverage. That meant big buyers and sellers in the financial markets could not force executives to be "accountable," and perhaps nobody else could, either. As Berle himself noted, "Major corporations in most instances do not seek capital. They form it themselves."[22]

In the absence of competitive markets and the political will to enforce disruptive antitrust policies, corporate liberals advanced an innovative idea: markets in and of themselves do not make an economy democratic. What else is a big corporation but an insti-

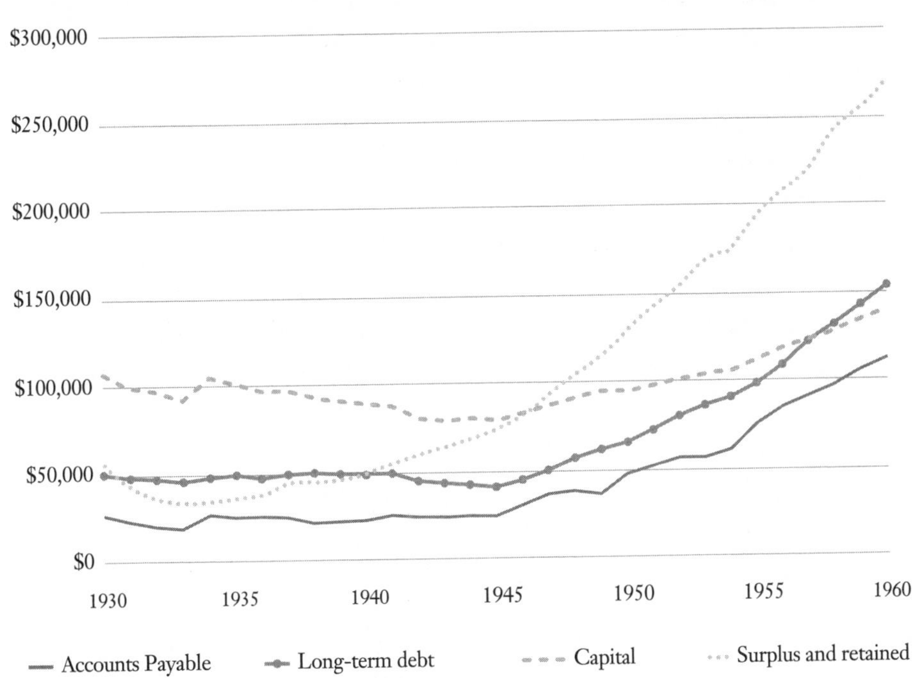

tution that replaces small-business owners and self-employed proprietors and the market exchange that went along with them? Berle called this a "twentieth century capitalist revolution" that, he believed, encompassed both the Soviet and the Western world. "In many countries, its instrument was one or another form of socialist organization. In the United States, the chief instrument has proved to be the modern giant corporation."[23] As he put it elsewhere, "The capital is there; and so is capitalism. The waning factor is the capitalist."[24]

Instead of the capitalist, there was the professional manager.[25] The manager, not the capitalist, could perhaps be trusted to act on behalf of a wide range of social interests in the absence of the accountability of market competition. It was precisely the end of competition and profit seeking that liberated the manager to seek higher aims—to seek the City of God, as Berle strangely put it once in a book where he compared 1950s America to the tumultuous moment in which Augustine of Hippo lived—at the end of an old world and the beginning of a new one. Once freed from the masters of Wall Street and the narrow-mindedness of ruinous competition, the businessman could become the business statesman. Or, at least, such was Berle's cautious hope.

Others were not nearly so cautious, convinced as they were that they lived in a new world where the old rules no longer applied.

With the kind of confidence that comes from having no opponents, business leaders and their liberal academic allies were freer to reimagine corporate capitalism in new and expansive terms. The language they used was not always consistent, but the message was typically the same: the political economy had entered into a new phase of development. "Many thoughtful persons have observed that the United States has evolved a wholly new form of capitalism," wrote Ralph J. Cordiner, president of General Electric.[26] "The modern corporation has undermined the preconceptions of classical economic theory as effectively as the quantum undermined classical physics at the beginning of the 20th century," wrote Gardiner Means in a widely cited article for *Science* in 1957. Means enthused over the development of "collective capitalism," even if he believed "we are still some way from understanding how it really works and what its imperatives are."[27]

John Kenneth Galbraith developed in those years his famous theory of countervailing power to explain that economic activity was coordinated through a self-generating system, by which groups such as trade unions, corporations, and consumer organizations checked one another's power.[28] "Competition, which, at least since the time of Adam Smith, has been viewed as the autonomous regulator of economic activity and as the only available regulatory mechanism apart from the state, has, in fact, been superseded," he wrote.[29] The "evident" alternative to competition, Galbraith asserted, was either regulation or planning.[30]

Beginning in the late 1940s, business leaders and their intellectual allies began developing their own form of economic planning, outlining a new form of capitalism in the speeches of business elites, in articles for management journals such as *Harvard Business Review* and *California Management Review*, in business magazines such as *Fortune* and *BusinessWeek*, and in the public relations campaigns and advertisements of top companies. Nothing so complete as a formal theory, it came to pass as the commonsense explanation of an economy that was no longer governed primarily by the laws of competition or the imperative of profit seeking, but by the expertise of managers.

A small group of Harvard sociologists had noticed this new business ideology threaded through advertisements, speeches, trade journals, and other corporate documents.[31] In 1956, they published *The American Business Creed*, a study that showed how the "managerial" strand of capitalism was in the process of supplanting the "classical" version—though that supposed classical version was always more of a myth than a historical reality.[32] "The managerial writers," the sociologists wrote, "see the break with the past as so sharp that the whole system is moving toward a new kind of homogeneity—of large professionally managed, socially oriented corporations."[33] It was an announcement of corporate power declared in the language of expert deliberation and tones of pragmatic realism.[34]

But it wasn't just academics who took notice. The editors of *Fortune* put the matter in a manner more fitting to the house style of Henry Luce's *Time-Life* empire. "There has occurred a great transformation, of which the world as a whole is as yet unaware," they wrote in *U.S.A.: The Permanent Revolution* in 1951, "the speed of which has outstripped the perception of the historians, the commentators, the writers of business books—even any businessmen themselves."[35] The task of the intellectual as much as the businessman was to discard the faded stereotypes fit for an earlier era and craft a new understanding of things. One key part of that project was to redefine the purpose of profits. "The great happy paradox of the profit motive in the American system," wrote the editors of *Fortune*, "is that management, precisely because it is in business to make money years on end, cannot concentrate exclusively on making money here and now."[36]

Others were more exuberant about the supposed obsolescence of self-interest. "The profit motive is, for most practical purposes, on its last leg as the hallmark of American capitalist motivation," wrote management writer Theodore Levitt, who would later popularize the term *globalization*. "The desire for personal and institutional approbation, recognition, security, and approval, and the fear of mutual self-destruction and political attack have created a new and complex set of underlying motives." A new kind of capitalism was overtaking the country, Levitt contended, one made in the image of "industrial statesmanship."[37]

Business executives and their intellectual allies gambled that there was yet another alternative: that if they could show convincingly that they exercised their power responsibly—that they used, as it were, undemocratic means to democratic ends—they could balance the expectations of a liberal, democratic society with an increasingly uncompetitive and hierarchical economy.

In 1948, leaders of the largest industrial firms in the United States found themselves in the unusual position of having to explain their financial success at highly publicized congressional hearings. Chairmen and executives from General Motors, US Steel, and General Electric, among other large corporations, came to Washington, DC, to answer charges that big business was making too much money and that its irresponsible profits—up more than 60 percent in a four-year span—were driving up inflation.[38] Business earnings, asserted one Republican senator, were "large enough to warrant the diversion of a considerable part of them into lower prices, higher wages, or both."[39]

Eager to nip in the bud the suggestion that they were reprising the role of the robber barons, executives produced financial statements showing how workers, consumers, and the public benefited as much as corporations from the 62 percent increase in profits between 1945 and 1948.[40]

This was a marked change in strategy. Not too many years before, when Franklin Roosevelt was still in office, a prominent coalition of business leaders formed organizations such as the Liberty League that cast their opposition to the New Deal as a defense of capitalist individualism and free enterprise against the looming threat of collectivism.[41] Now, a new generation of business leaders defended free enterprise in a reworked set of collectivist terms: they asked that the economic system be evaluated primarily by the good that business did for the public.

Marvin Coyle, a longtime General Electric officer, described profits as little more than a by-product of efficient production and only secondarily as compensation for investors.[42] Robert Dunlop, president of the Sun Oil Company—the company built by J. Howard Pew—agreed. "Adequate profits are essential for business and industry to fulfill their responsibilities to serve the general welfare," he told the committee. "Our interest in a competitive economy is not as an end in itself, but as a means to an end."[43]

Executives spoke in the language of business statesmanship as they sought to avert the critical eye of the public and government regulators. General Electric's Charles Wilson told Congress that the company's prices and profits did not "end with its stockholders." "Even more important is the indirect impact upon these individuals as members of our national economy, both in peace and in war." Profit was the food on which America had grown to a position of "unchallenged" leadership and usefulness in the world's economy."[44] The goal was to share the "benefits of progress," he said, as well as the benefits of efficiency, labor-saving machinery, and other wonders of modern industry with a variety of groups: customers, workers, owners, and the nation as a whole.[45] Wilson articulated the new, conventional wisdom about corporations when he famously told Congress a decade later, "For years I thought what was good for our country was good for General Motors, and vice versa. The difference did not exist. Our company is too big. It goes with the welfare of the country."[46]

If proponents of the new capitalism were correct that business leaders were no longer the errand boys for Wall Street, and if, furthermore, management had kicked the acquisitive vices of old-school capitalists, an understandable question came to mind: What right did executives have to maintain control of the most powerful economic institutions in the world? General Motors (GM), to take a prominent example, was the largest industrial corporation in the United States in 1955, with more than 575,000 employees and nearly $10 billion in yearly revenue. Some estimate that GM was responsible for more than 3 million jobs in total, if you take into account suppliers and employee service providers—which would represent about 5 percent of the civilian labor force.[47]

Increasingly, business leaders—even right-wing executives who made up the National Association of Manufacturers—no longer defended the narrow, sectarian interests of their particular class.[48] At least not so openly as they had before. Now they claimed to represent the interests of all members of society. They defended their power with claims that they were the only ones capable of making the corporation serve the public. And, in the process, they gave away a lot of money.

CORPORATE PHILANTHROPY, which was given a federal imprimatur with the Revenue Act of 1935, took off in the middle of the twentieth century.[49] By the time the New Jersey Supreme Court ruled in the 1953 *A.P. Smith Manufacturing* case that a corporation could make donations to colleges and universities even if there was no immediate benefit for the corporation, corporations were cleared to use business resources for purposes that did not immediately benefit shareholders.[50]

Corporate giving reached new heights in 1945 on account of the productivity of the war industries, but it subsequently plateaued. Six years later, corporations were making checks to tax-deductible charity organizations as they never had before. The *New York Times* heralded the new era with a headline: "New Giant in Giving: Big Business."[51]

The National Planning Association (NPA), a nonprofit organized by business and labor leaders, published a popular pamphlet in 1951 called *The Five Percent* (named after the IRS regulation that corporations could make tax-deductible donations of up to 5 percent of pre-tax income). The pamphlet was a toolkit for upper-level managers and directors to find ways to increase their giving and to find good reasons to do it. Management had "new obligations toward its stockholders," the NPA said, to reduce their tax burdens, which were becoming heavier in the 1950s.

And, besides, philanthropy had other benefits. A well-planned donation to a university for the creation of a new department or research center, for example, could benefit a firm's research and development. Corporations would also benefit by hiring from a pool of well-trained graduates. Other examples included Ford Motor Company's college scholarship program that supported the children of its employees. Or take the example of R. H. Macy and Company's contribution to Central Park in New York City that funded the creation of a cherry orchard around one of its lakes. "This contribution, although not large in financial terms," the pamphlet read, "is nevertheless appropriate and dramatic since it . . . creates a friendly attitude toward Macy's on the part of the city's residents and visitors."[52] Responsibility could come with rewards.

But *The Five Percent* was not concerned solely with self-interest. Corporations, the NPA claimed, had a social obligation to support educational, scientific, and welfare programs as their own and not leave them up to the government alone. Such expenditures were "social obligations" that corporate management had toward the communities in which they did their business.[53]

One major theorist of corporate philanthropy was a man named Richard Eells, a public relations researcher at General Electric and eventually a professor of business at Columbia University. He called on the company to give employees incentives and the time off to participate in local political campaigns and causes.[54] He was instrumental in directing corporate donations to local charities and community chests, private nonprofit corporations, and public arts projects. Between 1951 and 1957, General Electric increased its private giving by 232 percent. The same went for other major companies: Standard Oil of New Jersey by more than 192 percent, US Steel by 220 percent, and Corning by 288 percent.[55] As the following chart shows, corporate giving in aggregate increased dramatically throughout the 1940s and 1950s.

In practice, business leaders engaged in so much ad hoc problem-solving that any sampling evokes a chaotic scene of corporate do-goodery. A steel company picked up the tab for a rebuilt water system in east Chicago.[56] Ford, General Electric, and Chase Manhattan developed programs to encourage employee contributions to political parties.[57] Sears sponsored rural school programs such as 4-H and Future Farmers of America.[58] Eastman Kodak donated $30,000 to a local hospital.[59] Anheuser-Busch bought the St. Louis Cardinals baseball organization, outbidding an out-of-town group and preventing the team from moving.[60] When it came to these corporate social programs and contributions, decisions were generally made according to the interests, connections, and whims of upper-level management.[61] "You might wonder, if you were a conscientious newspaper reader," quipped Peter Drucker, "when the managers of American business had any time for business."[62]

Annual Corporate Philanthropic Giving
(in millions of dollars), 1935–1960

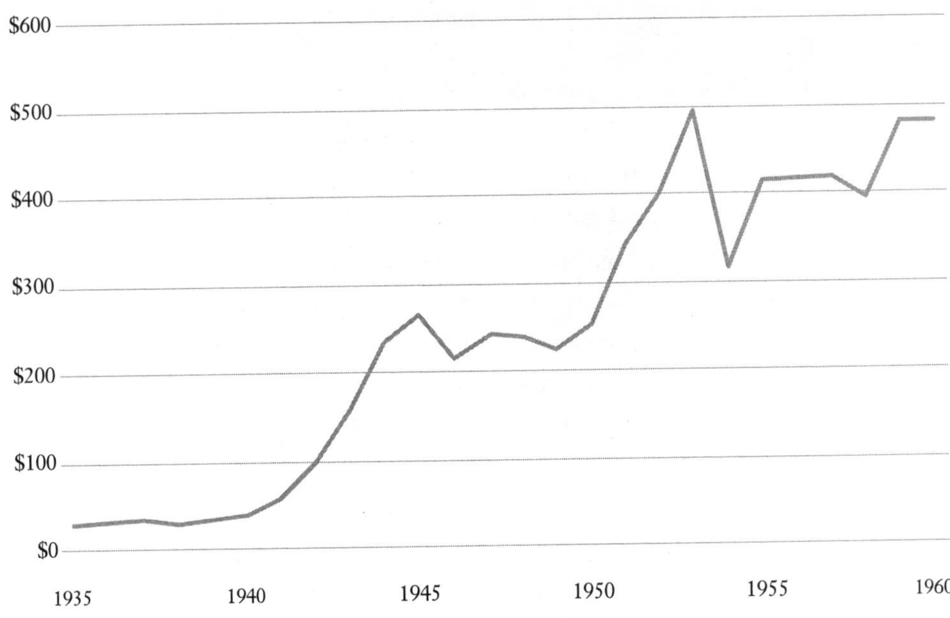

Richard Eells, from the ivory tower, argued that what could bring order to this chaotic scene was a business rationale for all of this activity. He advanced a "philosophy of corporate giving" in his 1956 book *Corporation Giving in a Free Society*. His case rested on conservative grounds, conceiving corporate giving as an instrument of corporate legitimacy. It "can be made the cogent ally of a free and competitive enterprise system," he wrote.[63] The purpose, Eells believed, was "strengthening the private sectors of society, protecting the nuclei or private initiative, and a progressive absorption of private responsibilities into the mechanism of the State." These were, undoubtedly, claims framed by the politics of the Cold War.[64]

The Cold War was a catalyst for mobilizing socially liberal efforts in business and giving urgency to the project of corporate theory. The rivalry between communism and capitalism motivated defenders of free enterprise to project a vision of the economy that fit with a liberal, democratic society.[65] Public relations experts worked to obscure the negative connotations of impersonal bureaucracy and instrumental power that the large corporation had long evoked.

If statesmanship was needed for business to defend its private system, there was left undeveloped a "complete pattern to justify corporate giving for philanthropic purposes." For Eells, this pattern included coordination with other firms, planned giving that corresponded with business goals over long periods of time, and a geographically national set of concerns.[66]

But instead of a coordinated plan for fulfilling social responsibilities, proponents of business statesmanship explained it as a form of professionalism. "The manager is becoming a professional," the editors of *Fortune* intoned, "in the sense that like all professional men he has a responsibility to society as a whole."[67] The special emphasis on the professional responsibility was a sign of the growing aspirations of the managerial class, propelled by the booming ranks of business schools, which funded journals, published books, used textbooks, and hosted lectures.[68]

Popular business publications were noticeably ambivalent about what business statesmanship meant. It could denote an attitude, a set of morals, a conscience or a soul, community leadership, anti-inflationary pricing, respect for employees, and a liberal record on civil rights, among much else. "Management, as a good citizen, and because it cannot properly function in an acrimonious and contentious atmosphere, has the positive duty to work for peaceful relations and understanding among men," said Frank Abrams, chairman of the Standard Oil Company of New Jersey.[69]

Liberal-minded paternalism was heralded as the panacea to the ideological conflicts that had plagued big business in the past. "An active social conscience," one midwestern manufacturer said, "and individual recognition of social responsibilities will compel us, as individuals, to test *every* managerial practice, measure *every* policy by a simple yardstick. Not 'What does it mean for me,' but rather 'What will this mean to my *workers* as *people*, to my *customers*, to my *suppliers*, to my *stockholders*, to the *community* in which my plant is located, to my *government*, to the *industry* of which I am a part, to the *economy* as a whole?' "[70] Management, under these terms, stood at the intersection of a range of different public interests: employees, stockholders, people in manufacturing-plant communities, dealers, customers, policy makers, and the public at large. In some cases, the expectations of groups such as suppliers, customers, and stockholders were relatively straightforward and revolved around financial interests. But, as Theodore Houser, head of Sears, Roebuck and Company, put it, "The relationships of a corporation with the community, the public and the government are less direct but not less real, and need to be given thought as a part of the broad spectrum of management responsibility."[71]

But how to maintain the proper institutional balance between the interests of different groups—between the public good and private profit? And how could such a balancing act be objectively judged?

—

PERHAPS NO OTHER INSTITUTION devoted more resources to reconciling the growing sense of social leadership with the principle of federalism than a think tank called the Fund for the Republic. A brainchild of Henry Ford II and led by one-time University of Chicago president Robert Maynard Hutchins, the Fund for the Republic originated in 1952 as an independent organization supported by the Ford Foundation. Its mandate was to support civil liberties and civil rights in the early Cold War in which both communism and McCarthyist anticommunism threatened both.[72]

In the latter years of the 1950s, the fund shifted gears and reorganized around what was called the Basic Issues Program, the most prominent of which was its study of the corporation. Large corporations, the program explained, "now employ three-fourths of the nation's labor force and hold considerable powers, explicit and implicit, over their employees."[73] Soon the Basic Issues Program was taken over by a spin-off organization called the Center for the Study of Democratic Institutions headquartered on the campus of the University of California, Santa Barbara.[74] The program hosted guests as diverse as philosopher Herbert Marcuse and law professor Henry Manne.[75] It organized regular seminars attended by intellectual and business luminaries such as Henry Luce, John Courtney Murray, Reinhold Niebuhr, Gardiner Means, Adolf Berle, Jr., John Kenneth Galbraith, Carl Kaysen, and Stuart Chase.

Formal committee members, including Galbraith and Kaysen, were given an annual stipend of $2,000 with the expectation of attending quarterly meetings and providing advice.[76] In the early years particularly, the program operated much like an academic seminar. The texts ranged from the English jurist Frederic Maitland's classic preface to the nineteenth-century German legal historian Otto von Gierke's study of political theory, to the internal memoranda of the DuPont chemical company—such as the one discussed at the beginning of this chapter. (Maitland and von Gierke were arguably the two hardest-working modern thinkers who strove to come up with a philosophically cogent yet historically plausible theory of the modern corporation. Their works remain the starting point for serious inquiry to this day.) The program also provided opportunities for the distribution of works-in-progress and the development of papers into publishable condition.[77]

As for nearly all think tanks, the ultimate goal was to shape public opinion and ultimately public policy.[78] Frank Kelly, a former speechwriter for Harry Truman and a longtime executive at the center, described the strategy of, on the one hand, creating new ideas and, on the other, introducing them to two target groups. The first was the "200,000 active citizens who read 'highbrow' magazines, go to civic meetings, write letters to editors, communicate with their Congressman, stir up political parties, etc." The second was a broader base of students, teachers, and members of the public who "regard themselves as 'responsible liberals' or 'forward-looking conservatives.'"[79]

The Basic Issues Program seminar on corporations was organized by the affable but at-times fiery Wilbur Ferry. The son of a successful automobile manufacturer who had been a leader in the Michigan Republican Party and an outspoken critic of the New Deal, Ferry went on to build a career that was distinguished from his father's in almost every way except ambition.[80] He started out his career as an associate of the public relations executive Earl Newsom and played a pivotal role in helping the Ford Motor Company navigate labor disputes with Walter Reuther and the United Auto Workers in the late 1940s.[81] Ferry's professional anti-unionism contrasted with the turn his later career took—a long tenure in the nonprofit sector characterized by criticism of corporate capitalism and American foreign policy. His class treachery prompted one journalist to call him a "happy heretic" and *The*

Nation to praise him near the end of his life as a "friend of peace and the dispossessed."[82]

Although less sanguine about it than business leaders and their fellow business school proponents, Gardiner Means and many of his colleagues at the seminar agreed with the broad outlines of the thesis of the new capitalism. "A crucial problem is the use of power in ways not justified by our concept of a functioning society because the concept derives from Adam Smith and doesn't fit the present reality," Means said at one seminar.[83] The corporate economy had jumped the bounds of the profit motive and the corresponding system of competitive individualism.

A new theory of the corporation was called for, Ferry contended, one in which accountability would play a vital role. "Reports on operations to stockholders and on good employee relations to the community are only partial accountability," he wrote. "They do not necessarily show how the corporation may be meeting the needs of society, as judged by criteria established by the community, not by itself."[84] Ferry believed that a responsible corporation should be subjected to the norms—and, crucially, to the governance—of democracy, whatever that might look like in the particulars.

The Fund for the Republic spent a portion of its $200,000 budget to enable the corporation program to pay fifteen scholars in fields of law, economics, and political theory to write essays on the relationship between the corporation and society.[85] But how to disseminate those ideas? Whether the transmission belt of the scholars' presumed influence would be federal regulation, new state charters, or something else, they did not say. Still less could they come to any agreement—speaking of common traits of intellectuals—about what form such regulation might take.

Take the case of national planning. It was the topic of one early seminar—a new political economic system of industrial production that would be a "necessity" in thirty years, Berle argued. The imperatives of national planning were full employment, full production, and technological progress. But Leland Hazard, a Pittsburgh manufacturer, objected that planning could become overly governmental and bureaucratic. "We have to tolerate less than perfect performance of our economy in a democratic society," he said. "Voluntary planning, by the institutions themselves, would be acceptable."[86]

Each time members of the group came close to consensus on a policy solution, they ran into the Cold War limits of political thinking. The program sponsored work on the development of a federal chartering system that would have reformed the governance and mandates of corporations—the same idea batted around by New Dealers and, before them, by Theodore Roosevelt's progressives.[87] Discussions about charters converged with more fundamental constitutional questions about how corporate power could be structured. There were proposals for the "constitutionalization" of the corporation; that is, the application of basic Bill of Rights protections for employees, customers, suppliers, and so on. Although constitutional due process might slow down economic growth, Wilbur Ferry admitted, "profits and efficiency are not the only desiderata" and "a way must be found to make the corporation genuinely responsive to its members, and that the power wielded by the organization over members requires a formal and effective check."[88]

But outside the Basic Issues Program seminars and the books and pamphlets published by the Center for the Study of Democratic Institutions, such ideas gained little traction. One Yale law professor at the time summed up the general feeling about the potential of making big changes to corporate charters or other such methods of reimagining governance when he wrote "corporation law, as a field of intellectual effort, is dead in the United States."[89] Public policy solutions in general tended to float toward the margins. As Abram Chayes, Harvard Law School professor and soon-to-be John F. Kennedy confidante, said at a seminar, "The state can't even appoint an honest meat inspector; how could it appoint a director to General Motors? Nothing in our experience leads us to think that the state could participate sensibly in a board of directors of a private corporation."[90] At one meeting, media titan Henry Luce argued passionately that public opinion is and should be the single most important form of accountability for corporate power and that the growing significance of public relations indicated a "continuously operative sense of responsibility" among management professionals.[91]

As time went on, seminar participants gravitated not toward public policy solutions but rather toward the strengthening of socially responsible norms and expectations among executives and managers. These doubts revealed an exasperation with the political processes of representative government—public, private, or somewhere in between. Skepticism about government impeded the project of corporate reform in general. The Fund for the Republic—and so many of its influential participants—left control firmly in the hands of elite managers, guided by their personal convictions.

WITHOUT REFORMS TO corporate governance, business statesmanship amounted to a peculiar gamble: that undemocratic corporate means could be used toward liberal or even democratic ends. And it was a more or less successful hand that elite business leaders played throughout the 1950s and 1960s.

Which is not to say that there weren't plenty of critics. The Cold Warrior and legal scholar Eugene Rostow concluded that it was all "bewildering balderdash."[92] Rostow wrote that the idea of business statesmanship revealed a deep corruption at the heart of liberal thinking, betraying a loss of confidence in regulation and in the "possibility of public oversight."[93] Another management scholar agreed. "If there are no legally enforceable responsibilities of management," wrote Edward Mason, "it becomes doubtful whether, over time, these responsibilities will be recognized."[94]

Perhaps the most high-profile critic was John Kenneth Galbraith, whose 1952 study of the changing nature of corporate capitalism became a best-selling book, *American Capitalism.* Galbraith was actually quite doubtful—even dour—about management's new fad of social leadership. He worried that it exposed business leaders to perilous scrutiny, essentially revealing the undemocratic power that they held. "Given the conviction that no man has the right to any control over the prices, wages, wealth or income of a fellow citizen, to admit possession of power is to concede guilt," Galbraith wrote. "For any one businessman to make such a concession is to invite the attention of the public and perhaps of the Department of Justice to his firm as a special case."[95] Economist Robert Heilbroner came near to the reality of the matter when he called business statesmanship a "more or less transparent defense of privilege masquerading as philosophy" and a "search for sanction cloaked as a search for truth."[96]

The quest for a socially responsible form of capitalism in the postwar era was ultimately a quest for authority. As Berle himself put it, "Modern corporate management has all the legitimacy it needs to run a cloak and suit store or a small business." What was trickier, and what the new capitalism demanded, was the exercise of legitimate power in ways that strained democratic norms. "Big business finds that it has a tremendous capacity to affect society in all kinds of ways, it has no legitimacy for that," Berle concluded. "It is painfully seeking a basis for a legitimacy that goes beyond the balance sheet."[97]

When Berle had written about the City of God, he imagined that a new generation of leaders might manage their institutions according to a new set of values and a higher range of purposes. As it was with the Christians of Augustine of Hippo's day, so it would be with the business statesmen—still living in an old, familiar, even conventional world but called to a more excellent purpose. Such men would constitute a new order of sainthood with the "moral and intellectual leadership" that alone was "capable of balancing our Frankenstein creations."[98] Unlike the young author of *The Modern Corporation and Private Property*, the Berle of the mid-century era had lost touch with how power worked. Or, perhaps, he had lost the nerve to face the unpleasant fact that the campaign to constrain managerial power, what the progressives and New Dealers—his generation—had fought for, had largely failed.

In the meantime, for corporations, asserting responsibility without the necessary authority on which it depended was an unsteady foundation. And it ultimately exposed business leaders to new risks—and to an eventual undoing that none of them could have anticipated. Liberal business leaders had little idea that by failing to justify the mantle of social responsibility, they would become vulnerable to new, vocal critics.

FOUR

Fighting for Jobs

Rochester, New York, had long been known as a regional home for big industry. By the 1960s, it enjoyed economic prosperity and social peace and one of the lowest overall unemployment rates in America. White liberals, in particular, prided themselves on Rochester's history as a center of antislavery politics and a home to such abolitionists and suffragists as Frederick Douglass and Susan B. Anthony. But that reputation suffered a damaging blow in the summer of 1964.[1]

It began with a Friday night street dance just north of downtown when a K-9 police squad arrived to remove an allegedly inebriated young black man from the event. In the ensuing scuffle, many in the large crowd claimed to have witnessed white police officers letting loose a German shepherd to attack the man, and in the chaos a young girl was also bitten. Officers flooded the scene, but the crowd rained glass bottles and rocks down on patrol cars and police helmets. The police chief pleaded alone with the crowd to disperse, but groups of white men arrived on the scene, and the police became sandwiched between the two increasingly aggressive and segregated crowds. Plumes of tear gas filled the streets to little effect. In the small hours of the morning, the crowd grew to about 2,000, overturning and burning cars and targeting white-owned businesses for destruction. The uprising continued for multiple days, causing hundreds of injuries and more than a million dollars in damage. New York governor Nelson Rockefeller finally sent in 1,000 National Guard troops to put down the rebellion, which he said amounted to little more than "lawlessness, hoodlumism, and extremism."[2]

Along with Harlem, Brooklyn, and Philadelphia, Rochester was the site of one of the earliest such conflagrations of the decade. From 1950 to 1964, Rochester received an influx of rural southerners, and its black population increased by more than 500 percent to about 40,000. But the new racial composition of the city did not result in changes in political representation. All positions of local governmental boards and offices were filled by white people, and there were very few black public employees. Even the local chapters of the NAACP and CORE were led by white people. Along with this imbalance in political representation, housing conditions were poor. Whereas white residents moved out of the inner city to subsidized suburban developments, African Americans had difficulty finding urban housing that was decent, unsegregated, or well maintained. And joblessness was high. African American unemployment was 14 percent—compared to 2 percent overall—and income inequality diverged dramatically along racial lines.[3] Such circumstances fueled anger and resentment. During the summers of the 1960s, uprisings and rebellions lit up not just Rochester but also Detroit, New York, Oakland, and many other places—more than 150 cities in more than 30 states—leaving dozens dead and causing tens of millions of dollars in property damage.[4]

Even as civil rights activists demanded that the state protect the rights and citizenship of black Americans (the Civil Rights Act of 1964 was passed that summer), they also called on big business to guarantee full racial inclusion in the system of corporate capitalism. Not just the livelihood of African Americans but the very stability and prosperity of major cities depended on whether equal opportunities would be found in industrial employment. The fight for work would put the social leadership of corporations to the test.

It's hard to date the beginning of the fight for black inclusion in American business. One might count slave rebellions or the flight of enslaved people to the North as legitimate starting points. In many ways, the fight for black freedom has always been a fight for economic justice. And there is arguably no more significant part of civil society than business—and no more important business institution than the corporation.

The integration of industrial corporations was a significant civil rights battleground because of the growing migration of African Americans from rural southern communities into northern industrial cities such as Rochester. The black population of Detroit, for example, went from 9 percent in 1940 to about 45 percent by 1970.[5] Hiring at corporations did not follow suit. The fight for black freedom, then, was always tied up, to one degree or another, in the fight for opening up good-paying union jobs to people of color. But when it came to broader areas of social life, the federal government refused to do much.

In the early postwar years, even as the civil rights movement made strides in the integration of public spaces and in the establishment of voting rights, the so-called urban problem—with periodic bouts of violence and rioting in cities such as Detroit and New York—haunted policy makers and became a chief concern for activists and social scientists. The key contributing factors to the urban crisis, most experts agreed, were unequal housing and employment. And the job numbers, which are much easier to track historically, show a pretty clear picture: the unemployment rate for black people in the postwar era was consistently double that for white people and, in many municipalities, much higher than that.[6]

President John F. Kennedy issued Executive Order 10925 in March of 1961, requiring that all federal contractors take "affirmative action" to employ workers without any regard to race, ethnicity, or religion. The order created the President's Committee on Equal Employment Opportunity, headed by Vice President Lyndon B. Johnson. "I don't think there's any more important domestic effort in which we could be engaged," Kennedy said at the opening meeting of the committee.[7]

But the committee's mandate was fairly limited. Kennedy's executive order did not require particular policies and procedures from business. It merely demanded basic compliance with nondiscrimination goals. The intention, of course, was to change the character of American business toward more egalitarian ends by demanding that those companies receiving government money to build roads and missiles and ships and other military projects enforce nondiscrimination policies. A Democratic US senator from Alabama, the segregationist Joseph Lister Hill, expressed the libertarian opinion that the committee was pure government overreach. It used, he said, the government's monopsonist position as the most powerful business contractor in the country to "vex and harass those doing business with the government to the point where orderly plant management and efficient production could well be impossible."[8] If Lister was worried about a government takeover, he should have been reassured by the fact that, in the words of Johnson complaining to Kennedy, "I don't have any budget, I don't have any power, I don't have anything."[9]

With few resources and a confusingly vague mandate, LBJ and his committee carried on with little fanfare during the first months of JFK's presidency. Kennedy's leadership was described repeatedly in the press as taking a "soft approach." The fundamental problem with Kennedy's equal employment efforts was that they did not extend into the arena of corporate governance or policies. As one scholar has put it, "They outlawed discrimination without saying what it was."[10] A vague and informal approach became the modus operandi of the Kennedy administration.

There were pragmatic reasons for this. Lacking an appetite for aggressive government action—the kind of action that would elicit the ire of southern Democrats—Kennedy was left with modest means. So when right after the equal employment opportunity order was signed, the government awarded a massive contract to the defense giant Lockheed Aircraft Corporation, a company known far and wide for its discriminatory practices, something had to be done. If the company kept up its Jim Crow–style segregated drinking fountains and racist hiring policies, Kennedy's agenda on civil rights would look like a sham. The NAACP, which had protested at Lockheed's main plant in Marietta, Georgia, wouldn't stand for it.[11] That's when a Kennedy family ally, attorney and sometimes fixer Robert Troutman—a Georgia native who helped reconcile the southern segregationist faction of the Democratic Party with Kennedy's campaign—stepped in to mediate between Lockheed and civil rights groups. "I'm a middle of the road fellow," he once explained, "I don't panic in either direction."[12]

Acting personally on behalf of the president, Troutman convinced the company to remove some of the most egregious Jim Crow practices in exchange for letting the contract go through.[13] Troutman and the Kennedy camp were so pleased with this method of informal negotiation and voluntary commitments—not exactly full compliance but some reforms that could be described as a step in the right direction—that they decided it should be institutionalized and made standard operating procedure for Kennedy's equal employment agenda.

The result was the formation in May 1961 of Plans for Progress, a program attached to the President's Committee on Equal Employment Opportunity and which coordinated with and cultivated buy-in from business leaders for civil rights reform—many of whom, such as the leadership of Greyhound more than ten years earlier, were hesitant or even deeply opposed. Troutman's basic idea, in the words of another administration official, was that "if you sign a Plan for Progress you ought to be excused from being bothered with the executive order."[14] The Urban League complained that having a "plaque on the wall attesting to their enlightenment"—which is to say, their signing on to Plans for Progress—would make it practically impossible to investigate or bring complaints against many companies.[15]

But if Troutman's idea was anemic when it came to enforcement, it was ambitious in scope. Just in the first six months, he reported to the president that nonwhite employment in participating companies rose by 10 percent.[16] Soon he recommended that 100 of the largest employers in the country—those that weren't even defense contractors—should sign on to Plans for Progress.[17] Yet, after a year in operation, the president's committee had not canceled a single contract on the basis of a discrimination complaint.[18] The program was fundamentally about celebrating and facilitating the voluntary commitments of companies, not about enforcing civil rights law.

UPRISINGS IN PHILADELPHIA, Rochester, and New York in 1964 compelled the passage of that year's Civil Rights Act, which went far beyond Kennedy's initial executive orders; the latter requiring equal opportunity only among government contractors. The new law criminalized discrimination in hiring for any company with more than twenty-five employees. But even still, the enforcement mechanisms for the law were weak, and the federal government failed to provide compliance criteria. Well into the 1960s, affirmative action remained a "fuzzy concept."[19] That was, in part, due to stiff business-executive opposition to anything that smacked of quotas.[20]

That's not to say that business had no interest in doing better on integration. The ordinarily right-wing National Association of

Manufacturers encouraged member companies to form connections with community organizations and to make an effort to hire black workers.[21] Many business leaders explained their support for private business initiatives this way: if we do not take charge and solve the unemployment problem in American cities, then it will only be accomplished on the government's terms. It would not be the last time that business justified corporate social responsibility programs in terms of opposing the growth of the social welfare state.

The idea driving many of these programs was that business institutions operated in closer proximity to the social problem that needed to be solved. If the contributing factor to the urban crisis was that young men weren't getting jobs, then getting those very people connected to and assimilated into industrial corporations was the solution. A top-down government program would only insert another layer.

Trying to hold together an aging New Deal coalition, President Johnson was unwilling (and unable) to abandon southern businessmen, who were too useful and, because they were so eager to avoid social unrest and bad national publicity, were also too easily bought to ignore.[22] They were also good at keeping things quiet, or what amounted to a more powerful version of the same thing—giving Johnson the not negligible achievement of negotiating the civil rights movement through southern white moderates—with a minimum of bloodshed. It was in keeping with LBJ's method of developing loose and voluntary networks that enrolled social and professional groups into a "depoliticized" solution to the problem of civil rights and to "press for a peaceful resolution of local conflicts."[23]

Johnson did what he did with all political actors: lure, buy off, and bully business leaders into line. As Johnson himself put it, speaking to a group of businessmen about business initiatives to hire the unemployed, "I wanted to come by here and . . . tell you how much confidence I have in your ability and your leadership to help me do something about these problems that I can't do by myself or I can't do with the other things that are available to me."[24] This kind of public-private partnership characterized many of the War on Poverty and Great Society programs over the course of the 1960s.[25] But such programs strained and groaned under the pressure of what was happening in many major industrial cities.

Consider the case of Walter Clark. He grew up on the west side of Chicago. An African American young man in the mid-1960s, he was newly married and had two young children. He found himself facing a set of challenging if not insurmountable obstacles. Clark never finished high school, and, with the exception of some experience in woodshop class, he had few credentials to recommend him for employment. What he excelled at was boxing: he was the open division champion of an amateur league in 1965 and had Olympic ambitions. "I could be a good amateur but maybe not a good pro," Clark admitted. "And I got a family to look after." But for many black men of his generation, the world of industrial capitalism—and the surest avenue to a living wage and social stability—was far from welcoming. And without training or a degree, it was almost certainly closed. He was only twenty-three years old, but few would blame him if he had begun to feel that life was slipping through his fingers.

Clark's fortunes turned the next year. And it wasn't that he was able to cobble together more part-time work, which he was accustomed to doing from time to time. He took a full-time position at International Harvester, the tractor-making giant, starting out as a drill-press operator. Through the company's New Start program, he joined a small group of job trainees, primarily black men but also poor white workers and others who had been referred to the company by local government agencies, social organizations such as the YMCA and Saul Alinsky's Woodlawn Organization, and the United Auto Workers labor union.[26] The New Start program was designed for the untrained, uneducated, and those unlikely to find substantive employment. It provided extended orientation meetings with human relations officers, veteran supervisors, and trainers who were supposed to help guide people such as Clark out of years of unemployment and into the expectations of a forty-hour workweek, including interactions with a supervisor and colleagues and the occasional need to work a double shift. A few weeks into the job, Clark himself started to hope that he might be able to pay for the college education of his two children. It was a humble beginning, but the future that International Harvester promised was auspicious.

New Start was a social-work program owned, operated, and supervised by a major industrial corporation. International Harvester itself described it as a kind of halfway house for what social scientists of the 1960s called the "hard-core" unemployed—so named because they were considered hard cases, excluded from industrial training and education and with few opportunities to make it into the labor force. The program was run by a racially integrated staff of instructors and counselors who had experience as engineers, machinists, and so forth. At International Harvester's main Chicago plant, they re-created in miniature version a conventional factory floor at which they gave hands-on instruction in the operation of machines, the handling of products, and other basic tasks. And, crucially, they instructed trainees in the ethics and norms expected of a modern industrial worker: show up on time, wear safety glasses, stay sober, and don't bring guns and knives to work.

The gap between the life experiences of the young men who showed up for New Start and the expectations of management was pretty wide—and in some cases unbridgeable. Classes started early, and although the staff served coffee and donuts, many trainees had never eaten breakfast before and didn't have alarm clocks. If someone didn't show up, a counselor would try to find that individual but usually without much luck in the unknown apartments of Chicago's poorest neighborhood. Court appearances and family conflicts were frequent interruptions. At one point, International

Harvester coordinated with community organizations to arbitrate a dispute between rival gangs—all of which had members in the program—and negotiated an agreement that would allow members to get to work without harassment or violence.[27]

The crisscrossing demands of doing business and doing social work made for some less than stellar outcomes for trainees. The case of Walter Clark and his fellow trainees in the first New Start class is illustrative. Aside from a few boxing scores in local newspapers, Clark shows up in the historical record only because of an article in a company magazine called *Harvester World.* Clark was the subject of a profile meant to showcase the accomplishments and promise of the New Start program. It was exceedingly paternalistic, taking special efforts to point out, despite his broken family and failures in high school, how eager and ambitious Clark was but also casting doubt, for example, on his hopes of sending his children to college—"perhaps premature," it concluded.[28]

A *BusinessWeek* story two years later, in 1968, reported that of the fifty job trainees the company took on in the pilot program, only six remained with the company.[29] Even as the program expanded to eleven factories and trained more than 800 workers over the next few years, problems such as drug and alcohol abuse, gang violence, medical issues, and incarceration were persistent among those enrolled.[30] On the basis of scant public records, it's not clear whether Walter Clark was one of the few who was able to stay with International Harvester or whether, perhaps, he went on to another industrial job—or whether something worse happened. What is clear is that despite the company's own ambitions to help solve the entrenched social problem of inner-city unemployment, it faced a steep learning curve of its own.

Despite these initial setbacks and persistent challenges, International Harvester celebrated the New Start program in its 1969 annual report to shareholders as evidence of the firm's commitment to social responsibility. Was this a defensive explanation—a way to justify novel if seemingly dubious uses of corporate resources to business-minded stock owners? Perhaps in some cases. Leadership tried to cultivate buy-in from everyone in the company: workers and middle management through the internal company magazine piece and also stockholders through the annual report. Both camps—motivated either by meeting performance expectations on the job or by maximizing financial investments as stock owners—were generally reluctant to support such programs.

To be sure, company presidents and chairmen throughout American history had used their bully pulpits and economic leadership to shape public policy and to influence social life. And especially from the 1930s onward, as we've seen, corporations themselves made regular gifts and contributions to nonprofits, funding not just social programs but also educational institutions, the arts, and civic associations. But in each of these cases, business was trying to reform areas of society that were literally outside the realm of business operations.

The case of International Harvester, however, amounted to a different set of circumstances: social reform engineered within the heart of big business itself. And the social-work program meant to accomplish what, exactly—a development for the good of society, or in the long run for profits, or for something else? Pulling back the layers of that question is what the history of corporate social responsibility—and, indeed, of the corporation itself—is all about. This ambition to develop programs inside the corporation to address social problems intensified not just at International Harvester but at almost every major corporation—especially those that were publicly traded—as the civil rights movement called powerful institutions to account.

Even as the smoke was rising from the inner city, Johnson formed a presidential commission headed up by Illinois governor Otto Kerner, Jr., which became known simply as the Kerner Commission. Its mandate was to investigate the sources of the urban crisis, to evaluate the state and police response, and to find long-term solutions.

At the top of the Kerner Commission's list of recommendations was jobs, and it's easy to see why. The final report's findings are still stunning to read, this many years later: 500,000 "hard-core" unemployed who "lack basic education, work not at all or only from time to time, and are unable to cope with the problems of holding and performing a job." It cited a Department of Labor study that found more than 25 percent of men of color between the ages of sixteen and nineteen were jobless—and 16 percent of those between the ages of sixteen and twenty-four were unemployed. It wasn't just that many of those who rioted were unemployed or underemployed, as the Kerner Commission argued; primarily, it was that the problem in the cities would not be solved without first addressing the financial impoverishment and general sense of hopelessness that widespread unemployment caused.[31]

The specific proposals that the Kerner Commission made with regard to jobs were lengthy. Many of them were just the kind of things you would expect: national policies focused on economic expansion and job creation, public and private investment in the cities, job-training programs, and streamlining the process by which corporations might hire those who lacked privileged backgrounds. Something real had to be offered, the commission said: "the previously hard-core unemployed trainee or employee must understand that he is not being offered or trained for a 'dead-end' job."[32] The commission recommended that 1 million jobs be created in the private sector, and, in order to make sure people of color would get a shot, a national job-training initiative should be funded by the federal government and operated much like the educational programs offered to military veterans through the GI bill.[33]

Meanwhile, far outside the conference rooms in Washington, DC, community groups also grappled with the jobs crisis. In Rochester, black church leaders partnered with the city's Protestant establishment to form the Rochester Area Council of Churches, a black-led organization that sought out the assistance of Saul Alinsky and his Woodlawn Organization in Chicago. With a background in labor unionism, Alinsky was good at building up political power by means of local activism. Rochester leaders were impressed by his accomplishments and by his tough approach, which one minister said was "confrontational but it wasn't violent. [. . .] We liked that." Alinsky signed on to assist with a two-year campaign of community organizing.[34]

The result was FIGHT, a community organization called Freedom, Integration, God, Honor—Today, which coordinated smaller associations, fraternal clubs, and churches around the city. Franklin Florence was elected as its chairman in April 1965. A Christian minister, Florence had a reputation for being a militant; he was young and had a strong personality and the charisma of a natural leader. The group started with housing, exposing slumlords and picketing their suburban houses, but soon moved toward corporate activism. With the urging of the local AFL-CIO, the Xerox Corporation formed a small job-training program called "Step Up" that it coordinated with FIGHT. The goal was to select people who had "good latent abilities whose environment has deprived them of the opportunity to develop these abilities." The program turned out to be a stepping-stone to a more ambitious agenda.[35]

Sporting a Black Power lapel pin and joined by fifteen other activists, Franklin Florence showed up unannounced in early September 1966 at the headquarters of Eastman Kodak and asked to "see the top man." They demanded that the company immediately waive traditional employment requirements for the poor and underemployed and begin a program to train 600 men and women over an eighteen-month period—all under the administration of FIGHT. "The poor must get jobs," Florence said, "industry must provide the training, and must provide leadership in this area."[36]

FIGHT was ready to stand outside and denounce corporate inaction to a gathered press, but to its surprise the group was brought at once to the president and to the chairman of the company. Kodak's leadership likely guessed that a welcome reception stood a better chance of sidestepping negative publicity for the time being. But if a conversation with the top brass was a propitious beginning to FIGHT's campaign for a jobs program, the president of Kodak, William Vaughn, made it clear that any commitments would be purely voluntary and unilateral. He offered the tepid gesture of accepting any "suggestions which FIGHT may offer." Whatever good faith that may have existed between the two organizations melted away as one FIGHT spokesman accused Eastman Kodak of "run[ning] the town of Rochester like a southern plantation."[37]

Kodak mattered to civil rights activists for the simple reason that it was the largest employer in town. The company employed 41,000 people compared to Xerox's 9,000. Only about 1,200 of Kodak's employees were black, according to the incoming company president, Louis Eilers. Critics claimed that number was even lower. But even the highest estimate put the percentage of African American employees of Kodak at around 3 percent. At the time, the black population of Rochester was 14 percent. This failure to integrate African American workers in a company that provided stable employment and generous benefits ($3,500 per employee according to the 1966 annual report) was not finally separable from an exclusionary and racist system of education and industrial training.[38]

Talks between the leadership of Kodak and FIGHT halted at one stumbling block: FIGHT wanted to administer the jobs program. That meant selecting candidates and overseeing their progress toward employment. From the point of view of Marvin Chandler, a black minister and activist, the organization needed to provide support for trainees as they transitioned into the labor force. "On a Monday morning," he recalled, "somebody's gotta call some guy who's not been used to having to get up at six o'clock on Monday morning and say, 'Get up outta bed, you gotta go to work.'" FIGHT wasn't going to abandon mostly young African American men to the whims and prejudice of Kodak. But the company wasn't about to give up control over the hiring process. "Florence wanted to set up a hiring hall," William Vaughn, the president and later chairman of Kodak, recalled, "and tell us what people to hire." In talks that stretched into the fall, the company's top brass almost uniformly rejected any discussion of sharing control. The real problem, Florence said, was that FIGHT had dared to challenge the "cozy paternalism" of the company. "They do not negotiate with anyone."[39]

The dispute over a jobs program was one part of a larger war over corporate power—and how big business would contribute to the jobs disparity that the Kerner Commission was studying. FIGHT had all of the legitimacy of a city-wide organization and the overwhelming support of the African American community. And the group was good at drumming up attention from the press, not just locally but increasingly at the national level. "Black leaders in every ghetto across the nation are watching the Kodak-FIGHT controversy," Florence said, and he was right. As the months stretched on, the two sides met in private repeatedly with the aim of coming to some agreement about the program, but any hope for cooperation dissipated. FIGHT stood firm—and informed allies in the community and supporters around the country. The company turned to a private foundation out of Indianapolis called the Board of Fundamental Education to create its own jobs program on its own terms, but Kodak's decision to bring in outsiders only generated sympathy for FIGHT—and angered Florence even more. He called it a fraud and a trick and a public relations "con game."[40]

Eventually, the company seemed to relent. John Mulder, an assistant vice president, stepped into what had become a PR nightmare as an unlikely negotiator. Appointed by Vaughn, the outgoing company president, to restart talks, Mulder had a personal connection to Marvin Chandler through the Rochester Area Council of Churches that provided friendlier backchannels by which to come to an agreement. Within a couple of days of meetings, Mulder and Chandler came up with the terms: Kodak would train and hire 600 workers within two years. FIGHT gave up the right to be the sole referrer for trainees, but the program would still be jointly administered by the company and the community organization. On December 20, 1966, both sides had a signed contract in hand.[41]

FLORENCE AND HIS WIFE and a small group of FIGHT leaders and their wives celebrated at a Christmas party at Chandler's house. It was a joyous occasion. At long last, the battle with the corporate Goliath had come to an end. Or so they thought.

The local *Democrat and Chronicle* had praised the deal with a laudatory front-page story, but the agreement barely lasted the length of time it took for the newspaper to go to print. The incoming president of Kodak, Louis Eilers, first learned about the agreement from a colleague who heard the news on the radio. When told that Mulder had signed a deal with FIGHT, he was enraged, exclaiming, "The hell he has!" After dressing down Mulder, Eilers called an emergency meeting of the board of directors. An executive committee asserted that Mulder never had the authority to sign the agreement in the first place. And they reacted suspiciously to the prospect that the company had obliged itself to employ a particular number of people on the basis of their socioeconomic status over a particular period of time. As one executive put it, the agreement gave too much power to FIGHT, and nearly everyone in the upper levels of management "detected the faint odor of a labor contract."[42]

At the celebratory Christmas party, Chandler received a call from a distraught Mulder, insisting that he come over—it was urgent. "I whispered to my wife, 'They've broken the agreement.' You could see it in John's face," Florence later recalled. "He looked like Christ must have looked when Peter denied him." With tears in his eyes, Mulder broke the news. Marvin Chandler remembered Florence's rage: "Franklin went *livid*, I mean absolutely livid." Chandler immediately called Eilers at home, but his wife refused to put him on the phone. Gathered around the television minutes later, the activists watched as the Kodak repudiation was reported on the eleven o'clock news.[43]

FIGHT called foul and accused the company of acting in bad faith. Florence led a rally of 150 ministers, nuns, rabbis, priests, and laypeople at his church who all signed a statement of opposition against the company. "We are disgusted and angry," he said. "Kodak's word is no good. Kodak's signature is no good." Soon realizing the window for negotiations had closed, FIGHT's strategy going forward was to avoid private renegotiations and put public pressure on Kodak to honor the original agreement. When Kodak repudiated the jobs program, the company not only aired its own internal dysfunction to the public but also failed at basic diplomacy. The company offered no chance for FIGHT to save face. And so its only option was to raise the stakes. "Equality can't be handed down as an act of charity," Alinsky would often say. "Equality comes from taking, or from getting, because the other side knows you have the power to take."[44]

In the weeks that followed, activists hatched a plan to raise the stakes by a campaign called "Focus on Flemington." The plan was twofold: disrupt the annual Kodak shareholders' meeting in Flemington, New Jersey, making the case for a community-organized jobs program and exercising the right of shareholder voting.

Activist shareholders up until the late 1960s had focused on financial interests, not social ones. Occasional conflicts between investors and executives could scarcely be avoided given the conditions of the corporate form, which separated the rights of ownership from the power of management. The Securities and Exchange

Commission (SEC) developed detailed and highly restrictive rules about what shareholders could and could not propose at shareholders' meetings—and any proposal was binding. Under ordinary circumstances, shareholders didn't have much to do with the day-to-day operations of the firm, and, in return, management used investors' capital in productive ways to generate profit, along with higher share prices and lucrative dividends. But when there arose a disagreement over business strategy or a campaign to force a merger or acquisition against the wishes of executives, shareholders often used their voting rights to fight for new directors or to replace management altogether.

Although intended to empower the judicious financial supervision of investors, the rules offered no specific language barring the use of proxy resolutions and shareholder activism for the purpose of social issues. As we saw in chapter 2, Bayard Rustin and James Peck had pushed the limits of SEC rules when they used their shares to publicize a desegregation campaign against Greyhound Bus Lines in the 1950s. By the time FIGHT activists had reached their impasse with Kodak, the notion of using the machinery of Wall Street for the cause of Black Power was still as untested as it was counterintuitive. But it was Lawrence Black, a Rochester minister, who suggested it. "What could be more in keeping with the American way?" he said. The idea was that churches, denominations, and individuals would sign over their shareholder votes to FIGHT officers. With those votes in hand, Florence would stand up at the shareholders' meeting and demand an answer for the company's failure on the jobs program.[45]

The Rochester activists turned Wall Street conventions on their head. Not only did they ignore the norm that if you do not like a company's management, you should sell your stock; they became stockholders with the intention of demanding change. And they did it without any expectation of making themselves wealthier. In speeches around the country, Alinsky used the idea to build public support. Activists had bought a few shares, but they needed more to make an effective demonstration. By March, they sent out a letter inviting national church bodies to support the group at the shareholders' meeting in New Jersey. "To all those who are appalled by institutional racism and irresponsibility toward the poor," the letter read, "this issue offers a concrete opportunity." The national attention gave Alinsky an opportunity to display his skill of incendiary rhetoric. "The only contribution the Eastman Kodak company has ever made to race relations is the invention of color film," he told the *Washington Post*.[46]

For organizers of FIGHT, racist condescension was one part of a bigger story about how business power controlled the Rochester community in general, but especially its black community, which had no influence on business decisions that profoundly affected their lives. Although the members of the group never laid out a formal theory of the corporation, in many ways they harkened back to an older view of corporate power: that corporations are not entirely private institutions—that they are, in fact, concessions of state power created for the good of society.

—

When preparations were made for the Eastman Kodak Company's annual shareholders' meeting in 1967, management had hoped that Flemington, New Jersey, would play to their advantage. The quiet, rural borough had been the location of Kodak's annual meeting for decades, and that year it promised an advantageous ground on which to face the controversy and national publicity that had been hounding the company for months. But the small town only made the protests that would envelop the meeting seem more pronounced. Flemington was overrun. State police, worried about the possibility of violence, set up a temporary headquarters for the occasion. Along with hundreds of state troopers, there descended on the town that weekend in late April hundreds of shareholders, a large national media contingent, and busloads of activists and protesters. "The war with Kodak," Alinksy said to a crowd of reporters when he arrived, "begins tomorrow."[47]

The annual meeting took place at a rural county high school. Classes were canceled that day, and the 1,000-seat auditorium was overflowing. In one of the first cases of heightened security at an annual meeting, guards checked the credentials of attendees to make sure they were, in fact, stockholders. About 800 demonstrators picketed outside the meeting, holding signs that read "Kodak Snaps the Shutter on the Negro" and "Kodak Out of Focus." As Alinsky, Florence, and the rest of the FIGHT delegation entered, pro-management shareholders shouted, "throw them out." As soon as William Vaughn, the company's chairman, approached the microphone to call the meeting to order and offer welcoming remarks, Florence stood and interrupted him. "Are you going to keep your word with the poor?" Taken aback, Vaughn called him out of order with the strike of his gavel. Florence was persistent, demanding that the company honor the agreement from December. "We will give you until two o'clock to decide," Florence shouted back. He and his FIGHT colleagues strode out of the meeting with the shareholders' boos and hisses fading to the sound of supporters outside and cheers and shouts of "Sock it to him!"[48]

Returning to the meeting hours later and asking whether Kodak would honor the agreement, Florence was met with shouts from other shareholders of "No! No!" When Vaughn confirmed that the company would not, Florence said, "We'll see you in Rochester." Outside the meeting, FIGHT announced that it was increasing its demands from 600 to 2,000 jobs and that it would lead a national pilgrimage of the poor against Kodak's headquarters on June 24, the anniversary of the 1964 Rochester riots. "Racial war has been declared on black communities by Kodak," Florence told the crowd. "If it's war they want, it's war they'll get."[49]

It was FIGHT's ownership of stock that had enabled its war with Kodak to continue as long as it did. The possession of stocks afforded certain rights, one of which allowed Florence and his colleagues to attend the meeting, ask questions, and make demands. There were others; given enough notice, the group could have submitted proxy resolutions for consideration at the meeting or their own candidates for director (though the former may have run afoul of rules that prevented shareholders from influencing everyday business operations). Even with thousands of votes in hand from religious denominations such as the United Church of Christ, the group fell far short of the threshold necessary to gain control of the firm. The annual meeting, despite the interruptions, was tightly choreographed, and there was never really any doubt about who was in charge.[50]

The war soon came to a close. The declaration of a march on Kodak for the anniversary of the Rochester uprising sounded too close to a call for violence—or, at least, an escalation that could lead to a dangerous confrontation. The urban rebellions were still on everyone's mind, and many in Rochester, including a council of churches that had long backed the group, believed that FIGHT had overreached. Alinsky, realizing that the window of opportunity was coming to a close, reached out to US senator Daniel Patrick Moynihan of New York for help overseeing renegotiations with Kodak. Within two months, both sides had made a compromise by which the company agreed to train unemployed workers and FIGHT would remain involved only in an advisory capacity. The activists achieved their main goal but not on the terms of their own choosing.[51]

Franklin Florence saw that the tactic of challenging Kodak's management by way of stock ownership (and the opportunities for control that it provided) suggested a new mode of political action. "We had a few Negroes in Rochester who said you can't win with the big boys. They said, 'go slow,'" he recalled in a speech in 1969. "We blacks in Rochester were tired of that tea sipping, safe Tom approach. We told those house Negroes to go back and tell [. . .] Master Kodak that we were going to overexpose their film and them with it." The fight with Kodak showed a new approach: enrolling big business into the cause of activists and community organizations. "You better start signing up Bendix, General Motors, Ford, Western Electric, the insurance companies, and TWA," Florence continued. "Organize and make them sign agreements." As one of Alinsky's associates put it, "We knew that if we could get Kodak in line every other business would follow."[52]

—

In response to the industrial jobs crisis, Lyndon Johnson did his damnedest to enroll big business in the cause of civil rights on a mass scale. He created the National Alliance of Businessmen, an association of leading corporate executives and other leaders headed up by Henry Ford II, then CEO of the Ford Motor Company and who canceled a planned African safari trip to take the position.[53] For a few short years, the organization served as the beachhead for encouraging corporate leaders to take on projects of hiring minorities and the disadvantaged. LBJ also formed an organization called Job Opportunities in the Business Sector (JOBS for short). The program worked not unlike the GI bill: companies would create job-training and hiring programs, and the federal government would reimburse them to the tune of $3,500 per worker. With $350 million budgeted, Johnson expected that the program would bring in 100,000 new jobs for the "hard-core unemployed" within a year.[54]

The National Alliance of Businessmen model followed on previous charitable initiatives that corporations organized in the past—such as Community Chests, which contributed to charities and social services at the municipal level through much of the twentieth century, morphing eventually into organizations such as United Way.[55] But the key difference from these earlier organizations was that corporations were operating and managing social programs within the corporations themselves. And, crucially, companies received federal funds to do so.

With Henry Ford II as chairman, the alliance set quotas for regions and cities, with higher quotas for denser population areas, and organized efforts to solicit pledges from company presidents to create permanent job openings for trainees, with bigger asks for larger companies. Branches in major cities were usually headed by a prominent business figure, and some municipal branches of the organization established phone banks to cold call business leaders and also sent out pledge cards.[56] As one management expert put it, "Companies that have launched training programs for the hard core have done so either because their chief executives believe they should do it or because of prodding by the Federal Government."[57] It was an extremely top-down approach. And it seemed to produce results. By 1971, the alliance boasted that associated companies had hired more than 700,000 disadvantaged workers.[58]

Big corporations that tended to pay competitive wages to skilled or professional labor (and which also tended to have a majority white workforce) now used different strategies to recruit new employees. General Electric, for example, sent a company-branded RV trailer out to small industrial towns such as Waynesboro, Virginia, and staffed it with a recruitment rep who helped people fill out paperwork in neighborhoods and parking lots. Lockheed Aircraft Corporation in Georgia proposed using gang leaders to reach out to recruits in cities such as Atlanta. Ford established community centers in Detroit explicitly for recruitment. Other companies used television and radio ads.[59]

What was it like for workers? They were in a difficult spot: at once the objects of both scrutiny and charity, they were also projects of self-help and social reform, given valuable opportunities, and made out to be the special beneficiaries of a mostly white management class. "We have been gaped at, photographed, and interviewed by almost every major firm in the country," one trainee complained. "It's to the point now that we ignore them. All this because we were the scene of a major riot. And now we are on display. We just want jobs and we would like to be left alone." Others offered more positive testimonials: "As far as I am concerned it's fine, one of the best things that could have happened to me. I was a loser and this program has made the difference with me."[60]

If a corporation undertook a minority-hiring program, people could be sure that the president and the rest of the top leadership wanted it. One survey showed, however, that not everyone in management was equally enthusiastic. A confidential 1968 study reported that 100 percent of top managers answered in the affirmative that "companies should make a special effort to hire and train Negroes for skilled jobs." But among middle and lower-level managers, that support dropped off dramatically, with only about half of the lowest rung of management supporting such programs.[61]

In some instances, one might be able to chalk up this disparity of support between upper and lower management to a deficit of enlightened opinion on the part of lower management. A manager on the line at Ford's River Rouge plant in Detroit was less likely to take such view of things than Henry Ford II. The dividing line, however, did not simply run between socioeconomic classes—executives tending to be socially liberal, lower and middle management more reactionary. The disparity could also be explained by the performance expectations placed on less powerful managers.

The case of the American Oil Company is instructive. Just as John F. Kennedy started implementing his equal employment opportunity policies, the company made it an informal goal in 1961 for its purchasing office to prioritize making contracts with minority-owned businesses. But according to one of the company's vice presidents, the company had little to show for it after ten years: "The purchasing managers just assumed that management wasn't serious."[62] Those in charge of procurement were still evaluated according to traditional measures of performance such as costs, quality, and speed, not according to social responsibility.

But after Blaine J. Yarrington became president of the company in 1969, he implemented policies requiring, for example, that vice presidents be held accountable for integration policies and that social responsibility goals be included in performance evaluations. "If a minority purchasing program is indeed to be cranked into the system, the men in the executive suite must do more than announce it by memorandum," he told a meeting of the Better Business Bureau. "Without communication—without follow-up—the program dies, and the blame cannot be put on middle management, whose members simply continue to perform as they have in the past—like good, profit-oriented managers."[63]

Left unstated but looming over Yarrington's explanation was that upper management was also caught in a web of performance expectations and governance norms. It, too, had to contend with a system that established who gets to make decisions and how. And waiting in the wings—though only watching from a distance at that exact moment—were investors and shareholders who, by American law and convention, still could exercise a controlling grip on large, publicly traded corporations. For the time being, however, federal jobs programs provided the cash incentives and the publicity to keep such governance considerations at arm's length.

But the civil rights movement was making more revolutionary demands on both the American state and powerful corporations—claims of political equality, full citizenship, and economic rights—that a few public-private partnerships could hardly meet. Even as big business was cajoled, enticed, and encouraged to do what it had never done before by bringing black workers more fully into industrial labor—and set many new employees on a path to the middle class—industrial leaders resisted the efforts of activists to transform the governance of corporations.

One black minister and community organizer from Rochester said that he and his fellow activists targeted firms that had a "good record of being a liberal, white company," precisely in order to push for something more that would change how governance worked. This strategy intended to shake the pretense that a corporation could be socially responsible even as its managers avoided accountability to the very communities and interests that they claimed to care about. The goal was to give workers, consumers, and community members a substantive role in the governance of large firms.[64]

Behind these blunt if not existential challenges to industry was a sophisticated conception of how to think about business power. And the activists wanted to unseat not just the privileges of shareholders but also the rule of elite managers and directors. The political theorist Robert Dahl registered the political idea of this movement. "Whatever may be the optimal way of governing the great corporation, surely it is a delusion to consider it a private enterprise," he wrote in his 1970 book *After the Revolution?* "Why should people who own shares be given the privileges of citizenship in the government of the firm when citizenship is denied to other people who also make vital contributions to the firm?" As one activist put it, the plan was to "change the dynamic of the thing."[65]

What neither management nor civil rights activists could see at the time, however, was that the dynamic might soon change in profound ways—turning on its head everything they knew about the American economy. A business movement would pioneer new strategies that would threaten the stability and long-term thinking that made possible any vision—whether top-down or bottom-up—of the social leadership of large industrial corporations.

FIVE

"A Bundle of Assets"

James Ling was an energetic and enigmatic entrepreneur who got his start with a small contracting business called Ling Electric. He took it public in 1955 by organizing a new corporation called Ling Electric, Inc., with a capitalization of 1 million shares, 450,000 of which he sold within the first three months by going door-to-door in the Dallas metropolitan area and from a booth at the State Fair of Texas. These were modest beginnings, but his prospectus boasted of a "planned national expansion program."[1] The experience transformed James Ling from an electrician into a speculator, and, at $2.25 per share, he raised more than $800,000 (minus expenses), most of which he used to acquire the assets and business of the old Ling Electric.[2] What was left of the original capitalization underwrote that promise of ambitious expansion, first in the acquisition of a handful of electronics manufacturing firms around the country, which included a capital-starved company called L. M. Electronics. Ling made it a subsidiary, renaming that company Ling Electronics (a small but significant change from Ling Electric, which he formed into a parent company called Ling Industries), and in 1957 he undertook an initial public offering of the newly acquired firm.[3] This process of acquiring firms, making them subsidiaries, and amassing capital by floating new securities of subsidiaries became a pattern that Ling followed repeatedly over the next decade or so. In the process, he transformed his operating company into a holding company.

Although the pattern remained consistent, Ling stretched the limits of what finance capital (and the law) would allow. Ling Industries went on a buying spree, increasing its sales by a dramatic twelvefold and its earnings by more than 600 percent.[4] Ling chartered his corporation in Delaware, registered with the Securities and Exchange Commission (SEC), and established a relationship with the investment bank White, Weld, and with the Mutual Life Insurance Company of New York.[5] These connections to the financial establishment gave Ling the resources he needed to test the limits of leveraging. He bought companies with short-term debt and cash and, with collateral from each transaction, sold long-term obligations that would enable him to clean out his short-term liabilities once again.[6] It wasn't quite a financial musical chairs routine, but it was close.

Highly leveraged businesses have come and gone, to be sure, but here was something noteworthy: a large industrial firm with an aggressive strategy premised on financialization—that is, the process by which financial instruments and, in particular, various forms of debt become ever more determinative of economic activity—and not on long-term manufacturing goals. The brisk march of quarterly earnings reports and bond schedules set a pace that not only made institutional stability impossible but also required that Ling and his C-suite colleagues conceive of the corporation in radically novel terms. The philosopher Aristotle once said that the soul is the form of a living thing. Here was a style of management that was committed to no particular form—that saw every asset as potentially fungible. This was a vision of the corporation that by its form and strategy would not easily assimilate and institutionalize the demands of civil rights activists. Could this kind of corporation have a soul?

Ling was on a trail first cut by the corporate raids and proxy fights of the 1950s, which were a high-profile and early chapter in a dynamic process of financialization that developed in the postwar era. Those rogue investors were followed by an intensified period of conglomeration in which financially limber holding companies went on a mergers and acquisitions spree by using unconventional accounting methods and cheap debt that lasted about as long as the bull market did. Over a twenty-year period from 1948 to 1968, more than 15,000 acquisitions were recorded by *Standard & Poor's Standard Corporation Records* and *Moody's Industrial Manual*, totaling assets at more than $67 billion.[7] In 1968, at the height of the conglomeration craze, 84 percent of large mergers were of the conglomerate type, and such acquisitions accounted for more than $11 billion.[8] The merger wave reached its crest with more than 200 large firms and nearly 2,500 manufacturing corporations acquired in 1968.[9] Both the volatility and volume of the financial markets grew rapidly.[10] A total of 500 million shares changed hands on the New York Stock Exchange in 1956. By contrast, annual volume reached more than 2.9 billion shares by 1968.[11] "The stocks of young companies," wrote business historian Robert Sobel, "were coming to market where they shot up to twice the offering price in a matter of minutes."[12]

But Ling was probably the most prominent conglomerator of his day. His next target was Temco, a Dallas aircraft manufacturer much larger in size than Ling Industries. Then in 1961 Ling made a hostile tender offer for 150,000 shares of Chance Vought, a defense contractor whose sales dwarfed those of the newly formed Ling-Temco.[13] With the approval of shareholders, the merger bestowed one final name on this shape-shifting collection of firms:

Ling-Temco-Vought, Inc. (or, LTV for short). By 1964, LTV was 186th on *Fortune*'s list of the largest industrial corporations, and by the end of the decade it would peak at number 25.[14] LTV's path to the top came by way of an insatiable commitment to diversification. "Our concept would be that we would continually and on a sustained basis seek diversification," he said in a speech in 1969. "I guess you now would call us a conglomerate, although we did not know that such a word existed in those days."[15]

As they prowled American industry for acquisition targets, LTV looked for companies with above-average management, valuable assets, and relatively low share price. The way diversification worked in practice, for LTV and many other companies, was highly varied. An ice-cream producer could buy a textbook company. A machine manufacturer might absorb a technology developer.

"We make no claim to understand the industry," wrote John W. Johnson, a public relations executive at LTV.[16] LTV looked not for how it could contribute to an acquired firm but for how the new subsidiary could increase LTV's profits.[17] As Ling put it, "We have literally undergone every corporate reorganization and realignment that can be devised by mere mortals."[18] A risky way of doing business, the strategy only worked as long as the stock market kept pace with interest rates.

That delicate balance tipped sideways at the end of the decade. The stock market did not keep pace with interest rates. The Dow Jones Industrial Average stumbled and then fell precipitously, from a height of about 8,000 points in 1965 to about 4,500 in 1970, a period in which the corporate bond yield rose from 4.5 to 8.5 percent.[19] At the same time, LTV came under scrutiny from the Antitrust Subcommittee of the US House of Representatives and the Antitrust Division of the Department of Justice. In 1969, the Department of Justice filed an antitrust suit against LTV, demanding that it divest its holdings in Jones & Laughlin, the sixth largest steel producer in the United States.[20] In the process, the market had become skittish about conglomerates. The declining share price of LTV and its subsidiaries led to a concomitant collapse in the collateral for its corporate loans, turning its financial outlook upside down. By 1970, Ling was forced out as president and chairman, and LTV embarked on a long and slow process of financial reorganization that began with the layoff of 40 percent of its staff.[21]

The turmoil on Wall Street spilled out into the political world of the late 1960s. Slow to start, the engine of policy making began firing on all cylinders. The SEC asserted its regulatory authority as chairman Manuel Cohen called on the US Senate to enact regulations to tighten up rules surrounding tender offers and to require disclosures of finances and intent on the part of those seeking corporate takeovers.[22] Just as the SEC had tightened the reins on proxy contests in the 1950s, so the Williams Act of 1968 put the SEC in the middle of the conglomerate craze. Cohen told senators that the cloak of secrecy, which hid not only the intentions of activist investors but also their financial sources and obligations, led to manipulations of the stock market and disadvantages for the everyday shareholder.[23]

Louis Wolfson, the corporate raider from the 1950s, got caught in the dragnet as the SEC sought to rein in disreputable investing. As "bad a trumped-up Soviet-style criminal case as we ever had," the libertarian legal theorist Henry Manne called Wolfson's conviction on charges of securities fraud, chalking the prosecution up to the bias of a Democratic presidential administration.[24] As for the SEC's attempt to provide greater supervision of the conglomerate craze, Manne argued that it was an administrative state that would do far more damage to the economy than would corporate raiders or self-dealing investors. "The chief results," he wrote in a *Barron's* article in 1967, "will be the protection of inefficient corporate managers and the financial injury of American shareholders."[25] This impulse to regulate was another example of the liberal tendency to value fairness over the proper functioning of markets.

Manne cited his friend and colleague George Stigler, an economist who in the 1960s developed the concept that the federal regulation of securities markets not only was a failure of public policy but also lacked any economic justification.[26] By analyzing market performance in a series of years before and after the establishment of the SEC, Stigler claimed that no economic benefit had been derived from the regulation of the stock market. The market did a pretty good job of regulating itself, and the added government regulation was simply a drain on industry. The legacy of the New Deal, he asserted, was built on little more than "a promiscuous collection of conventional beliefs and personal prejudices."[27] It was, Manne wrote, an "unholy alliance of regulators and inefficient corporate managers."[28] Or as he put it in another article at the time, "Once we leave the workable ground of competitive prices, we are stuck in the morass of 'fair' or 'adequate' price, and other useless metaphysical notions. As yet no economist has figured a scientific way of giving content to those empty concepts. It is strange that a Commission dedicated to making capitalism function successfully would even try."[29]

Despite the regulatory moves that the SEC made in 1956 and again in 1968, free marketers cheered on the financialization of those decades and heralded it as a harbinger of the victory of markets over managers. But this was an overstatement. Corporate raids and the conglomeration wave did not signal a structural shift in the political economy of the corporation so much as they represented a change in managerial strategy that took advantage of cheap debt and market liquidity.

That the declines of 1969 came exactly forty years after the Crash of 1929 was not lost on the national press. John Kenneth Galbraith, an elder statesman of liberal economic thinking, drew a comparison between the two versions of a "self-destroying speculative boom."[30] He reserved his harshest words for James Ling, whose theory of redeploying funds he dismissed with derision. "The madness is thinking that people who combine corn starch factories with aviation plants are geniuses," he told the *New York Times*.[31]

In place of a business statesmanship model that downplayed the significance of profits, Ling proposed a method that was based on a short set of financial gains. As he told *Fortune* in 1969, "When you get right down to it . . . the general objective is to build shareholder values—which should be coupled with the other objective of increased earnings per share." This market-oriented strategy corresponded to a radically new vision of the corporation that held firms to be nothing more than a "bundle of assets subject to 'redeployment,' i.e. corporate structures are simply one of the means of managing assets," as *Fortune* put it.[32]

When Ling looked out on the massive conglomerate that he had constructed and at the changing business scene of the 1960s, what he saw was a financial triptych of cash flows, stock price, and debt obligations. Any modern executive, of course, would have been attentive to such accounting numbers. What set Ling apart is that he saw the corporation not in terms of anything in particular that it produced or the services that it provided, but almost exclusively in terms of finances. As he explained in a letter asking for additional funds from his underwriters at Lehman Brothers in 1965, "We, the parent company, in effect, would be acting as the banker . . . [and] would be in the most enviable position to make a number of constructive moves with such a large cash balance."[33]

Ling may have been exceptional in the 1960s, but it would be dismissive to call him an aberration. The lessons of a financialized managerialism that Ling and Wolfson pioneered were assimilated in the broader business community. Consultants at McKinsey and Company and at the Boston Consulting Group learned lessons from Wolfson's and Ling's experiences and repackaged what they learned for routine management of less daring publicly traded firms.[34] Within a few years, raiding and proxyteering were business as usual.

HENRY MANNE WATCHED the conglomerate wave of the era with fascination, and he became particularly interested in Louis

Wolfson's career in corporate raiding as recounted with journalistic flair by David Karr in his 1956 book, *Fight for Control.* It was on Manne's mind in 1965 when he wrote what became one of the most widely cited law review articles of the twentieth century. Manne theorized that if traders only behaved more like Wolfson, there would emerge a market made up of profit-maximizing investors who would buy or sell stocks on the basis of the efficiency of management—thus signaling to managers to shape up or ship out. Manne called this the "market for corporate control." He wrote, "It would seem that the average market price of a company's shares must be the 'correct' one."[35]

Why would the share price accurately reflect the efficiency or inefficiency of a corporation? One reason was that people with reliable information were motivated to participate in the market and, by their transactions, spread that information around. Another reason was that the managers, Manne surmised, would be properly motivated to avoid getting unseated from their positions. Prices increase insofar as corporations are run effectively, thus increasing the cost of a merger or hostile takeover, and share prices decline when confidence is low, thus making the removal of upper-level management more feasible.[36] It is worth noting that there were no empirical data to back up Manne's contentions; it was an exercise in rationalism pure and simple.

Manne opposed the concentration of corporate control in the hands of self-interested managerial elites, but he did not seek to do away with the big, hierarchical institution. He also did not want to make corporations represent the interests and social views of shareholders democratically, as civil rights activists and shareholder citizens had wanted.[37] They were interested not just in liberal norms but also in democratic processes such as deliberative meetings, consensus-led policy making, and elections of representatives who could be held accountable. Manne argued that common shareholders should not have the ability to vote at meetings. Shareholders should never engage in a battle with management about business decisions and policy; they should simply sell their votes and walk away. And, if it came down to a fight for control of the corporation, he continued, these fights are not "likely to involve any fundamental difference of opinion among shareholders on ultimate goals."[38] The ultimate goal being, in this case, the maximization of profits. Shareholders, he insisted, are not citizens.

This was a vision of market accountability stripped of anything approaching a democratic purpose. For Manne, the market was the end—the *telos* of almost all things. Manne's liberal colleagues greeted such free-market ideas not so much as points to be debated but as grotesque objects of fascination—or, at best, unusual exceptions to the hegemonic liberalism of the day that assumed, more than it argued for, the necessity of government planning and managerial expertise.

This fundamentalist view of markets—that they penetrated and permeated every institution, including the corporation, that they were efficient, that they were the only way to decentralize power, that they were the only means to disseminate information about the economy—shaped the way Manne thought about everything. His 1966 book, *Insider Trading and the Stock Market*, was Manne's most developed attack on the New Deal regime of corporate governance. A takedown of contemporary stock market regulation to the political foundation, it reexamined the Pecora hearings and the reasoning that went into the creation of the SEC regime. To no surprise, he thought the New Deal was a failure because it did not take seriously enough the power of markets. "Economists think with a different tradition behind them," he wrote. "Theirs is perhaps the most scientific of the social sciences. Here the word *scientific* must connote objectivity and moral detachment, as well as systematic verification of results. Economists tend to view any controversy as reflecting a platonic, ideal conflict."[39] Mutual fairness and individual morality, he said, were not germane to economics. (Neither was "systematic verification of results," but somehow that never seemed to trouble Manne.)

Insider trading was an important test case for him because of its association with self-dealing and white-collar crime. His argument was that insider traders provide a desirable service to financial markets by transmitting reliable information about the status of the management and the future of the firm. If executives, acting on privileged information, sold stock in their firm, they were providing *information*. So what if they made a bunch of money off of the deal? Consider it a form of compensation from the rest of the investing public.[40] "Information is not a free good, and we should not assume, without more information than we now possess, that its distribution is generally capricious, arbitrary, random, or uncontrolled," he wrote. "Rational, self-serving individuals will not blithely or willingly allow information of tremendous value to pass freely to individuals who have no valid claim upon it."[41]

For Manne, the stock market itself was an exercise in the "marketing of information." As information is allocated in a market-like system of exchange, what investors knew, for example, about the value of James Ling's conglomerates was regularly updated. And, in his case, the LTV empire was extremely valuable, its securities appreciating in value for years—until it collapsed. Or, as Manne might have put it, correcting prices signaled new and different information about the company. "The stock market is, par excellence, the arbiter of the value of information," he wrote.[42]

The logical extension of Manne's theory of insider trading was that the SEC regime was a fundamentally flawed project. A few years later in a lecture at New York University, he attacked the New Deal vision of how to keep corporations accountable. "Among securities lawyers today only the uninitiated take the idea of shareholder democracy seriously," he said.[43] So what if SEC disclosures and other shareholder protections were democratic? They were inefficient, he insisted. The requirement that corporations file accurate, publicly available information with the government simply served as a tool for entrenched interests to perpetuate their hold on power. In Manne's mind, society was power all the way down. That is, unless there were markets. "The whole 'disclosure philosophy' as a basis for securities regulation is close to being a fraud on the American investing public," he said, "providing unwarranted benefits to government officials, securities lawyers, accountants, financial analysts, and printers."[44]

In the space of about ten years when he was a professor in law at St. Louis University, the University of Wisconsin, and George Washington University—from the mid-1950s with his first book reviews to the 1960s with his articles in leading economics and law journals—Manne had laid his analytical axe to the root of corporate liberalism. He attacked corporate social responsibility, corporate democracy, and corporate ethics—the corporation driven by anything other than economic logic. In place of the categories of power and responsibility, he asserted the objectivity of economic science. And, in contrast to a regulatory system of corporate accountability, he erected a defense of the deregulated market as a system of responsibility. The result? "I was probably the most reviled law professor in America . . . and to experience it as an academic was not fun," he said decades later.[45]

For years, Manne had been saddled with his ties to the "Chicago school," the libertarian way of thinking about economics developed in and promoted by the business and law schools and the economics department at the University of Chicago, where Manne himself studied law. It was an epithet of derision that leading liberals used to label the libertarians and conservatives whose work lay outside the margins of respectable opinion. That began to change, however, by the late 1960s, and the increasing popularity of Milton Friedman and Friedrich Hayek served as a kind of litmus test.[46] Manne remembered one moment in particular at a meeting of the Association of American Law Schools. "I remember I was starting up an escalator in a hotel and there were two young professors I didn't know in front of me, except that I overheard that they were talking about me," he said in an interview in 2012. "One of them said to the other one, 'Aw, no, he's not a conservative kook; he's like Milton Friedman.' At that point, I knew that the world had changed. If it had reached the level where Milton's popularity and influence was now resurrecting my reputation, it was of big importance."[47]

Manne made his radically new conception of the corporation seem like common sense. He cast corporate raiders from the 1950s and their successors such as James Ling in the 1960s into the leading men of a new chapter in the history of the corporation in which aggressive, but rational, economic agents created a market for corporate control that was based solely on the maximization of shareholder value. Manne was writing a creation myth for a new form of capitalism that would so efficiently disseminate economic information through financial markets that the corporation would be transformed. But transformed into what, exactly? A network. Every agent—from executives and chairmen on down to middle managers and workers—would be held accountable to the imperatives of economic efficiency and the interests of shareholders. Not an institution in sight. But even if such libertarian ideas were slowly becoming respectable among academics, they remained solidly outside the mainstream of the rest of society. For a new generation of Americans that sought to trace (and contest) the tangled lines of political power through every institution—from the family and the church to Congress and the boardroom—this narrow ideal of market accountability seemed to miss the point entirely.

SIX

The Rise of the Corporate Guerrilla Fighter

In the early-morning hours of November 11, 1969, explosive devices went off in three of the largest skyscrapers in midtown and downtown Manhattan. Although no one was killed when the homemade time bombs ripped through the offices of Chase Manhattan Bank, General Motors, and Standard Oil of New Jersey, the explosions set off a minor civic panic. City officials struggled to contain the ensuing disruption of copycat threats that emptied out dozens of office buildings in subsequent days. In a letter to the press claiming credit, the perpetrators condemned by name CEOs who "run the system" and the giant corporations of America that profited from war, pollution, and mindless consumerism.[1]

Just one among several acts of corporate terrorism that rocked New York in the fall of 1969, this series of protest bombings was meant for spectacle, not bloodshed—or so claimed the self-described revolutionaries who wired together clocks and dynamite. Attacks on business and government buildings increased in scope and frequency across the United States in the early 1970s and together represented the return of militant radicalism to America. The radicals who torched bank lobbies and blew up office spaces announced to the world a message also shouted by a growing chorus of social and political activists: that the corporate order forged in the Progressive Era and reconstituted by the New Deal should no longer be taken for granted.[2]

Undermined by the scandal of the Vietnam War—a conflict that hauled in record profits for many firms and exposed corruption at the highest levels of state—confidence in American institutions withered during the 1970s. In the mid-1960s, 70 percent of the public told surveyors that business did a good job balancing profits with the public good, and more than half expressed trust in big-business leaders. Ten years later, those numbers plummeted to less than 20 percent.[3] One activist group accused the largest companies in California of "corporate apartheid" for excluding women and minorities from leadership positions. Whistleblowers at top manufacturing firms exposed cover-ups of dangerously faulty products. Activists and muckraking journalists churned out reports on ever-expanding corporate misconduct, including one firm's production of napalm and cluster bombs and another's role in the CIA-backed coup against Chile's president Salvador Allende. The economist Robert Heilbroner called it "My Lai massacres in the boardroom." "What we have here is a business version of the principle behind the Vietnam War," he wrote, "the imposition of casualties on other peoples in the name of [. . .] profits." By decade's end, *Fortune* published an exposé of what it called the "corporation haters"—activists who not only tarnished the reputation of business but were supposedly trying to put an end to capitalism full stop.[4]

IN THE YEARS leading up to his infamous crime, Sam Melville, the 1969 New York bomber (who later died in Attica Prison in a prison riot), had a handful of odd jobs, including one delivering *The Guardian*, a Marxist-Leninist publication. A center of student movement activism with deep ties to the Old Left, the weekly paper published a call that same year for direct action. "We need to find ways to lay siege to corporations," wrote the activist and historian Staughton Lynd. He urged students to besiege big business in coordinated but multiple ways. Some could buy stock and work from within. Others could protest outside. And still others could organize labor strikes or interrupt corporate recruitment events on college campuses. The paper published a list of major corporations, from Westinghouse to General Motors, and the dates of their annual shareholders' meetings. The message was clear: it was time to act against big business.[5]

While labor unions had long agitated for better working conditions, and civil rights activists had just a few years earlier taken direct action against segregated businesses, this was something new. There came in the late 1960s and 1970s a strain of activism that shocked America's CEOs—a shock later brilliantly rendered as a kind of family breakdown by the great Philip Roth in *American Pastoral* (1997). It focused on major, publicly traded corporations and coordinated a variety of social and political interests: civil rights, yes, but also gender equality, consumer safety, environmental pollution, workers' rights, and more. This constellation of interests, if properly organized, presaged an unprecedented mass movement. That was just what the community organizer Saul Alinsky had in mind when he spoke of mobilizing both the student movement and middle-class shareholders to reform big business. "Corporate America says that . . . it's our American duty to participate; but, in fact, they won't allow it," he told a Yale Law School student. "We propose to bring reality into line with that rhetoric."[6]

Such annual exercises in rule-following became dramatic sites of conflict between management and insurgent activists, just as they had with Kodak in Flemington but now on a much larger scale. The protests "shattered that old tranquility," *Time* magazine reported. AT&T, Boeing, Chase Manhattan Bank, Bank of America, Gulf Oil, Union Carbide, CBS, and many others were besieged. One observer noted the range of tactics: angry confrontations and disruptions at shareholders' meetings; picketing, sit-ins, and demonstrations at corporate offices; bombings or bomb threats and sabotage; the harassment of employment recruiters at university campuses; and increasing use of shareholder resolutions for purposes of social and political interests. The Conference Board, a liberal trade group, put out a guide for industrial leaders on how to control annual meetings in the face of defiant protesters. Their advice? Control the narrative ahead of time by publicizing corporate benevolence. Maintain control by tightening up security and speeding along the agenda. The head of the Dow Chemical Company advised his colleagues to "keep your cool," but "don't ever be afraid to over-prepare for a confrontation." Veteran New Leftist Staughton Lynd said, "Why . . . do we continue to demonstrate in Washington, as if the core of the problem lay there?" It was the year of the corporate guerrilla fighter.[7]

The antiwar movement brought the highest-profile campaigns against the largest names in postwar industry. And for its involvement in the Vietnam War, Dow Chemical Company suffered perhaps the most significant blow to its reputation and challenges to its power.

In 1965, Dow Chemical won a $5 million contract from the Department of Defense to produce napalm, a gel-like incendiary substance made from gasoline, benzene, and polystyrene (otherwise known as Styrofoam) that became widely used as an antipersonnel weapon by US forces in Vietnam. Napalm, which was sticky and burned at extremely high temperatures for long periods, quickly became a symbol for the cruel violence and wanton destruction wrought by American troops. In the spring of 1966, a group of antiwar protesters picketed the company's Manhattan offices while holding signs such as "Napalm Burns Babies, Dow Makes Money" and calling for a boycott of Saran Wrap (Dow's best-known consumer product up to that point). In the summer of

1966, twenty protesters were arrested while part of a mass sit-in at the same building.[8]

Direct action against the company only intensified in the final years of the decade. Activists targeted Dow's recruitment of college upperclassmen at more than 180 campuses. Students at the University of Minnesota, for example, staged a sit-in that trapped a campus recruiter for more than five hours; at Harvard, students did the same for more than seven hours. A group of Roman Catholic leftists known as the "D.C. 9" broke into Dow's offices in Washington, DC, in March 1969 and spilled human blood and destroyed equipment and files. Their open letter addressed to "the corporations of America" condemned Dow and other war-production companies that "under the cover of stockholder and executive anonymity," said the statement, "exploit, deprive, dehumanize, and kill in search of profit." By the end of the decade, the company was the target of more protests and activist campaigns than any other up to that point.[9]

When questioned on the ethics of producing something as destructive as napalm, Dow diverted the moral culpability to the government and clothed itself in the language of patriotism. The company's president told *Time* that the production of napalm wasn't about making money. "As long as the U.S. is involved in Viet Nam [sic]," he said, "we believe in fulfilling our responsibility to this national commitment of a democratic society." The chairman later said, "I am proud of doing my duty."[10]

After two years of protests, boycotts, and sit-ins, peace activists came to the same conclusion that Rochester's FIGHT organization came to in their conflict with Kodak: they had to go to the annual shareholders' meeting. It was the Medical Committee for Human Rights, a civil rights organization with strong ties to Martin Luther King, Jr., and originally formed to provide medical services for Freedom Summer volunteers in 1964, that organized the shareholder campaign against Dow Chemical. Provided with a handful of shares as a gift from a young Yale law student, Geoffrey Cowan (who would play a pivotal role in corporate protests just a couple of years later), the committee hoped to use its modest stockholdings to take advantage of Securities and Exchange Commission (SEC) rules in order to press for changes at the company. The results were less than modest—at least at first.[11]

Quentin Young, a medical doctor from Chicago and sometime personal physician to Martin Luther King, Jr., was the chairman of the Medical Committee. He proposed an anti-napalm resolution to Dow Chemical, calling it a "matter of such great urgency that we think it is imperative not to delay."[12] The company rejected his request for a proxy resolution because it didn't arrive within the legal deadline of sixty days prior to the annual meeting. A group of interfaith clergy attended the shareholders' meeting in May 1968 and urged management to allow for a vote on the production of napalm, a chemical agent, they said, that "goes beyond what is humanly tolerable in time of war." Dow's chairman, Carl Gerstacker, told the protesters to spend their time elsewhere—to change government policy and not American business. As Dow hunkered down, campus protests heated up. (The elder student-movement activist Howard Zinn called the American use of napalm manufactured by Dow "one of the cruelest acts perpetuated by any nation in modern history.") The company refused to budge. Instead, its public relations firm produced a newsletter for executives called *Napalm News*, which kept managers informed on the latest information about campus protests and corporate demonstrations.[13]

Dow's general counsel made an empty promise to get back to Quentin Young later that year. After the Medical Committee wrote again in January 1969, Dow responded with an unconvincing combination of claims. The group's resolution, they said, touched on "ordinary business operations" and so attempted to manage the everyday decisions of the company. Dow also claimed that activists singled out the company for symbolic purposes only and that the proposal was primarily for purposes of "promoting a general political, social, or similar cause." In this, the Medical Committee followed the same playbook that FIGHT pioneered. Both, it was true, violated SEC regulations going back to the creation of Rule 14a-8 barring proposals that circumvented management—and later clarifications that disallowed purely political shareholder resolutions. Playing from the same playbook as Kodak, Dow rejected the proposal. Young appealed to the SEC, which backed up the company's rejection. The Medical Committee appealed to the US Court of Appeals for the District of Columbia, and then the case went to the US Supreme Court.[14]

The high court eventually dismissed the case because Dow stopped producing napalm in 1969, for which the activists claimed victory. The company probably overbid on the Department of Defense project just to avoid the continuation of a public relations nightmare. But this corporate protest had a significance that went beyond the particular business decisions of Dow Chemical. For one thing, the appeals court issued a strong statement of support for the rights of shareholders to vote on matters of broad social and political importance. It was a check on managerial autonomy and, said the opinion, on "management's patently illegitimate claim of power to treat modern corporations with their vast resources as personal satrapies implementing personal political or moral predilections." Liberal US senator Edmund Muskie, a Democrat from Maine, introduced in 1970 the Corporate Participation Act, a bill that would have protected shareholder proposals that involved economic, political, racial, religious, or similar issues. "Americans are becoming increasingly aware of the need to solve our common problems through available channels," Muskie said at the introduction of his bill. "Expression of these concerns can and should be permitted through corporate democratic processes." Congressional and judicial sympathy for activists made the SEC more open to shareholder resolutions that touched on political issues throughout the 1970s.[15]

Critics of the Dow protests and sarcastic business journalists often said the activist campaign was misplaced—a case of youthful zeal without knowledge. They pointed out that the manufacturing of war products only accounted for a small part of the company's operations. Why not aim the fire of popular passion against a more substantial defense contractor such as Lockheed Aircraft, which produced more than $1.5 billion in equipment for the US government in 1966? Why single out Dow—only seventy-fifth on the list of defense contractors?

The answer to these questions is a key to understanding the strategy behind many of the corporate protests of the era. Activists singled out corporations that checked a handful of boxes: they were visible to the public (that is, they were known by brand or products), they were vulnerable to consumer markets and therefore sensitive to attacks on their reputations and to boycotts, and they were publicly held and thus accountable at least in a symbolic sense to the demands and votes of shareholders. Combined with more traditional activism such as labor strikes, each of these forms of protest provided some potential for insurgents to challenge the autonomy of management and to lay hold on the gears of corporate governance.[16]

THE DOW AND KODAK protests exploded during a time when mass social movements were remaking modern America. Shots across the bow of the managerial establishment, they spread "a cloud of suspicion and distrust over all we have achieved and hope to achieve," complained General Motors chairman James M. Roche. Even as executives pledged their personal commitment to the liberal ideals of business statesmanship, activists made corporate institutions targets for nearly every conceivable cause. Leaders such as Dow Chemical's Carl Gerstacker questioned the motives of activists. "If you really want to put your energies to something," he asked of anti-napalm protesters, "why don't you devote it to seeing that it is declared illegal?" Why target corporations? Why now?[17]

These are questions worth considering. After all, activists and policy makers had been successful at transforming the relationship between big business and the state in the previous decade or so. And they did it through laws. The Civil Rights Act of 1964, to take an obvious example, or the Clean Water Act of 1972, to take a less obvious one, forced business to adapt profit-seeking to imperatives of equality and environmental protection.

A clue to these shifting tactics can be found in the career of Ralph Nader. The son of Lebanese working-class immigrants who saved enough to start their own small business, Nader followed what should have been a predictable path to American success: first Princeton University and then Harvard Law School. But by the time he was set to earn his JD in the late 1950s, Nader was far more interested in social and political issues that affected Native Americans or the statehood of Puerto Rico than in contracts and torts.

In 1958, Nader wrote an article for the *Harvard Law Record* called "The American Automobile: Designed for Death?" There he laid out an argument that would occupy his work for much of the 1960s and make him a national political figure. Many of the more than 40,000 automobile deaths each year, Nader wrote, weren't really matters of chance or bad luck as the euphemistic label "accidents" implied. They were the result of negligence on the part of engineers and automotive manufacturers. A weak steering wheel, a dangerously thin glove box door, a sharp hood ornament, a collapsible roof—all of these turned a stylish family car into a death machine. Many vehicle dangers, Nader believed, could be mitigated or eliminated with the right rules and regulations. "Coping with dangerous automotive design," he wrote, "does not involve the framing of new concepts of responsibility for the manufacturing of products for the national market." They were matters of public interest that were already well established by the Progressive Era.[18]

Nader adapted his article for publication in *The Nation* the next year under the title, "The Safe Car You Can't Buy," and followed up with the groundbreaking 1965 book, *Unsafe at Any Speed.* The book traced the major design failures of popular vehicle models and the negligence of their manufacturers, the details of which he gleaned from hundreds of lawsuits. Nader indicted not just the failure of business, but also the failure of government to regulate an industry that had become the most powerful in American business. "A great problem of contemporary life is how to control the power of economic interests which ignore the harmful effects of their applied science and technology," he wrote. "The ability to ignore criticism, rather than to meet the issues raised, is one measure of the immunity to public responsibility that has characterized the automotive industry's position on safety matters."[19]

The following year, Nader appeared at multiple hearings convened by the Democratic US senator Abraham Ribicoff on the topic of automobile safety. Ribicoff, the former governor of Connecticut and longtime critic of the auto industry, had complained in 1965, "Should the industry always be lagging behind, waiting to be told what it has to do?" He took officials from Big Auto to task for prizing profits over safety. Nader found in Ribicoff an important ally before Congress and the national press. He condemned car makers for indulging in a "stylistic orgy of vehicle induced glare" while refusing to disclose necessary information about defects and hazards.[20]

For his trouble, Nader became the target of one of the most notorious campaigns of corporate intimidation of the twentieth century. During the first months of 1966 when he testified before Congress, he was repeatedly followed, approached by women who attempted to lure him into compromising situations, and called at odd hours of the day. His landlord was called and asked if he paid his bills on time. His stockbroker was approached and asked questions about his personal life. So were an old editor and a former law professor. After high-profile reporting from the *New Republic* and the *Washington Post*, General Motors (GM) admitted that it had been investigating Nader. Ribicoff hauled James Roche, the chairman of GM, before the committee where Roche did his best to argue that the company was not trying to intimidate a congressional witness—a federal crime if it were the case. The next year, a private detective hired to investigate Nader admitted in court documents that a GM lawyer had asked him to "get something somewhere on this guy" and to "shut him up." And in 1970, the company handed over $425,000 as a part of a settlement with Nader. He immediately put the money into a handful of advocacy organizations.[21]

Congress passed in 1966 the National Traffic and Motor Vehicle Safety Act, which established the National Highway Safety Bureau, the first federal agency created to enforce basic car safety standards. This was a major victory for Nader—probably the most significant of his career—and a culmination of nearly ten years of work. But it also represented a turning point for him, and not just in terms of his notoriety or name recognition. It was the beginning of a new consumer movement, which, as he wrote in an essay for the *New York Review of Books*, rested on the conviction that "consumers are being manipulated, defrauded, and injured not just by marginal businesses or fly-by-night hucksters, but by the US blue-chip business firms whose practices are unchecked by the older regulatory agencies." With settlement money and honoraria from speeches, he hired a small group of "Nader's Raiders," young lawyers who specialized in regulatory compliance, investigation of big business, and whistleblowing. Nader became the face of consumer interest.[22]

Not focused narrowly on safety and fraud, Nader's consumerism engaged in a new and expansive kind of political activism. For one thing, public interest activism didn't operate within conventional political party structures. "Nader's activities have done more to publicize certain specific evils of corporate power than all Democratic politicians put together," historian Christopher Lasch would write in 1971. But in the wake of his scuffle with Big Auto, Nader's work increasingly reflected the concerns and strategy of the larger movement of corporate protest. After 1966, he began to think about car safety as one aspect of the larger problem of corporate power.[23]

It was Robert Dahl, political theorist at Yale University, who summed it up best in a book edited by Nader and Mark Green called *Corporate Power in America*. Two axioms should govern new campaigns to gain control over corporations, he said. The first was that every large corporation should be thought of as a "social enterprise," whose existence can only be justified by public or social purposes. The second was that every large corporation should be thought of as a political system—an entity whose leaders exercise great power and control over other human beings. "If the large corporation is a social enterprise and a public political system," Dahl wrote, "the government of the corporation should be very much a public matter."[24]

By the time of the 1966 congressional hearings, Nader was already in the process of making a pivot from activism focused on winning discrete victories over specific business decisions—such as the requirement of seat belts in every car—to seeking control over the governing structures of big business. Consider his words from his testimony on GM's attempt to intimidate him:

> I am responsible for my actions, but who is responsible for those of General Motors? An individual's capital is basically his integrity. He can lose only once. A corporation can lose many times, and not be affected. [. . .] The requirement of a just social order is that responsibility shall lie where the power of decision rests. But the law has never caught up with the development of the large corporate unit. Deliberate acts emanate from the sprawl-

> ing and indeterminable shelter of the corporate organization. Too often the responsibility for an act is not imputable to those whose decisions enable it to be set in motion.[25]

The question that faced Nader—and a new generation of activists on the left who wanted to move beyond the politics and methods of the liberal establishment—was how to shine a light "where the power of decision rests."

Nader's pivot came in 1970. He assembled a press conference in Washington, DC, that February to announce the Campaign to Make General Motors Responsible. Nader's history with the automaking giant all but guaranteed that the protest would receive ample media coverage. But it became the highest-profile corporate protest of the era precisely because the campaign targeted the largest and most identifiable corporation in the United States. The goal was to expose the "fiction of shareholder democracy" that continued to "plague reality," Nader said. "Campaign GM will appeal to the nearly million and a half shareholders of the company. It will appeal to these shareholders as citizens and consumers." General Motors was a strategic target because its vast shareholding public, its popular and important products, and, perhaps most important, its secure place at the top of the Fortune 500 made the firm a perfect stand-in for American business as a whole. As one of the organizers put it, "We couldn't do anybody but General Motors. It had to be GM."[26]

Announced just in time for the company's annual meeting in May in the city of Detroit, Campaign GM was an initiative of the Project on Corporate Responsibility—one of the many corporate activism groups that sprouted up in the early 1970s. The project was organized by a handful of young law school graduates: John Esposito, Joseph Onek, Geoffrey Cowan, and Philip Moore, all of whom had either been associated with Nader or involved in corporate protests with FIGHT or the Medical Committee for Human Rights. The idea of Campaign GM began with

Moore and Cowan, both of whom had been impressed by public interest law, a movement in law schools of students and professors who sought to use the credentials of the bar to advocate for social change.[27]

The plan at first was simple: publicize critiques of GM's management and try to install outside critics on the board of directors. They turned to Nader originally with the idea of having him run as a director, but he declined because he was still in litigation with the company. But he agreed to support the campaign anyway. Nader gave them ideas for resolutions, suggestions about social issues to focus on, and a long list of social connections. Like Alinsky's idea of "Proxies for People," the goal was to get support from large institutional investors, such as universities, banks, churches, insurance companies, and unions, and from those with small holdings, such as students, depositors, laypeople, policyholders, union members, and other constituencies. But with less than four months between the announcement of the campaign and GM's annual meeting, there was precious little time to build an organization of mass shareholder activism.[28]

The original plan was to purchase a small number of shares in order to submit a proxy resolution that would address the firm's violation of safety and clean air laws. The insight that propelled the activists was that corporations are political institutions; to change their behavior is to change public policy. But the campaign grew into a general referendum on the abuses and failures of big business in America. "G.M. may be the host for a great public debate on the role of this giant corporation in American society rather than a wooden recital of aggregate financial data," Nader said. Donald Schwartz, a Georgetown law professor and counsel to the Project on Corporate Responsibility, said that the activists had "analogized corporations to the state." In order to change economic policy, then, they had to oppose "corporate policies not as outsiders, but as participants in the process."[29]

Campaign GM submitted nine resolutions to the company,

starting with matters of corporate governance—how the company was run and who gets to control it. The first resolution was to put three directors on the board who would represent consumer, minority, and environmental interests. The second would amend the corporate charter to create a permanent committee for corporate responsibility that would include labor, environmental, academic, consumer, civil rights, and religious representatives, among other groups. The committee would have a mandate to examine issues of consumer safety, labor, public transportation, social welfare, and stakeholder participation and submit its findings annually to shareholders. Other resolutions sought in quite particular circumstances to change the way GM did its business. One would force GM to allocate a "fair proportion" of its dealer franchises to members of minority groups and diversify its employment more generally. Other resolutions followed along similar lines, committing General Motors to support public transportation, consumer safety, and worker safety.[30]

Following the pattern of Greyhound Bus Lines in the 1950s and of Kodak just a few years earlier, General Motors rejected all resolutions put forward on the grounds that they pertained to social causes and not business operations. Even after activists appealed to federal regulators, the SEC threw out most of the proposals—retaining only two. It was a blow to Campaign GM, but the resolutions that the SEC retained were the most substantive. One was the expansion of the board of directors to include members that would represent public interests. The group supported three candidates, each with representative biographies: the minister and civil rights activist Channing Phillips, the liberal consumer activist Betty Furness, and the scientist and environmentalist René Dubos. The other resolution approved by the SEC proposed a "shareholders committee for corporate responsibility" that would include representatives from the United Auto Workers, environmental groups, consumers, academics, and religious institutions, among others. But, in a further weakening of Campaign GM by the SEC, the two resolutions, if approved by shareholders, would be recommendations to the board of directors, not mandatory directives.[31]

Campaign GM was shrewd in its public relations efforts—and the group did what it could to overcome the SEC's decisions by raising awareness for the cause. They took out a full-page advertisement in the Sunday edition of the company's hometown newspaper, the *Detroit Free Press*, soliciting donations and proxy votes from shareholders. It explained the proposals that were to be put to a vote at the annual meeting as well as the other resolutions that were previously rejected. The campaign sought to make General Motors "more responsible to the community as a whole" and that "all corporations must serve interests larger than their shareholders." Such language was not meant to persuade the management and shareholders of General Motors. It was meant to provoke. And it contributed to the narrative that had caught the imagination of the press that this was a David-and-Goliath story: a group of young, idealistic Washington lawyers with just a few thousand dollars to their names, standing up against one of America's largest corporations.[32]

—

By the end of April, Campaign GM expected to lose the vote on both resolutions by overwhelming margins, and despite this, its members believed they were making gains "on all fronts." So said Philip Moore, a twenty-eight-year-old graduate of Harvard Law School who was the energetic head of the Project on Corporate Responsibility. They redefined victory not in terms of shareholder votes but in raising public awareness and obtaining public support. They received support from elected officials including Senator Edmund Muskie and a group of sixteen members of Congress.[33]

The annual meeting, which took place in Detroit on May 22,

provided the biggest forum yet for reformers. Supporters of Campaign GM dominated the questions and comments over a grueling six-hour period, but the voters stood with management. The two proposals—to expand the board by three and to create a corporate responsibility committee—were defeated by 97 percent of the vote (a result not too different from most shareholder proposals at the time).[34]

More than three hundred activist supporters showed up to the meeting. They were described by reporters (about 130 journalists were present) as bright and energetic, mostly young and generally well dressed, but with long sideburns and hair and wearing casual ties and miniskirts. They passed out campaign literature to other attendees. Longtime holders of small shares were typically resentful. The company, fearful of scuffles breaking out or, worse, the threat of a bombing, hired local police and private guards to patrol the meeting. A few weeks before, the Honeywell shareholders' meeting was canceled after fourteen minutes when, due to protests, managers were unable to maintain control.[35]

After a statement from management defending its record and concern for the public's interest, supporters of Campaign GM questioned business leaders for hours from the floor of the meeting. They pressed GM on issues of pollution and consumer safety. A United Auto Workers spokesman gave an endorsement of the protesters, adding that management had lost confidence with shareholders. A dramatic moment came when Barbara Williams, a young black law student from the University of California, Los Angeles, asked, "Why are there no blacks on the board?" James Roche, the chairman, replied, "Because none of them have been elected." "I expected better of you," she shot back. She asked the question again. "No black has been nominated, and no black has been elected." Asked in the same way a third time, Roche said, "I have answered the question." To which Williams replied, "You have failed not only the shareholders but the country." She sat down to cheers and whistles. This interaction between Roche and

Williams was unprecedented in the history of the corporation, if not only for her status as a young woman of color standing up to a powerful white man, but also for the substance of her question—that minority people must be represented in the upper levels of business leadership.[36]

The company responded to these pleas for change on its own terms. Later that year, Roche announced the creation of a public policy committee that would report directly to the board of directors and advise them on public issues. A gesture toward "corporate citizenship" it may have been, but the move was criticized by Moore, who said it was afflicted like the rest of the company with a kind of parochialism. No African Americans, women, or representatives from the consumer or environmental movement were on the committee. Likewise, GM appointed Leon Howard Sullivan, a black minister and civil rights activist from Philadelphia, to its board in January 1971—another victory, Moore said. "General Motors would never be the same," Sullivan recalled in his memoir, *Moving Mountains*, "Nor would other large corporations in America who would open their doors to African Americans in leadership positions." Best known for his codes of conduct called the "Sullivan Principles," he used his position to pressure the company and other large industrial firms to change their policies on discrimination, particularly as they pertained to business in South Africa.[37]

GM's concessions were criticized as symbolic and the bare minimum—and rightly so. But the company took other, more substantial actions before the next year's annual meeting: financing low-income housing in two cities, depositing $5 million at black-controlled banks, and committing $188 million to antipollution efforts, among other things. Even still, Nader, who was in the process of constructing a small fortress of public interest lawyering at his Center for the Study of Responsive Law (founded in 1968) and Public Citizen (in 1971), wasn't impressed. He called GM's concessions "genuinely preposterous" and "pretty cosmetic." That deepened a rift over strategy that had been growing between Nader and the organizers, particularly Geoffrey Cowan, who admitted that they wanted not to be "identified with Ralph" going forward. The mechanical Nader, who tended to favor the precision of litigation over the messiness of popular movement politics, thought Campaign GM had lost focus. The group needed to get a strong grip on the gears of power, but all they got was a pep rally—or so he thought. "They wanted me to go to Detroit," Nader recalled. "I said I wouldn't do it. Oh, how they bitched and moaned." As for the showdown between GM officials and activists, Nader said, "They ran it like a Gene McCarthy campaign. Before it was over they saw for themselves that that wasn't the way to do it."[38]

The corporate protests were successful at getting big, publicly traded corporations to make commitments and change business decisions. Some activists wanted to remain focused on racking up these small victories. After all, Kodak *did* create a large job-training program. Dow *did* stop producing napalm. And there were dozens of other victories, many of them not very well publicized. The activists of the late 1960s and 1970s forced big business to shed the ideology of business statesmanship and build in its place an organizational structure of public relations and social outreach.[39]

Forcing corporations to change business practices was one thing. But rewriting the rules of how those business decisions got made was another. Over and again, activists aimed for both but only ended up with the former. Even as activists sought to treat corporations as private governments—as social and political institutions—they were stuck in the intractable position of playing the role of the consumer, investor, or worker. All of these were market roles that engendered economic relationships of property or contract. It was a far cry from the stated goal of the Project on Corporate Responsibility: "to work toward a reform of the corporate system that will give the public interest a permanent and persuasive voice in the corporate decision-making process." Even the most successful campaigns were only as successful as the shareholder regime and consumer markets would allow.[40]

NADER AND HIS FRIENDS weren't the only ones taking aim at General Motors. Others—whose influence would surpass Nader's—came from the political right, from scholars such as Henry Manne and his friend, Milton Friedman. Friedman wrote an essay in the *New York Times Magazine* called "A Friedman Doctrine—The Social Responsibility of Business Is to Increase Its Profits."[41] Although Friedman did not single out any particular corporate executive or activist, the context was made clear by the editors, who framed the piece with photos of James Roche, Campaign GM organizers, and other movement leaders. According to Friedman, corporate social responsibility was a fundamentally flawed project because it conflated economic action with political action. These two spheres ought to remain separate, he argued, because the logic of the market is the only immediately and commonly available coordinator of human activity. Politics is far less efficient than the price mechanism, invites conflict rather than consensus, and, when called upon to determine economic decisions, acts as a handmaiden to socialism. Friedman reserved his greatest opprobrium for liberal business leaders, such as Roche, who failed to stand firm against the corporate protesters and who gave heartfelt speeches on corporate citizenship. "This may gain them kudos in the short run," he wrote, "but it helps to strengthen the already too prevalent view that the pursuit of profits is wicked and immoral and must be curbed and controlled by external forces."[42]

Friedman's article took on a second life in subsequent years as a classic text for critique in national newspaper op-eds and college courses. A regular feature of business ethics textbooks and to this day a staple of MBA course syllabi, the essay articulated in a succinct and accessible way the conservative opposition to the idea of corporate social responsibility.[43] Friedman presented the relationship between shareholders and corporate leadership as a relationship of agency in which the only fiduciary duty of the managers and directors is to create profits. Profits—and little else—are the responsibility and area of expertise of business leaders. Using the language of social-choice theorists, Friedman argued that activists, such as those involved in Campaign GM, were rent seekers who wanted to take control of corporate institutions in order to divert profits for their own personal interests.[44] Any executive who capitulated to such schemes, he explained, was in effect imposing taxes on shareholders.

Although Friedman's manifesto didn't advocate a particular kind of managerial strategy, it did provide a justification for the maximization of corporate investments and an ideological shield from the more substantial proposals for corporate reform. On one point Friedman and Nader agreed: corporate social responsibility only made sense if the corporate system of governance was redesigned to empower community representatives and experts who participated in a substantive decision-making process. Friedman was fond of pointing out that business school graduates and their other colleagues in management did not possess the expertise to solve social issues.[45] Both leftists and libertarians agreed on that much. Friedman once countenanced substantive reforms to the way corporations were governed, but by the late 1960s, he had abandoned such reform ideas.

The emerging New Right and the New Left both used concepts such as "the system" and "corporate liberalism." Historians coming out of the University of Wisconsin and the progressive intellectual community of Madison issued a searing indictment of the corporate imperial state in the form of powerful historical revisionism. Liberalism wasn't about restraining big business and its abuses. Or so they argued. Rather, at its core, twentieth-century liberalism was imperialist, corporate, racist, and undemocratic. "Both in its nineteenth and twentieth century forms," wrote the New Left historian James Weinstein, "liberalism has been the political ideology of the rising, and then dominant, business groups." The corporate protests were fueled by this belief that from Theodore Roosevelt to Lyndon Baines Johnson, liberalism primarily served the economic and social interests of big business.[46]

The corporate protests advanced by way of two primary beachheads. One sought to force particular concessions from business in areas such as consumer safety, environmental pollution, and racial inequality. The other focused on reforming corporate institutions from the inside out—transforming corporate governance into a democratic stakeholder system that, either by direct votes or by representatives, would include a range of interests and communities. It was this latter approach to corporate activism that took on a greater significance as protesters came to understand the difficulty of holding business management accountable. It turned out that forcing social commitments from management was far easier than the more arduous process of making sure that those commitments were met equitably and transparently.[47]

SEVEN

Making Social Responsibility Corporate

Business leaders struggled to weather the storm of corporate protests in the late 1960s and early 1970s. They were ill equipped for the intensity of the opposition and bewildered by the ever-widening range of demands for social change. National and well-publicized activist campaigns created some of the first of what we might recognize as modern public relations crises. "We have in effect been cut off from a segment of society, the size of which is indeterminate, which has blocked us out emotionally," Dow Chemical's board chairman, Carl Gerstacker, said in 1970.[1] It's hard to overestimate the effect it had on executives to see collegial, even sometimes festive (or, at least boring) annual shareholders' meetings transformed into shouting matches and high-security battlefields as they had seen at Kodak and Dow and General Motors and dozens of other companies. "Only tangible and prompt action will quiet [General Motors'] persistent detractors," *Time* magazine predicted.[2]

The Conference Board had other ideas. A liberal trade group representing the largest corporations in the United States, it put out an educational pamphlet in 1971 called *Handling Protest at Annual Meetings*. It was a guide for executives on how to keep their house in order in the face of sometimes paralyzing public protests and direct action. However emotional the issue or militant the activism, the pamphlet advised, there were effective ways to mitigate the damage—and control the situation. Problems would always arise when executives and their public relations officers allowed the annual meeting to diverge from matters that pertained to business and to become a public forum for things that could not be so easily controlled, such as environmental pollution or racism. "The annual meeting has not been the ideal place for meaningful debate or dialogue on the question of a company's social responsibility," the pamphlet asserted.[3]

Given that the corporate protest movement was premised, in part, on making annual shareholders' meetings more deliberative and democratic, this was a particularly bold form of question begging. *Handling Protest at Annual Meetings* even entertained the possibility that under the enabling corporate laws of Delaware, which governed many publicly traded firms, companies could do away with the annual meeting entirely—the loophole being that mail-in proxy ballots would serve as a substitute for shareholder input. But the Conference Board also recognized that many financial investors—a far more respected and significant constituency to executives—would be displeased with that move and would, as one investor put it, "soon be on our way to Washington for legislation to prevent them from doing so."[4]

The clash between protesters and executives was, among other things, a kind of culture war—with two sides working from diametrically opposed premises and motivations. And while many professional managers were more circumspect about what they told the press, many longtime shareholders voiced severe frustration. "Why, they are just a bunch of youngsters who are hardly past diaper age," complained one longtime General Motors shareholder and retired electrical engineer.[5]

Besieged corporations waged their own counterattacks in the press and in official publications sent to stockholders. But even as they pushed back, many industry leaders had come to believe that the proper response to the social protests was to claim the mantle of social responsibility, leading and developing it on their own terms and to their own benefit.

—

SINCE ITS FOUNDING IN 1942, the Committee for Economic Development (CED) had served as a bridge between business and the state. Many corporate leaders were on the board of trustees, including the director of Eastman Kodak and a senior vice president at DuPont.[6] Many of its officials, such as its first president, who administered the Marshall Plan, had significant experience in government—from cabinet positions to head of the CIA.[7] In 1971, the committee published a widely read guide for business on social responsibilities.[8] If one wanted to know the mind of the business establishment in the early 1970s, the CED was not a bad institution to listen to.

The guide told a powerful and uplifting story about the progress that had been made with respect to the social role of corporations. It reaffirmed a few basic points. A corporation was responsible to five constituencies whose "interests and welfare" were identified as "inexorably linked": employees, stockholders, consumers, suppliers, and community neighbors. Corporations ought to make contributions to nonprofits—what it called "enlightened self-interest." Good ethics pays, in other words. Stockholders, in the long run, the guide asserted, benefited from both nonprofit gifts and socially responsible business practices. New measures of profit were needed to incorporate social contributions into quantitative models. In the meantime, management had to show leadership—and not leave social responsibility up to the whims of business statesmen. "Exceedingly good managerial judgment will be required to achieve the right balance," the guide stated, "between the internal constraints on corporate leadership and external social needs and pressures."[9]

It might be tempting to see the CED endorsement of the social role of corporations as a natural development of the corporate liberalism that had defined much of the elite managerial class since the New Deal generation—and, indeed, a culmination of an elite business concern to show social leadership. But the guide—and the CED's endorsement of corporate social responsibility—came in response to the civil rights movement and the urban crisis of the late 1960s, though those circumstances are only obliquely referenced. The two-sided way in which the CED responded to the social movements of the era reflected intersecting strategies. On the one hand, keep the social movements at bay and do not concede organizational power. On the other, embrace the practices and rhetoric of social responsibility on the corporation's own terms.

This top-down character of corporate social responsibility ran counter to what the social movements and protesters demanded—democratic control. But the pressure from the Left did not simply demand that businesses take action on social issues. The protests also had the corrosive effect of undermining the legitimacy of big-business leaders in the United States.

That's an important distinction to make. The protests, along with rising labor militancy, declining corporate profits, and a general loss of trust in institutions, contributed to a legitimacy crisis for corporate America. Many journalists and scholars have written about the rise of corporate lobbying in the 1970s and 1980s. The so-called Powell Memo, written in 1971—the year of publication of the CED guide—by soon-to-be US Supreme Court justice Lewis Powell for the US Chamber of Commerce, outlined a conservative strategy for how big business could respond to what Powell called attacks on the American free-enterprise system.[10] Many scholars have pointed to the Powell Memo as the incubator of a kind of corporate political spending that has only intensified since the 1970s. In response to a rising generation of left-wing activists, organizations such as the American Enterprise Institute and the Cato Institute began promoting free-market ideas about deregulation and other business interests.[11] The truth—and what has been mostly overlooked—is that corporate lobbying and corporate social responsibility emerged around the same time. Both came in response to an embattled inner circle of executives who saw the decline of industrial capitalism coming in the United States and did everything they could to weather the storm.[12]

—

THE LANGUAGE AND PHRASES that historical actors used can sometimes be revealing, expressing a thread of insight that, when tugged at, draws out the meaning of a moment. Consider that the phrase "corporate America" entered the lexicon in the late 1960s and early 1970s. As it was typically used by critics on the left, the phrase expressed the sense that big business was generally unified in its own set of interests, that it had splintered off from the rest of American society, and that it was actively undermining liberal democracy.

Consider, too, that the phrase "corporate social responsibility" began to circulate at the same time. This phrase was first used by a much different set of people: economists, managerial theorists, public relations experts, and then, and very soon, business executives and industry spokesmen. It expressed an almost diametrically opposed ideal to "corporate America"—that business would use its vast resources and managerial expertise to address and mitigate what was going wrong in American society. Major corporations had grown so large and powerful that they had outpaced liberal democracy, so the thinking went, but they could nevertheless make a trade-off between public good and private profit, sacrificing some of their industrial-gotten gains for the good of the country.

Critics might have seen it as a Faustian bargain. A lot of business leaders called it a natural development. But many theorists had for years been making a case for the necessity of corporate social responsibility. One was a business management professor named Keith Davis who called it the "iron law of responsibility." His 1966 textbook (which took off in popularity in the 1970s), *Business and Its Environment*, shaped the way a rising generation of business managers thought about the way corporations related to the broader social world. His central insight, which quickly became a form of conventional wisdom among business school professors and the students who took them seriously, was that "the avoidance of social responsibility leads to gradual erosion of social power." This was the iron law: "Those who do not take responsibility for their power ultimately shall lose it."[13] The implication was that any major firm that ignored the imperatives of social responsibility was running an existential risk that regulators, communities, and the public at large would turn against it. Davis and his coauthor put it this way:

> One fact is certain; businessmen cannot withdraw into isolation and avoid the social-responsibility issue. Neither can they claim that business is amoral and exempt from considerations of responsibility. The simple fact is that business is a major social institution, and as such it is importantly involved in social values. . . . As stated by one top manager: "We must sense and be responsive to the social demands of the public as well as the marketplace and recognize the social consequences of economic decision-making."[14]

Business and Its Environment was remarkably successful, going through three editions in its first ten years of publication. The book reiterated what Davis had previously written about in blunter terms in 1960. "In the last analysis it is always the businessman who makes the decision. The business institution can only give him a cultural framework, policy guidance, and a special interest."[15]

That is not to say that he and his colleagues invented the concept of corporate social responsibility out of whole cloth. Mainline Protestants at the National Council of Churches—a group of denominations that always had strong ties to government and business leaders—sponsored the work of an economics professor named Howard Bowen and published his book *Social Responsibilities of the Businessman* in 1953. Bowen defined the *doctrine of social responsibility* as the "voluntary assumption of social responsibility by businessmen" that might serve as a "practicable means toward ameliorating economic problems and attaining more fully the economic goals we seek."[16]

Bowen's book was one of the first to try to flesh out the conceptual language of business responsibilities, but it focused primarily on the individual business leader and on the problems of economic planning. It was, in short, rudimentary, but it reflected a lot of the ideas of business statesmanship that had been floating around in the immediate postwar era.[17]

The number of academic books and articles on the topic exploded in the late 1960s and 1970s. Clarence Walton, an academic dean and, later, a university president who came to be called the "Father of Business Ethics," wrote a successful book titled *Corporate Social Responsibilities*, which was published in 1967. "Growing evidence indicates that the modern corporation is consciously placing public interest on a level with self-interest and possibly above it," he wrote in the midst of the urban crisis and blossoming jobs programs.[18]

Walton imagined that the professional manager could be a mediator between the social and economic interests that intersected the business firm. But he criticized those who thought that social interests could be incorporated into a general profit-seeking strategy. There were trade-offs that had to be realistically dealt with. But, then, what made the executive the responsible officeholder? Walton argued that the separation of ownership and control had created an avenue for executives to take up social responsibilities.

Another key textbook was *Business and Society* (1971), written by a longtime management professor at the University of California, Los Angeles, named George A. Steiner. He put all of the onus and creativity on the manager, eschewing anything that smacked of structural change. "The assumption of social responsibilities is more of an attitude, of the way a manager approaches his decision-making task, than a great shift in the economics of decision-making," Steiner wrote. "It is a philosophy that looks at the social interest and the enlightened self-interest of business over the long-run as compared with the old narrow, unrestrained short-run self-interest." Already, theorists of corporate social responsibility were feeling around, stumbling toward a new way of thinking that would reconcile profit seeking and responsibility taking.[19]

—

THE VISION OF corporate social responsibility theorized by management professors, spoken about by business leaders, and spurred on by social movements played itself out in thousands of different stories in the 1960s and early 1970s. Some were dramatic, full of conflict and consequence. Most were small and unremarkable. Businesses large, medium, and small constructed a vast array of programs. All of them belong to the history of corporate capitalism.

The Xerox Corporation, the same company that started job-training programs in Rochester in the 1960s, created a "social service leave" program in 1972, which gave twenty-one employees several months of paid leave to volunteer at a socially beneficial nonprofit, government, or religious organization. Employees such as middle managers, accountants, and high-level executives participated in the program for varying lengths of time: some two months, others as long as six months. One sales rep taught math and building-trade skills to inmates at two prisons in the Massachusetts Department of Corrections. A nurse volunteered at a children's hospital in Kansas City. A vice president worked at a community services organization helping low-income black families achieve home ownership.[20]

IBM shook up its traditional philanthropy program beginning in 1972 with a new Fund for Community Service. The program gave full- and part-time employees the chance to request money for community projects—in broad areas of "social welfare, health, medicine, education, science, civic affairs, and culture."[21] The program had the effect of distributing IBM's corporate largesse to more diverse and decentralized groups around the country. Among other things, it made for good PR: for years the company advertised the Fund for Community Service in *Ebony* magazine, highlighting the stories of black employees who used company money to fund test kits for sickle-cell anemia in Huntsville, Alabama, and bus repairs for a track-and-field team of disadvantaged youth in Durham, North Carolina.[22]

The Chrysler Company funded an education program called "Women on Wheels" to offer classes to women about car maintenance and repairs. In 1972 and 1973, 18,000 women took the course at car dealerships around the country.[23] American Airlines helped fund the creation of August Martin High School in Queens, New York, in 1971, which offered courses in aviation with the intention of recruiting African American pilots.[24] The food company Borden budgeted $1 million in 1971 on a drug-treatment and education program for residents of Franklin County, Ohio.[25] Sun Oil, Shell Oil, Philip Morris, Aetna, General Motors, and Atlantic Richfield all developed programs to deposit cash in minority-owned banks.[26]

This was the birth of the modern corporate social responsibility movement. Corporate social responsibility was no longer the domain solely of business statesmen who doled out corporate charity from their proverbial expense accounts; instead, large companies created formal organizational structures for dealing with environmental, consumer safety, and social issues. One study in 1975 found that 60 percent of more than 200 of the largest firms had a high-level executive or committee whose job was to direct social programs such as the employment and training of disadvantaged workers or the mitigation of air and water pollution. Another study found that more than 60 percent of companies on *Fortune* magazine's list of the largest US firms had developed social policies on "urban affairs" and the environment.[27]

It was a sea change in the way American business understood its social role. Harvard Business School offered regular courses for students on such topics as "Black Power and the Business Community." The University of Virginia's Darden School of Business founded its Center for Applied Ethics in 1968. In 1971, the Affiliation of Concerned Business Students was formed to promote socially responsible causes among business students. The journal *Business and Society Review* was founded in 1972 with the editorial position that "we believe it is possible to develop a new commercial bargaining system that works for all people."[28]

But even as the movement for corporate social responsibility picked up steam in the early 1970s, those who filled the ranks of management remained ambivalent and divided about what, exactly, business was obligated to do. A study from the Stanford School of Business found that just 20 percent of firms were committed to taking "an aggressive role in solving social problems." And although half said that business "should become more heavily involved in social problems," those firms had no specific program for how to do that—and 20 percent of those surveyed said that social responsibility amounted to little more than "being profitable, paying taxes, and supplying jobs."[29]

There were divisions within firms, too. One survey of hundreds of managers at large, multidivision firms found that operating managers tended to be much more skeptical about programs designed to hire more women and minorities and about other social causes such as cleaning up air and water pollution.[30] One corporate director at Standard Oil of Indiana wrote, "Rhetoric is an inexhaustible resource that the chief executive officer can squander freely without noticeable impact on the bottom line. A great deal of it is dispensed in lieu of costlier action, and most employees know it."[31]

By 1973, *BusinessWeek* had discontinued its "Business Citizenship Award," which the magazine had sponsored annually since 1969. The reason? An article titled "How Social Responsibility Became Institutionalized" quoted an official with the US Chamber of Commerce who said, "Corporations are bored and disgusted with 'good works.'" The mood among corporate social responsibility managers had turned "gruesome," he said. As *BusinessWeek* put it, "It is obvious that something has changed in the attitude of business toward social goals that were considered unimpeachable only a few years ago."[32] Urban communities and disadvantaged workers had soured on what they came to regard as the instrumentalization of job programs for PR purposes. As *Business and Society Review* asked in 1974, "Whatever happened to the National Alliance of Businessmen?"[33] *BusinessWeek*'s answer was that voluntary programs focused on equal employment and pollution can become institutionalized through civil rights and environmental regulation. Corporate social responsibility programs today, explained the publisher of *BusinessWeek*, "are not as innovative as much as they are legislated."[34]

Without a clearly defined sense of what corporate social responsibility actually meant and, most significant, without a structure of governance that made management accountable to certain social obligations, the future of the movement was left unsecured. And perhaps it is a historical irony that just as industrial capitalism was becoming more responsive to a wider range of social interests, it was about to stumble—and soon fall.

In his 1966 book, *The Effective Executive*, management theorist and advice-giver Peter Drucker developed the theory of the knowledge worker. This type of worker, which he defined as "the man who puts to work what he has between his ears rather than the brawn of his muscles or the skill of his hands," used to be few and far between, vastly outnumbered by manual workers.[35] Where the latter produced real, physical things (or at least took part in a larger production line that produced real, physical things), knowledge workers "do not produce a 'thing,'" Drucker wrote. "They produce ideas, information, concepts."[36]

The rise of the knowledge worker registered a shift in American capitalism. Between 1966 and 1986, the share of nonfarm workers employed in manufacturing jobs declined by more than one-third.[37] During that same period, the number of workers who were union members plummeted by 38 percent.[38] A shrinking manufacturing sector meant the very jobs that companies had sought to train disadvantaged workers for were increasingly scarce. And the logic that justified such programs—that entry into industrial work would give stability and self-respect to those caught in the crossfire of the urban crisis—collapsed under the weight of economic reality. As a slumping manufacturing sector fled for the lower taxes and cheaper labor of the Sunbelt, a city such as Philadelphia lost 64 percent of its manufacturing jobs; Chicago 60 percent.[39]

Observers at the time such as sociologist Daniel Bell read these trends as signs of a deep social change. His 1973 book, *The Coming of Post-Industrial Society*, highlighted different aspects of this emergent era: the eclipse of a "goods-producing" economy by the service sector; the rising significance of professionals and technicians; the "centrality of theoretical knowledge" and technocratic control; and the increasing importance of technological innovation.[40] As Bell indicated, the nascent post-industrial society had already cast doubts in many people's minds about the credibility of big business. "A feeling has begun to spread in the country that corporate performance has made the society uglier, dirtier, trashier, more polluted, and noxious," he wrote. "The sense of identity between the self-interest of the corporation and the public interest has been replaced by a sense of incongruence."[41]

Where Bell offered a more academic extrapolation, futurologist Alvin Toffler was much less reserved. His best-selling 1970 book, *Future Shock*, predicted a world where much of society would suffer from a sense of psychological paralysis wrought by the speed of innovation. Toffler, who also became a corporate consultant, predicted that the citizen of the future, "instead of thinking in terms of a 'career'" would "think in terms of 'serial careers.'"[42] A "frenzied reshuffling" would soon overtake the economic institutions of America as corporations were baptized into a constant churn of mergers and de-mergers, liquidations, and restructurings.[43]

Although economic indicators are only one part of this story, they convey this sense of crisis. The United States went through

Unemployment and Inflation Rates (in percent), 1970-1980

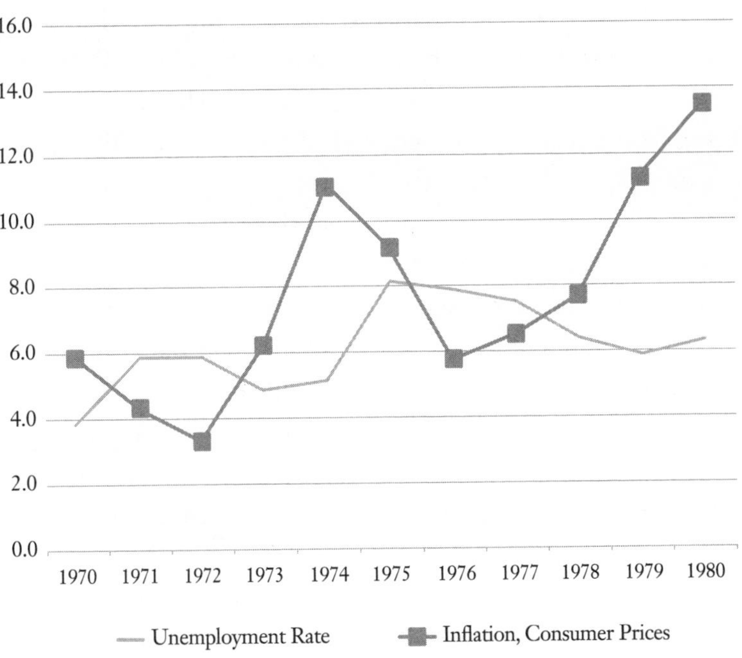

a recession in 1969 and 1970, and again—this time much more

severe and prolonged—between 1973 and 1975. Richard Nixon put an end to the convertibility of US dollars to gold, effectively shuttering the Bretton Woods system that had ensured the dominance of the American financial system across the globe. That, combined with the oil crisis, in which an OPEC oil embargo pushed the price of crude up 300 percent, precipitated a stock market crash. In 1974, GDP declined by 6 percent.[44] As labor strikes became more frequent, a deepening "crisis of profitability" plagued big business for the better part of two decades.[45] The rate of unemployment lurched up and floated between 5 and 10 percent during the same years that inflation more than doubled.[46] By decade's end, President Jimmy Carter diagnosed a "crisis of confidence" as the root cause behind a constellation of cultural and economic adversities.[47]

The economic turmoil of the 1970s, with stagflation and other economic shocks that effectively put an end to the industrial prosperity that the United States and other Western countries had enjoyed since the 1940s, transformed the way that people thought about corporate power and the way that executives were able to exercise it.

It wasn't just that big business had lost some credibility. That much was true, despite the desperate attempt to shore up legitimacy through social responsibility programs.

More significant, the strong and growing economy that allowed executives to use ever-expanding corporate resources for such projects had come to an end. Repeated recessions and high inflation eroded that largesse. The large, industrial multidivisional firm had given executives wiggle room to balance big-growth divisions with flagging ones; conglomerates had done the same but on an even larger scale, shoring up losses in one industry with profits in another.

Toffler imagined a future of financialization—of the chaotic and creative destruction pioneered by James Ling featuring near-constant mergers, acquisitions, and restructurings—that would lift the US economy. In the process, it would change practically everything business leaders knew about financial and managerial strategy. The new evangel of corporate America: every asset must be lean, mean, and flowing with cash, its status subject to the quarterly earnings call and a few simple metrics such as return on investment and share price.

With the financialization of the corporate economy, the status of the executive was about to undergo a tectonic shift. What Adolf Berle, Jr., had identified fifty years before as a wall of separation between ownership and control—which had allowed management to exercise remarkable power over economic institutions—was becoming porous. Increasingly, management had stock options and other incentives that made it more invested in the interests of stockholders. As Wall Street entered an extended bull market, activist investors and private equity firms demanded higher rates of return from executives. New forms of management strategy shaped an emerging business culture—and vice versa. This was not simply the victory of dollars and cents or a structural change to the financial economy but also a transformation of the ethical imaginations of Americans, from CEOs to consumers, according to a new cultural logic of market performance. Power and responsibility were fading away and an uncompromising imperative to squeeze a dollar out of every asset (and every institution, profession, even every career) was taking command.[48] The language of markets spread like a contagion throughout the political culture, fracturing notions of the common good—and of social responsibility—and justifying policies of deregulation.[49]

In 1974, neoconservative writer Irving Kristol would lambast American corporations in the pages of the *Wall Street Journal* for engaging in "clever public relations games" while fudging account books and concocting sophisticated Wall Street ploys in order to keep their stock prices up. Executives, he wrote, "are intensively and sincerely interested in 'the social responsibility of corporations,' and are quite willing to contemplate 'bold initiatives' in training the ghetto poor, solving our urban problems, etc. In other words, they are eager to assume responsibilities for various and remote tasks they probably cannot accomplish, but loath to shoulder the responsibility for doing what can easily be done: i.e., giving the public a true picture of the condition of their enterprises." It is, he summed up, a "neat prescription for corporate suicide."[50]

EIGHT

"There Is No Such Thing as a Corporate Responsibility"

The corporate protests created a market for Henry Manne. Once dismissed by colleagues as a "conservative kook" and relegated to the margins of academia, the forty-three-year-old University of Rochester professor found new audiences for his scathing criticisms of Ralph Nader and the Campaign to Make General Motors Responsible. "It is high time," he told a public audience in 1971, "that we stop treating corporate activists as simply nice young idealists and start realizing that they are irresponsible gadflies who deserve to be publicly chastised."[1]

Manne crisscrossed the country doing just that. He gave speeches defending the profit motive and delivered the message that the proposals of the "anticorporate zealots" were, among other things, fascist.[2] He appeared in public debates with Nader and with other leaders of Campaign GM.[3] At the White House Conference on the Industrial World Ahead in 1972, he traced the ideology of corporate social responsibility through the New Deal back to Progressivism and Populism. It was, he said, a defunct concept that would lead to the destruction of the market system.[4] Activists were afflicted by a "paranoid delusion of vast power and responsibility," he asserted.[5] *BusinessWeek* called him Nader's "most outspoken critic."

When he wasn't engaged in polemics, Manne was an advisor to business leaders. He was a consultant to General Motors and other large corporations facing scrutiny, providing advice for how to deal with the social issues that activists raised.[6] He wrote position papers and crafted the language that eventually wound up in the speeches of important business leaders such as the chairman of GM, James Roche, who declared that corporate social responsibility was a catchphrase of the "adversary culture" that was tearing the country apart.[7]

For years, Manne had chased public significance, penning newspaper columns, public lectures, and controversial books, though always overshadowed by his friend and mentor Milton Friedman, advisor to presidents and writer of best-selling books. But the corporate protests gave him the big break he had been looking for. Manne planned to launch an organization modeled after the American Civil Liberties Union (ACLU)—this one for the defense of free enterprise—that would engage in activities such as suing regulatory agencies and lobbying against licenses. A prolific writer, he made plans for a magnum opus: a takedown of the economic theory of New Deal liberalism and New Left activists that had done so much to undermine public confidence in free markets.[8]

Manne brought an incandescent devotion to free enterprise into everything that he would do over the next ten years. "I stand in awe of what the free market can do," he said in 1971.[9] Such a doxology to markets would have sounded unusual to most Americans at the time—the motto of an unbalanced if not unsound mind. But by the beginning of the next decade, that ideology would be the de facto creed of a country that had rebuilt its society around Wall Street.

A new activist Wall Street made benchmarks the driving imperatives of business: return on investment, quarterly earnings, and share price. A giddy "shareholder value" movement pushed for massive deregulation, the offshoring of American jobs, and the marginalization of corporate social responsibility.[10] "Any management—no matter how powerful and independent," wrote the finance expert Jack Treynor in the 1980s, "that flouts the financial objective of maximizing share value does so at its own peril."[11] Manne and the rest of the right-wing economics movement provided the policy proposals, ideas, and new common sense that made it all seem perfectly natural and desirable.

Rarely does an activist, or an academic for that matter, enjoy a series of changes that so closely matches his vision of the world. But Henry Manne's great gamble, one that he had made years before, was hitching his wagon to an insurgent corporate culture that took its cues from Wall Street markets.

Manne's mentor, Aaron Director, was the main founder of a school of thought that had become known as law and economics. The field started out as a descriptive methodology, but it developed to incorporate prescriptive views as time went on, especially when it came to the corporation (which it construed as an organization with extremely porous boundaries and essentially no meaningful independence from markets). Scholars working in the field proposed economic models as a normative method of legal reasoning for practical use in courts and regulatory administrations.[12]

By the 1970s, law and economics was no longer confined to Chicago. Not only had it made its way into top schools such as Harvard and Yale, it was also embraced by a range of scholars who were not so conservative or as motivated by ideological libertarianism as those in the Chicago school.[13]

Richard Posner, who went on to join the faculty of the University of Chicago Law School and to become a federal appellate judge, picked fights with top scholars and pointed out economic flaws in revered legal scholarship. He published widely in a range of fields and created his own economic consulting firm called Lexecon. As Steven Teles has put it in appropriately economic terms, Posner's work "produced a positive externality for the movement, by increasing the demand for its scholarship and removing blockages to its supply."[14] Posner's book *Economic Analysis of Law*, published in 1973 and almost universally described as monumental, signaled that the economic approach to legal questions could no longer be ignored.[15]

The spread of law and economics had a cascading effect for a rising generation of economists who had to come to their own conclusions about the form and function of the large corporation. The great irony is that the message of neoclassical economics—that voluntary accidents of haggling in unregulated markets are the best society can do—ended up being attractive to those whose interpretations were enforced, and in a sense defined, by powerful state institutions—including, most significantly, the courts.[16] Economics failed to persuade most scholars and policy makers, at least in the short term. But it turned into a forceful set of tools for winning lawyers and judges. Older legal and economic thought focused on the differences between firms. But law and economics scholars in the 1960s and 1970s sought to show that corporations were essentially structured and governed by market logic.

Two examples of this emerging view deserve some attention. Armen Alchian and Harold Demsetz, both libertarian in their predilections and longtime members of the Mont Pelerin Society, wrote an important article in 1972 called "Production, Information Costs, and Economic Organization." They argued that corporations exist on an ongoing basis because of constantly renegotiated contracts. This had significant consequences for the way they thought about corporate power. "It is common to see the firm characterized by the power to settle issues by fiat, by authority, or by disciplinary action superior to that available in the conventional market," Demsetz and Alchian wrote. "This is delusion."[17]

The corporation, in their view, should be seen simply as a team constituted by contracts and exchanges that are not much different from what is coordinated in the market. That is to say, the employer-employee relationship was basically the same as the consumer-retailer relationship. "Telling an employee to type this letter rather than to file that document is like my telling a grocer to sell me this brand of tuna rather than that brand of tuna."[18] Although it was a bizarre analogy that was based on a fundamental obliviousness to the social conditions of working life, Alchian and Demsetz produced a powerful theory of the firm as a "specialized surrogate" for a market in which managers are able to more efficiently supervise and surveille contracted employees.[19] In an aside, Alchian and Demsetz floated the idea that shareholders could be seen not as joint owners but as investors who don't necessarily have a proper role in governing the firm.[20]

The economists Michael Jensen and William Meckling developed this view further in one of the most influential economics papers of the late twentieth century. A firm, they argued, was not a concession of power from the state. They argued that the behavior of a firm—including how it relates to its employees—is basically the same as the behavior of a market; that is, "the outcome of a complex process of equilibrium."[21] There was essentially no difference between the "inside" or "outside" of a company.[22] The corporation, in this understanding, was not a concession of the state and it had no owners, not really. In Jensen and Meckling's words, the corporation was just a "nexus of contracts." It followed that there was no reason to treat a corporation as anything different from any other group of individuals or any individual.

These and other theorists applied economic analysis to law in order to critique prevailing liberal theories that considered corporations as creations of the state, or, at least, independent from the market in some way. But in the process of seeing past liberalism, they found themselves seeing through the corporation entirely. There was nothing left of the organization. Not really. "The truth is that there is almost no aspect of corporateness," Henry Manne wrote, "that could not be acquired—although in a very cumbersome fashion—by the exercise of freedom of contract, a freedom not generally considered a gift from the state."[23]

—

IN THE YEARS WHEN FIGHT was ramping up its campaign against Kodak in Rochester, Manne was there, too, and he proposed to the University of Rochester the creation of an entirely new law school that would be built around an economics curriculum. Starting a new program from the ground up created opportunities for tailoring the faculty, administration, and curriculum to fit this vision. But this idea of a new kind of legal education required not just new intellectual connections but also new institutional structures, and most of these Manne formed through his own salesmanship and networking.[24] A school of law and economics also promised a measure of influence exceeding that of other institutions. "[N]o other social discipline can begin to match the relevance and importance of economics for the training of modern lawyers," he wrote to W. Allen Wallis, the president of the university and a fellow Chicago alum. "The idea should be to infuse the entire curriculum with economic sophistication."[25]

Manne personally felt burned out in his quest for a conventional academic career. "The educational world is such a mess today from the libertarian point of view that a cleansing is certainly long overdue," he wrote to Pierre Goodrich, the right-wing businessman and founder of the Liberty Fund.[26] He became captivated by the idea of establishing an educational institution that would serve not only as a beachhead for law and economics in universities but also as a center through which lawyers, judges, and business professionals could be brought around to the free-market viewpoint. Manne embraced a vocation as an "intellectual entrepreneur," operating within the field of law while also seeking to change the intellectual content and the practice of legal education.[27]

Manne may have been disillusioned with a traditional academic career path, but his ambitions had not narrowed; they had widened. He wanted to build institutions of influence and learning at the intersections of law, government, and business. The "economic sophistication" of his curriculum would provide graduates with opportunities in public policy and in-house legal work. If Manne's school could feed graduates into the ranks of large corporations, then business would see the value not only in training economically literate lawyers but also in the cultivation of pro-business ideas. It would be a mutually beneficial relationship. As he wrote to Goodrich, "A single generation of lawyers from one school dedicated to true liberal values could turn the American legal system back into a productive and desirable channel."[28]

Public interest lawyering was taking on new dimensions and greater influence among a generation of young, liberal law school graduates in the 1960s and 1970s. "A source of intense interest for the present generation of law students is the small number of practitioners outside government or corporate law practice whose prime goal is the promotion of significant social change," wrote a group of Yale law students in 1970. With support from liberal institutions, new public interest organizations took up causes of civil rights, the environment, and, in particular, the failure of regulatory agencies to mitigate corporate abuses.[29] The conservative legal movement, with which Henry Manne and company were comrades in arms, was mobilized primarily in opposition to public interest law.[30]

If nonprofits such as the Ford Foundation and elite institutions of higher education such as Harvard and Yale law schools fostered liberal and public interest law, Manne hoped that allies within big business could be called upon to support free-market ideas in law.

In letters to Wallis and Goodrich, Manne outlined the plan for a conservative takeover of legal education. "I have no interest in founding 'just another law school,' and certainly no interest in furthering the statist characteristics of our leading schools," he wrote to Goodrich. "Nothing would make me more proud than to be able to name our law school the Pierre F. Goodrich School of Freedom Under Law."[31] Manne's vision of law was all-encompassing, and he hoped for an institution that would bring a free-market approach to government, law, and business.

The funding and institutional support for a law school never materialized at Rochester, but Manne found another path by starting a summer economics program for law professors. "I got the idea that perhaps I could train people to be able to read what I had written," he recalled. "That was part of my idea in doing this and part of it was to establish a law school connection to the University of Rochester, but it developed a life of its own."[32]

The first summer seminar for law professors began in 1971, and the seminar was offered annually for the next twenty-five years. Manne secured the funding to give $1,000 stipends to each participant and pay for their travel and accommodations costs. That first cohort of professors was an important one. He carefully selected faculty members from elite law schools for purposes of branding and advertising. And he shrewdly recruited legal experts who were already sympathetic to and interested in the mission. Manne didn't want someone who was there to "argue about ideology or first causes."[33] "Pareto in the Pines," as it came to be called, needed the credibility that came from those who first bought into the program.[34]

There was a sheen of academic neutrality that varnished the economics seminars. It was important to Manne that they were perceived as educating professors in the objective science of economics, not in some ideology. But, after a few years, law and economics critics such as Arthur Leff were left appalled by the program's politics and surprised by its popularity. He wondered at the fact that Manne's "summer indoctrination session in economics" was "continuously over-subscribed" to the point that "his little Pareto-in-the-Pines has its own long and distinguished alumni group rivaling that of more conventional 'legal' alma maters."[35] The way Manne came to see it was that if he couldn't start his own law school, he could at least "wholesale" his understanding of law to professors who could then "retail" it to students.[36] And it seemed to be working. He had a long list of applicants every year and consistent support from a dozen major corporations who were interested in promoting a more business-friendly approach to antitrust.[37] In time he would see more than 650 law professors go through his program.[38]

But that experience taught Manne that there must be new ways of influencing the law—ways that were untried and untested. The summer program demonstrated the importance of professional networks in gaining broad-based acceptance of new ideas. As Steven Teles has shown, early participants at Rochester such as Ralph Winter from Yale and Douglas Ginsburg from Harvard took the law and economics perspective back to their respective law schools and to their respective scholarly agenda. Surrounded by liberal orthodoxy, they planted the intellectual seeds of free-market ideas that eroded faith in the institutions of twentieth-century liberalism. The Manne program did a lot to develop a core of law and economics professors at law schools such as the University of Virginia and the University of Southern California.[39] "It created a group of true believers," said Michael Graetz, a University of Virginia law professor. "If you look at key first generation people of a certain age cohort of that time, you'd find that they had been through the Manne school at some point."[40]

In 1974, with support from Soia Mentschikoff, a Chicago alum and dean at the University of Miami, Manne founded the Law and Economics Center (LEC) in Coral Gables, Florida.[41] This was a milestone in the development of the field of law and economics because it "served as a kind of clearinghouse or association for people interested in the field," as Manne put it, but it was also a platform by which he would disseminate a free-market perspective.[42] The center continued the work of educating law professors in conservative economic ideas through short-term courses, but its agenda became increasingly ambitious. This was somewhat paradoxical because the institution that hosted the LEC was fairly marginal, at least compared to the Yale Law School, which had surprisingly that same year finally offered Manne a job.[43] That offer was a milestone in terms of the mainstream recognition that it offered him, but Manne realized by that time that it would be easier to influence the legal establishment from the outside rather than the inside.

> The relative weakness of the University is paradoxically an advantage in that same regard. At a stronger University or law school, where I would not be the most prominent professor, it is very unlikely that I could promote a program of this sort without considerable resistance and interference from other members of the law faculty, the economics department, and from the University administration.[44]

In an era when think-tanks were becoming prominent within American political and intellectual life, the Law and Economics Center was one of the most successful at spreading conservative ideas. The center hired researchers and brought aboard big names such as Friedrich Hayek, James Buchanan, and Ronald Coase for visiting professorships or lectureships. They published research for specialists and popular audiences. In association with the libertarian Liberty Fund, they hosted conferences.[45]

Manne took his playbook with "Pareto Under the Palms" and expanded it into something even more ambitious. His summer Economic Institute for Federal Judges was an all-expenses-paid vacation and educational program that had at one point hosted one-fifth of the federal judiciary.[46] The *Washington Post* sounded the alarm in 1980 that ninety-three judges had attended the programs of a right-wing institution bankrolled by more than 100 corporations.[47] Despite controversy over the appearance that big business was influencing the opinions of powerful federal judges, Manne maintained that the courses were non-ideological. He solved, he claimed, the appearance of impropriety by funding the judges' program solely through the donations of foundations and no longer through corporate funds. Later that year, a judicial ethics committee gave its approval to continued operation of the program.[48]

What was most striking about the judges' program was the far reach of its influence and Manne's ability to navigate his institutional ship through polarizing political winds. In the span of about twenty-five years, more than 450 federal judges attended the program, including Clarence Thomas and Ruth Bader Ginsburg.[49] Even the liberal Ginsburg walked away from the seminar with appreciation and later congratulated Manne on the program. "Cheers to Henry, innovator and dean nonpareil," she wrote in 1999. "As a student in two of his seminars, I can affirm that the instruction was far more intense than the Florida sun."[50]

The pleasant Florida sun was one part of the formula that made the program work. Combined with fine food and drink and recreation afforded by the beach or golf course, the summer program attracted participants with more than just microeconomics. Manne was a "zealous proponent of overconsumption of fine food," one alum recalled.[51] "Naturally, one remembers stone crab, pecan pie, and great snorkeling more vividly than macroeconomics," said another judge of the Ninth Circuit, "but the amenities improved the absorption rate of the substantive matter."[52] This combination of wining and dining was important for the success of all of Manne's programs. "Some who attended Manne's 'summer camp' got a good rest or a good tan, but most came away with more," said Ronald Cass, a Chicago alum and former dean of the Boston University School of Law. "Most found something in the economic analysis that changed the way they looked at a problem or a group of problems."[53]

The effectiveness of the summer program, however, was not a trick of crabs and snorkeling but of the care and shrewdness of Henry Manne. The chance to mingle with senior scholars and Nobel laureates such as Milton Friedman, Friedrich Hayek, and Paul Samuelson was enough to pique the interest of most judges and law professors.[54] As George Priest, the longtime sponsor of the Federalist Society at Yale Law School, put it, Manne paid attention consistently over the years to the content of the conference and the positions of the attendees. "None of the many Manne conferences that I attended were ideological directly. There was no clear or, to my mind, subterranean agenda," he wrote. Manne provided for a balance, but not "too much balance." "Commonly, extremely prominent liberal economists would attend—such as Paul Samuelson and Ken Arrow," he remembered. "Though both are irrepressible, their positions were often cabined by topics far from familiar to them." Manne would bring in liberal academics to the judges' program to teach sessions on "safe topics." A liberal economist teaching supply and demand presents very little danger compared to having such an economist teach on antitrust or regulation. "That," Priest wrote, "Henry Manne would never allow."[55]

By 1980, Manne had fully embraced the role of the outsider, but he was no longer frustrated about it. Precisely by becoming an effective outsider and making clever use of institutions, he was able to promote previously marginal ideas into the mainstream. Entrenched within the emerging conservative movement, the LEC had a budget exceeding $1.5 million raised from right-wing organizations, such as the John M. Olin Foundation, but also from major corporations, such as AT&T, Ford Motor Company, and US Steel.[56] He felt like he was well on his way in establishing "Hoover East," as he came to call it—an academically and politically more significant version of California's Hoover Institution but on the East Coast.[57]

By the time the LEC was ten years old, it had become a major force in the conservative movement. Milton Friedman wrote to

Manne in the summer of 1984 to congratulate him on the anniversary and note that the field of law and economics had become dramatically more significant partly as a result of his efforts. "The consequences are reflected not only in scholarly articles in journals and the establishment of new journals devoted to the field," he wrote, "but also in court decisions by judges who have participated in your economics institute for Judges or for Law Professors."[58] Manne would use Friedman's praise for the all-important task of fund-raising, an enterprise that he excelled at both with corporations and with foundations.[59]

While law and economics was adopted in law schools at the University of Virginia, the University of Southern California, and in guarded ways at Yale and Harvard, Manne's project at the University of Miami was the most recognizable and most overtly ideological of all these institutions. Manne, however, was always in the market for expanding his vision of what the LEC could be. He brought the LEC to Emory University for a time. Initially with significant support from the conservative John M. Olin Foundation and from the university administration, Manne had plans to purchase a large building on the outskirts of the campus that would help make the LEC the premiere free-market institution on the East Coast.[60]

He eventually landed a final institutional home at George Mason University. James Buchanan and Gordon Tullock, libertarian social-choice theorists who were also friends with Manne, invited him in 1985 to meet with the school's president, who was looking for someone to head the law school that the university had recently acquired. It was a match. "He committed enough money that I could buy out a lot of the existing faculty and fire those that didn't have tenure, and I did," Manne said. "I got rid of fourteen people in one year and hired eleven new people, twenty-five personnel actions without a single faculty meeting. Nothing like that has ever happened in the history of higher education. By the second year, we were already an important law school, and embarked on implementing the Rochester program at Mason."[61] Manne's contempt and disregard for faculty governance went a long way toward compiling a team of conservative economic specialists who were highly motivated but likely undervalued in the liberal academy. He built up an institution that was focused on public policy and specialized in feeding graduates into government and business.[62]

Perhaps Henry Manne's most high-profile opportunity to respond to the rising tide of activists who were calling on corporations to embrace new forms of social responsibility came in 1976. At the behest of John Durkin (a junior US senator from New Hampshire who had made a name for himself as a public interest activist particularly in areas of consumer protection and corporate fraud), Warren Magnuson, the powerful Democratic chairman of the Senate Commerce Committee, convened hearings that summer to discuss new proposals relating to corporate rights and responsibilities.[63]

It was a significant moment. Both sides of the brewing corporate social responsibility debate had the chance to state their case, from conservative members of the American Enterprise Institute and the Hoover Institution to liberal faculty at elite law schools.[64]

Although debates over corporate reform had been ongoing throughout the decade, the proximate cause was a new proposal from the Corporate Accountability Research Group. Led by Ralph Nader and his associates Mark Green and Joel Seligman, these public interest activists proposed a new Federal Chartering Act that would make large corporations more responsive to a range of social concerns and more accountable to the federal government.[65] The case for a new federal incorporation system was laid out in a controversial book published by W. W. Norton, *Taming the Giant Corporation*, which showed how corporations had become out of control and untethered from the vision of a democratic political economy.[66] The legislative proposal was practically an omnibus of liberal ideas for how to reform corporations, including more democratic shareholder voting processes, increased social disclosure requirements, and an employee "bill of rights."

The hearings that June 1976 were tense at times. Among certain populist Democratic members of Congress, such as Oklahoma's US senator Fred Harris, the Nader bill had stirred a lot of interest, and many at the hearings were sympathetic to its general aims.[67] But among those on the conservative side who had been called to testify, Nader and his ilk were poster boys for muddled economic logic and a special kind of threat to the free market. If there were an individual most disposed to dislike and disregard Nader's perspective, it was likely to be Henry Manne. And if there were one to see Manne as a cynical mouthpiece of the corporations that funded the Law and Economics Center, it was probably Nader. The crux of Nader's argument was that corporations had grown to become something much bigger and more powerful than they were when America's corporation laws had been written. The imperative was to bring the law up to speed with reality.

But Nader knew that wasn't entirely persuasive. "There are some observers who say that size itself makes no difference," he said. "These observers are usually relegated to academic groves in South Florida."[68] As Henry Manne's turn came to testify, the presiding senator joked, "Since Mr. Nader referred to the Southern Florida experts, we will permit you to testify." "I should have thought my suntan would make it clear to everyone that it was I to whom Nader was referring," Manne said.[69]

As the libertarian *Reason* magazine reported with exasperation, the liberal Democratic US senator Vance Hartke was the only member present, and even he left the chamber just a few sentences into the prepared statement, leaving Manne talking to an empty dais and a handful of aides and spectators. Halfway through, Hartke returned and proceeded to interrupt with a series of questions that were occasionally aggressive, if not rather insulting. The ensuing back-and-forth revealed Manne as defensive and Hartke dismissive. Was it "useless to attempt to 'work through the system' bit by bit?" *Reason* asked. "Or is the conclusion that the free-market position is finally getting on the map, since only people who are getting scared pull such shenanigans?"[70]

The effort represented by Nader and company to "democratize" the corporation was an "attempt to solve a nonexistent problem," Manne said.[71] He laid out the rudimentary sketch of libertarian economic theory, including in particular the efficient market hypothesis as well as his own long-held views on how the price of shares reflected accurate information about the value of investments and the efficiency of corporate management. "Some market mechanism," he said, "must be available to ensure managerial efficiency and to replace less productive managers with more efficient ones." The point was this: shareholding was simply an economic act, not a political phenomenon. To alter the structure of corporate governance by bringing non-economic interests to bear would distort market mechanisms, produce massive inefficiencies, and result in general economic catastrophe.[72]

Vance Hartke pressed Manne on whether corporations have responsibilities with regard to pollution. "Senator, individuals can have responsibilities to society; corporations are not such beings as can have responsibilities or souls or spirits or anything of that sort," Manne said. Hartke was incredulous. "There is no such thing as a corporate responsibility," Manne repeated. Upon closer inspection, he said, a corporation dissolves into a collection of contracts and utility-maximizing individuals. It was a misnomer, he contended, to infer that institutions have responsibilities at all; "the ultimate unit of analysis is individuals have incentives, constraints, motivations, responsibilities, and can be dealt with in those fashions." "I think you are going to find yourself in such a minority that we don't have to worry much about this testimony," Hartke retorted.[73]

The ensuing back-and-forth quickly foundered, with Hartke accusing Manne of being an anarchist and having a "callous approach" and Manne defending rather tactlessly the usefulness of economic metrics for the valuation of social goods, including human life. Such lines of thought were fit for seminars at the Law and Economics Center and not so much for hearings on Capitol Hill.

It is safe to say that Henry Manne's appearance before the Senate Commerce Committee was a poorly received attempt at rebutting Ralph Nader's justification for corporate reform. But it is also fair to say that Manne was unlikely to find a particularly receptive audience in the Senate regardless of the rhetorical persuasiveness of his performance. The experience confirmed for Manne something that he had already learned; namely, that the best way to evangelize for his cause was not at elite institutions directly, be they Ivy League law schools or the US Senate, but indirectly through non-mainstream if still well-funded institutions that could cultivate and spread libertarian ideas. What perhaps escaped Manne's notice for the time being was a small but determined group of people who also appealed to the market and worked outside the mainstream—but who wanted to find a way to reconcile corporate America and social responsibility.

NINE

Nothing to Ask Permission For

In 1968, a liberal-leaning Boston synagogue asked the investment-management firm it dealt with, Thomas O'Connell Management and Research, to adjust the congregation's portfolio to exclude any firms profiting from the war in Vietnam. At the time, investment managers usually didn't receive requests such as that—and likely wouldn't know how to respond. It turned out that disentangling good profit-seeking from the bad was a far more difficult task than it seemed at first.

There was the problem of ethics. What, after all, did it mean to have socially responsible investments? And did a broker, portfolio manager, accountant, or someone else get to decide? Such questions blurred the lines between politics, ethics, and capitalism, creating awkward and challenging situations for investment professionals, who usually lacked the training to make such judgments. But there was also the problem of information. Even a seemingly straightforward request such as withdrawing investments from any companies with Department of Defense contracts was not one that most fund managers were prepared to fulfill. They simply lacked the necessary data.

Enter Alice Tepper. A junior securities analyst at Thomas O'Connell, she was a liberal activist chosen to construct a "peace portfolio." "I'd just returned from a six-month stint on the [Eugene] McCarthy [presidential] campaign so the request was passed on to me," she later said.[1] It took a few months. But once she put together the portfolio, her investment group placed a small advertisement for "peace stocks" in a national newspaper and received more than 600 interested responses by mail.[2]

The experience led Tepper to found the Council on Economic Priorities (CEP) in 1969, an organization that replicated and expanded on what she did as an analyst at Thomas O'Connell. The timing couldn't have been better. As protests heated up against firms such as Dow Chemical and General Motors (the Campaign to Make General Motors Responsible was organized in part by a fellow Eugene McCarthy staffer and friend of Tepper's named Geoffrey Cowan), Tepper's group received financial support from religious activists and, soon, from the Rockefeller Family Fund, the Carnegie Corporation, the Ottinger Foundation, and labor unions and other funds.[3] Dubbed one of the "New Independents" by *Vogue* magazine, Tepper and other young public-interest activists would receive glowing profiles from prominent magazines and newspapers such as *People* and the *New York Times*.

With a volunteer staff mostly made up of students working out of a Washington, DC, hotel, CEP had humble beginnings. But by 1970, the organization was putting out its monthly *Economic Priorities Report*, profiling corporations, and highlighting corporate social responsibility campaigns. It also published a groundbreaking study, *Efficiency in Death: The Manufacturers of Anti-Personnel Weapons*, which described the development of weapons such as cluster bombs and flechette-firing rockets designed primarily to kill and maim people and provided information about the finances, leadership, and consumer-facing brands of companies who produced such weapons.[4] The book helped show to the public that it was not innocent of the activities of such nefarious corporations as Dow Chemical and the wider military-industrial complex that profited from war.[5] The organization tried to capitalize on influential readers and supporters in mainline Protestant churches and other religious groups, nonprofit foundations, colleges and universities, labor unions, and a small number of socially conscious mutual funds.

Over the years, the CEP would publish books that showed systemic discrimination against women and people of color in the commercial banking sector and that examined the social policies of the 100 largest companies.[6] But its most popular book was *Shopping for a Better World: A Quick and Easy Guide to Socially Responsible Supermarket Shopping*, which provided to socially conscientious consumers information for responsible shopping that was organized either by the social issue (apartheid, for example, or animal testing) or by types of products (baking mixes or canned meat).[7]

The CEP aimed to squeeze corporate actors at two points: investment capital and consumer markets.[8] The rising significance of institutional investors had been recognized by Peter Drucker, who warned in 1976 of the arrival of "pension fund socialism."[9] A growing consumer movement focused primarily on safety issues but expanding to other areas of social concern from the 1970s to 2000s would transform the way high-profile brands managed their reputations. To both consumers and investors, the CEP pursued a pedagogical strategy: act as a clearinghouse of accessible and useful information about corporate conduct in order to inform the public's decisions about how to spend money.

This strategy of shaming business into acting better through damaging public disclosures was not exactly new—a tradition of using "publicity" in lieu of direct regulation went back to the Progressive Era (and would stretch forward into contemporary activism over human rights abuses, for example). Where Tepper and her colleagues advanced something truly innovative was in the development of new forms of accounting that tracked and publicized the social responsibility or irresponsibility of each industry or corporation.

In an era when the specter of a corporate "social audit" would hover over 1970s American business, Alice Tepper believed that a more accurate social accounting—and the better business behavior it encouraged—did not have to cut into business profits. "Peace stocks," Tepper told the Associated Press in 1969, "can be a good investment."[10] This was her contribution: not just that principles of corporate social responsibility should be applied to investing, but also the idea that socially responsible investments could and would naturally be profitable—even more profitable than conventional stocks. "Public accountability on the part of corporations," she told *Playboy* magazine in 1970, "will lead to an increased awareness of the need to be socially responsible for the simple reason that it will be good business."

The early movement for corporate social responsibility had faltered over the question of the authority of management to trade profits for the promise of the public good—and over the capability of management to decide what constituted the public good. But socially responsible investing—and the style of corporate social responsibility that it would engender over the next several decades—offered a way out of this impasse by answering questions of political power and moral judgment through market solutions. Young activists such as Alice Tepper made an alluring promise: with better accounting practices, the struggle between public good and private profit could be harmonized to the benefit of all. Still, there persisted a conflict between what many activists and corporate managers said was good for the world and what was good for women and babies.

Social workers and nutrition experts had known about the problems with baby formula for a long time. It was a lifesaving substitute under the right conditions, but it was expensive and required the use of safe drinking water. For many in the developing world in the 1970s, disposable income and clean water were in short supply. Products such as Enfamil and Similac became deadly contributors to a public health crisis when poor mothers used unsanitary water or diluted the formula in order to stretch their supply.

Derrick Jelliffe, a professor of population and family health at the University of California, Los Angeles, was one of the first to identify a worldwide "protein gap" between the rich and poor. In a series of influential articles in the late 1960s and 1970s, he traced this inequality to the entrance of women into the workforce in developing countries such as Chile and Uganda. Jelliffe blamed multinational corporations for tearing the traditional family apart. Industrial work took women out of the home. Western-style consumer culture, advertised in newspapers and on radio, idealized women's independence. The result was a disruption of traditional patterns of child-rearing, a rapid decline in breast-feeding, and the increase of health problems, including malnutrition and infant mortality. "It is harsh, but correct, to consider some of these children as suffering from 'commerciogenic malnutrition'—that is caused by the thoughtless promotion of these milks and infant foods," he wrote. Pointing to a recent collection of muckraking reports on corporate misdeeds that was edited by economist Robert Heilbroner, Jelliffe saw such corporate marketing as one part of a larger industrial trend in which social responsibility was sacrificed for profits.[11]

A Ralph Nader–inspired movement came in 1973 when the *New Internationalist*, a British leftist magazine, reported on the baby formula crisis. In an article called "The Baby Food Tragedy," two leading nutritionists pointed to advertising and promotional techniques used in Africa and the Middle East to target new mothers while they were recovering in the hospital. Ralph Hendrikse, a director at Liverpool University, said there was an urgent need for international consensus on appropriate advertising. "In Bangkok, I saw a mother who was just about to leave hospital with a baby that had just been born and she had on the locker beside the bed, a tin of Nestlé's milk and a small bottle with Nestlé written on it which, I was told, is given to all mothers before they leave hospital," said David Morley, an expert in tropical child health at the University of London. "I think that the sellers of these milks would like to paint the idea to us that it is a responsible campaign." The next year, a nongovernmental organization (NGO) called War on Want published *The Baby Killer*, a twenty-page document that popularized these findings. "The baby food industry stands accused of promoting their products in communities which cannot use them properly," the report read, "of using advertising, sales girls dressed up in nurses uniforms, giving away samples and free gift gimmicks that persuade mothers to give up breast feeding."[12]

The impact of *The Baby Killer* was global. War on Want distributed copies in the United Kingdom and advertised in newspapers such as *The Guardian*. A group called Third World Working Group translated it into German and published it in Switzerland with the provocative title *Nestlé Kills Babies*, provoking a libel suit from the corporation that stretched on for years and generated a great deal of publicity. In 1976, documentary maker Peter Krieg released a film called *Bottle Babies*, which focused on the impact of Nestlé's baby formula products in Kenya. As one academic observed at the time, the film was "probably responsible for enrolling most of the persons and groups who support the Nestlé boycott."[13]

The first activist action in the United States began not with the Nestlé Corporation, which was the largest producer of baby formula in the world, but with a handful of American companies—Abbott Laboratories, Bristol-Myers, and American Home Products. It was the Interfaith Center on Corporate Responsibility (ICCR), an organization representing dozens of Protestant and Roman Catholic groups and founded in response to Campaign GM, that brought resolutions to these companies' annual meetings in early 1976. Along with the Sisters of the Precious Blood, a women's religious community from Ohio, their efforts to pressure corporations by means of shareholder resolutions earned publicity in the United States. Dubbed "ecclesiastical Ralph Naders," these groups recognized the potential influence that voting shares held in the endowments of religious institutions such as monasteries, denominations, and colleges might have in American business. Tim Smith, one of the leaders of the ICCR, imagined the Christian church as a massive shareholder. "For too long, the church has kept its stock portfolios in one pocket and social ethics in another," he said. "Finally, it discovered that it could no longer remain a social schizophrenic."[14]

These religious activists, whom *Fortune* magazine called "Marxists marching under the banner of Christ," were instrumental in forcing the baby formula issue. The ICCR introduced resolutions at the annual meetings of Bristol-Myers, Abbot Laboratories, and American Home Products asking the companies to present their consumer education programs and to provide information on the promotion of baby formulas in developing countries. Although these resolutions failed at the corporate ballot, the ICCR and the Sisters of the Precious Blood forced Bristol-Myers to settle out of court over litigation that accused the company of lying about its sales and marketing in developing countries.[15]

But the big target was Nestlé. On July 4, 1977, the Minneapolis-based Infant Formula Action Coalition (INFACT)—which for months had been organizing public demonstrations against the local Nestlé office and used handmade messages such as "Nestlé cares for profit more than people"—announced the launch of a boycott. The Swiss company posed significant challenges to American activists because it was not subject to the same securities laws or shareholder markets as American companies such as Bristol-Myers or General Motors. Storming a shareholders' meeting was not an option. INFACT's campaign, which spread internationally among a variety of groups, took the fight to consumers. But even the consumer market campaign was not straightforward. Nestlé did not market its baby formula products in the United States. Other aspects of the firm's business had to be targeted. Nestlé was a conglomerate made up of a variety of companies in different sectors of food production and service. This variety gave the corporation its stability. But, in the case of a boycott, conglomeration became a liability because of the broad range of products that consumers could avoid purchasing. INFACT targeted products ranging from Stouffer's frozen dinners and Nestlé's chocolate to Cain's coffee and Libby's frozen vegetables.[16]

Nestlé officials met with INFACT representatives in the fall of 1977 along with other activists in the corporate responsibility movement such as the ICCR. The company offered minor concessions, such as promising that it would no longer have sales reps dress as nurses in hospitals. But activists said these promises didn't represent a fundamental rethinking of the baby formula problem. Nestlé officials subsequently bungled a US Senate hearing in May 1978, where the Democratic senator from Massachusetts, Edward Kennedy, pressed an industry representative. "The US Nestlé Co. has advised me that their research indicates this is actually an indirect attack on the free world's economic system," responded Oswaldo Ballarin, president of Nestlé Brazil. "A worldwide church organization, with the stated purpose of undermining the free enterprise system, is in the forefront of this activity." To laughter and applause, Kennedy interrupted Ballarin. "You do not seriously expect us to accept that on face value," he said. "It seemed to me that they were expressing a very deep compassion and concern about the well-being of infants, the most vulnerable people on the face of this world." He questioned whether the company could be trusted to be socially responsible when "economic incentives are in conflict with public health."[17]

The boycott continued, and in 1980 Nestlé's earnings were down by 16 percent, and sales slumped in the United States. Sensing that things had gone on long enough, the company formed an office with fifteen staffers to handle corporate social responsibility issues. Nestlé sent out mailers to most US clergymen—about 300,000 at the time—defending its record. A memo written in

1980 by a Nestlé vice president, Ernest Saunders, shows a company besieged. "It is clear that we have an urgent need to develop an effective counter propaganda operation," Saunders wrote. He was particularly pleased with *Fortune* magazine's publication of "The Corporation Haters" in June 1980, a Red-baiting article that cast the baby formula activists as promotors of communism. A confidential internal memo showed that Nestlé had secretly helped fund the Ethics and Public Policy Center, a new right-wing think-tank, which reprinted and distributed the article. The effectiveness of this campaign was short lived, however, because Saunders's memo eventually ended up in the hands of Morton Mintz, a reporter at the *Washington Post*, who published an exposé, "Infant-Formula Maker Battles Boycotters by Painting Them Red," that detailed the secret arrangement.[18]

As activists from the War on Want, INFACT, ICCR, and other international committees laid the groundwork for the World Health Organization's adoption of an International Code of Marketing of Breastmilk Substitutes in 1981, Nestlé was in emergency mode. The code set clear limits on how companies presented their baby formula products to consumers and how health care systems educated mothers. It also called for a strict international system of monitoring so that any malfeasance on the part of manufacturers, distributors, or hospitals could be identified.[19]

The boycott of Nestlé continued up until 1984. After one-on-one negotiations, activists and Nestlé jointly announced victory and the end of the boycott. The World Health Organization (WHO) code established for the first time a system of governmental accountability for multinational corporations. The code, which was opposed solely by the new Reagan administration, represented a change in how corporate decisions could be made, what managerial accountability meant, and how social responsibilities were understood. Administered by an international Nestlé Infant Formula Audit Commission chaired by Senator Edmund Muskie, the voluntary code set up multiple layers of transparency and adjudication, and, perhaps most important, it held the threat of a future boycott over the company. "Global justice was to be achieved through an ethical form of regulated capitalism," as historian Tehila Sasson puts it.[20]

The voluntary WHO code and the audit commission represented a form of corporate social responsibility from the ground up that had real teeth—and staying power (the WHO code is still being audited and enforced). But this achievement was hard won, complicated, and costly. At the time, many forward-thinking strategists and institutional investors wondered whether financial pressure could be wielded in more efficient and exacting ways.

In an age of protest, many religious organizations and philanthropic foundations began taking steps to divest from defense contractors and from industries contributing to environmental pollution, racial segregation in the United States, or apartheid in South Africa. This shift in the use of finance capital and this transformation in philosophy—away from simply seeing investments as sources of capital for an organization's use and understanding them as instruments of change in their own right—took time.

The organizers of the Campaign to Make General Motors Responsible, for example, received support from several religious organizations and foundations, but they were disappointed to learn that the Carnegie Foundation and the Rockefeller Foundation both decided to throw their voting stock behind management during the proxy season of 1970. In fact, no major foundation stockholder supported Campaign GM, including the four largest among them: Charles Stewart Mott, Charles F. Kettering, Alfred P. Sloan, and Richard King Mellon.[21] As noted later by Campaign GM's legal counsel, Donald Schwartz, all four foundations were formed by officers or directors of General Motors.[22]

The liberal leadership of the Rockefeller Foundation, for one, was quite sympathetic to the activists. The former concluded, however, that the far-reaching and ambitious proposals of Campaign GM were "unwieldy and impractical," as foundation president J. George Harrar put it in a statement. "But we are not prepared to let the matter rest there."[23] Harrar criticized GM's management for being overly dismissive of Campaign GM and called on business leaders to "assert an unprecedented order of leadership in helping solve the social problems of our time." He promised that the Rockefeller Foundation would reconsider its philosophy of investment because "more is at stake than our role as a stockholder."

Other nonprofit funds such as the Ford Foundation had begun in the late 1960s to rethink their approach to money management, developing what came to be called program-related investments: "laying aside the structure of maximum return in order to endow risky projects with social potential."[24] But when it came to stockholdings, the Ford Foundation also found itself generally supportive of corporate social responsibility but lacking both a consistent policy and the necessary information to make judgments about controversial shareholder resolutions. By 1973, according to an internal report, the foundation was taking a case-by-case approach to socially responsible investing.[25]

Other institutions faced similar difficulties. Religious organizations—primarily mainline and liberal Protestants and Jews—were at the forefront of corporate activism. The ICCR was an early organizer of Protestant, Catholic, and Jewish faith leaders, denominational fund managers, and religious foundations. The National Council of Churches formed the Corporate Information Center, which began publishing in 1971 a monthly magazine called the *Corporate Examiner*.

Such religious organizations represented a significant source of influence not only because they were motivated by ethical and moral considerations and because they were naturally well suited to organize churchgoers into activists, but also—and perhaps primarily—because they had a lot of capital and investments in securities. One oft-cited and controversial book from 1969 by an eccentric scholar of religion and "free-thinking" activist, Martin A. Larson, called *Praise the Lord for Tax Exemption*, took the American religious establishment to task for its excessive wealth and estimated that churches possessed more than $100 billion in assets and collected and disbursed more than $22 billion annually—leaving it unsurpassed by any other sector, save, of course, the federal government.[26] A Rockefeller Foundation internal report of 1971 estimated that $4 billion in ecclesiastical assets might be reinvested in alternative companies because of new concerns about social responsibility.[27]

The churches became increasingly active, in part because of pressure from the outside. In what was probably the most high-profile protest against the Protestant establishment in the United States at the time, a black civil rights activist named James Forman walked into Riverside Church, the great United Church of Christ building built in New York by Standard Oil monopolist John D. Rockefeller, and interrupted a Sunday morning service. The pastor tried to drown out Forman by having the organist blast the church with another rendition of "When Morning Gilds the Skies," but after a few minutes the clergy, choir, and laity ceded the pulpit to Forman, who delivered his so-called Black Manifesto to the hundreds still assembled in the Neo-Gothic nave. "Riverside Church must pay extra reparations to black people through the National Black Economic Development Conference, for the money of John D. Rockefeller is still exploiting people of color all around the world," Forman said.[28] Many sympathetic church leaders balked at the demand for reparations, choosing instead to support the cause of civil rights and racial reconciliation in their own way.

The Episcopal Church, for example, introduced a resolution at the GM annual meeting in 1971 calling on the company to cease manufacturing operations in apartheid South Africa.[29] Because of apartheid, too, and other matters, the United Presbyterian Church targeted Gulf Oil by use of shareholder resolutions, and the United

Church of Christ organized a boycott of the company. The United Methodist Church formed a committee to establish social criteria for investments, and its Women's Division used stockholdings to advocate for "such matters as fair employment, equitable conditions of work and other major concerns of social justice."[30]

Similar stories could be told about most major institutional investors. In response to student activists who in 1969 demanded that Princeton University separate its endowment from colonial and apartheid investments in South Africa, Rhodesia, Angola, and Mozambique, the university formed a committee to study the issue, which recommended that university administrators express concerns to companies doing business in those countries, financially support programs that help black people of southern Africa, and, among other things, offer courses in race relations. Notably, Princeton asserted that selling of its securities would "severely impair" the university's "effectiveness as an institution."[31] In response, students involved in a so-called Radical Arts Troupe put on a presentation called "When the Blue Chips Are Down, the Tiger Shows His Stripes," which depicted the committee's chair as a "white master and his black worker in South Africa, and a Princeton trustee serving as the 'middle man,'" according to the *Daily Princetonian*.[32]

The fissures of the corporate protests ran through all the major institutions of higher learning in those years. Dartmouth University and Union College were forced to reckon with their investments in Eastman Kodak because of the FIGHT-Kodak dispute. Amherst College, Brown University, and the University of Pennsylvania supported Campaign GM. The Council for Financial Aid to Education estimated that the largest seventy-one universities held $7.6 billion in investments, which the Rockefeller Foundation internal report said represented "considerable potential economic influence for social change in our economy."[33] "It is increasingly clear," said J. Richardson Dilworth, chair of Yale University's finance committee, "that there is going to be more concern with social conscience in the investment decision—unless we are to go back to the cave age."[34]

Pension funds were another matter. Often managed by institutions such as unions that were prodded into addressing political and social issues, the reserves of non-insured pension funds increased fifteenfold between 1965 and 1985.[35] Management guru Peter Drucker called the explosion of pension fund balances an "unseen revolution" in his similarly titled 1976 book because of the socialization of ownership that such conglomerations of finance capital represented: employees, the self-employed, and public workers owning a rising portion of the equity capital of American business.[36] One expert estimated that institutions in 1970 owned nearly 40 percent of the stock of the nation's major corporations.[37] By the early 1980s, experts estimated that the pension funds of corporations and of state and local governments held about $1 trillion in assets.[38] By 1980, the AFL-CIO formed a council to determine social responsibility criteria for its investments.[39]

And just as Alice Tepper put together a "peace portfolio," other socially motivated investors concocted their own brew of mutual funds meant to make the world a better place. J. Elliot Corbett and Luther Tyson, two United Methodist ministers, formed Pax World Fund in 1971, which combined antiwar ethics with traditional Methodist opposition to alcohol, tobacco, and gambling.[40] So, too, Howard Stein at the larger investment-management company the Dreyfus Fund formed the Third Century Fund, which focused not so much on screening out the bad but finding and investing in companies with a stated mission of improving the environment, for example, or race relations.[41]

But back in the proxy season of 1971, little progress had been made at the Rockefeller Foundation. When Campaign GM came back with additional shareholder resolutions, the nonprofit again supported management (though abstaining on two issues: corporate disclosure and apartheid in South Africa), only providing moral support to activists. "No consensus has emerged," explained the foundation's 1971 internal report, "and there is as yet no agreement on what the goals of a sensitive and well-meaning institution should be, much less on how those goals might be achieved. In one of the areas of primary importance—the development of an investment policy that will encompass both social and financial considerations—no commonly accepted yardsticks have been developed. The whole concept of a 'social audit' is still in its infancy."[42]

THE QUEST FOR a social audit was a search for some systematic or objective form of accounting that would relieve socially responsible investment managers from the time-consuming and frequently vexing process of making decisions about where to place their funds on a purely ad hoc or case-by-case basis. After all, researching proxy votes took a tremendous amount of time—especially when every major publicly held corporation might have dozens of resolutions for shareholders to evaluate each year. Researching a particular company's ethical conduct would take even more time—far more than many organizations were capable of devoting, especially since much business conduct (with regard to pollution, for example) was not always publicly known.[43]

But the allure of the social audit—and of other forms of social accounting from the 1970s to the present day—was not just that nonfinancial information could be integrated into what the public (especially the investing public) could know about big business. The social audit also held out the tantalizing possibility that ethical problems could be made legible on an accountant's ledger as simply and clearly as a profit-and-loss statement. It suggested a convenient way out of the corporate social responsibility impasse. Struggles over institutional power—and over what was right or wrong—could be transformed into a seemingly objective form of knowledge ready-made for investors to use to make the world a better place.

The idea of the social audit wasn't original to the 1970s. Thirty years earlier, a Stanford business professor named Theodore J. Kreps had written a monograph on the possibility of measuring "social performance," as he called it, for the New Deal–era Temporary National Economic Committee. And economist Howard Bowen theorized in his 1953 book, *Social Responsibilities of the Businessman*, that outside social auditors could provide an objective "social point of view" of major corporations.[44] But the social audit became more than a theoretical possibility in the 1970s when an increasing number of institutional investors began to ask for actionable information about where socially responsible investments could be found. "Disclosure," one observer said at the time, "is a more salable idea that tends to attract more institutional support."[45]

Seen from the vantage point of the accounting profession, the problem of social responsibility was interpreted as a problem of measuring and processing information—which is just what many institutional investors wanted. David F. Linowes, a professor and longtime CPA at a major accounting firm, believed that what he called social performance could be rendered into accounting terms analogous to other categories of business performance. "As I see it, it will be as common as the profit-and-loss statement and the balance sheet," he told the *New York Times*. "It will undoubtedly be on file with a government regulatory agency and it should be part of every company's annual report."[46] Management and futurist prognosticator Alvin Toffler predicted that "accounting itself is on the edge of revolution and is about to explode out of its narrowly economic terms of reference."[47]

Linowes was one of the most prominent advocates of the social audit in the late 1960s and early 1970s, which he believed would only make business more efficient and profitable in the long run. "The worst present-day corporate abusers of the environment and of humanity look best on their current profit and loss statement," he told a meeting of the American Accounting Association in Baton Rouge, Louisiana, in April of 1972. "The business executive can no longer look to dollar profit measurement alone as an adequate reflection of his effectiveness." He insisted that, in the long run, socially irresponsible behavior would cut into profits and lead to inefficiencies.

The social audit, so the thinking went, would make clearer in the short term who was doing good—and thus who would go on to do well financially. What, however, did doing good exactly mean? Linowes advocated for something called a "socio-economic operating statement" that would tabulate "those expenditures made voluntarily to improve the welfare of employees and the public, product safety, or environmental conditions."[48] The examples he had in mind were just the sort of programs corporations had been developing during those years, such as training programs for minority workers or the handicapped, donations to black colleges, or use of more expensive lead-free paint. But he also argued that costs associated with inaction or irresponsibility should be tabulated as well: postponement of the installation of a new safety device or damage done to the environment because of strip mining.[49]

Such categories of responsibility and irresponsibility reflected the concerns of contemporary social movements then gaining ascendancy, but the methods of accounting neutered the political dynamics of those movements. Indeed, the tendency of the social audit was to extrapolate matters of ethics and power into the abstract quantification of numbers—and, particularly, of dollars. Historically, such forms of social accounting and statistics have often been governed by what one writer referred to as an "investmentality," which has led professional number crunchers to put a dollar figure on a human life, for example, or on the annual cost of alcoholism or other social ills.[50] So, too, Linowes could hope that standards of measurement in the "social field" would soon achieve the objectivity and predictability of "the same units of measurement employed in business."[51]

In the early 1970s, accounting firms such as Abt Associates began offering social audits to corporate officers for internal decision making.[52] Ernst & Ernst started compiling the "social disclosures" of companies on an annual basis. Outside watchdog groups such as Alice Tepper's CEP published their own form of social accounting reports. The managers of Dreyfus's Third Century Fund tracked a selected twenty industries.[53] Much of the information gathered for such audits came, however, from the very companies being audited (or, in some cases, from government data or lawsuits). Many firms were motivated to provide information in order to reap the public relations and investment rewards.[54]

The sort of quantified tabulation of corporate social performance—at least the kind that David Linowes wanted—wouldn't come in the 1970s. What reform-minded accountants got instead was mostly corporate self-disclosures, which were typically far more prosaic in character. General Motors began publishing annual reports on its social programs in response to Campaign GM—a report that continued to be published up until 1994.[55]

But the main venue for such disclosures was the corporate annual report. According to an Ernst & Ernst report, the percentage of companies that included social disclosures went from 60 percent in 1973 to about 91 percent in 1976—with the length of the disclosure varying from one to four and a half pages.[56]

General Electric first began providing information about its social responsibility programs in the annual report of 1970, and in subsequent years it provided annual updates from the "Public Issues Committee," which was then finally replaced by a "Public Responsibilities Committee" in 1979 and which continued to review, General Electric reported, "management's responses to public issues affecting the Company." But communications about social responsibility withered. By the time Jack Welch—whose fanatical commitment to shareholder value transformed the company in the late twentieth century—took over as chairman in 1981, the committee had four lines in the annual report.

Some reformers, doubtful of the credibility of corporate self-disclosures and anxious about the fact that executives were losing the appetite for social responsibility, insisted that a more objective form of the social audit was needed—something with regulatory teeth. One key figure here is Juanita Kreps, secretary of the Department of Commerce under President Jimmy Carter. In 1977, Kreps announced that her department intended to develop what she called a social performance index that would track how corporations performed with respect to minority hiring, environmental pollution, consumer responsiveness, or purchasing from minority-owned firms.[57] Each year, the Department of Commerce would publish a set of standards that could be used to evaluate the social effects of business behavior, and the department would then publish the results of those measurements in an annual index. At first, the CEO lobbying organization Business Roundtable and the liberal trade group Conference Board, for example, participated in the development of this index.[58]

But business opinion quickly turned. "The word 'index' seems to have triggered some psychic alarm system, for it seems to connote a report card of sins and virtues," Kreps said. And even though she insisted that the central goal of the index was to "advance the development of procedures that would enable a corporation to judge its own social performance," the idea of a government-sponsored evaluation of the social conduct of business sparked alarm.[59]

At a hearing arranged to consider the appropriation request of $428,000 for the program, several congressmen expressed profound opposition to Kreps's proposal because they believed it would only contribute to inflation. "Somebody, somewhere, ought to point out that a corporation is simply a pass-through organization, that passes through all their costs to the consumer," said one North Dakota representative, voicing a particularly Henry Manne view of the corporation. "This attitude that some politicians think it is so great to 'Let's sock it to the corporation'—all they do is sock it to the person on the end of the line that is already getting hit by high prices."[60] The Business Roundtable likewise turned against the program, the executive director telling Kreps that most CEO members believed the idea was "impractical, unworkable and unfair." She soon quietly dropped the proposal.[61] Looking back years later at her time at the Department of Commerce, Kreps said "I had the unhappy experience there, as I have elsewhere, of proposing things before people are ready to accept them."[62]

That grim assessment was undoubtedly true. The political timing *was* bad. Jimmy Carter's presidency would soon be on the rocks, the result of a confluence of political and economic crises that he was unwilling or unable to master. Proposed a few years earlier, at the dawn of the decade when social movements and activists might have mobilized support around the program, the social performance index would likely have received congressional support against the objections of executives and lobby groups. But the defeat of the index—and problems that hampered the social audit, too—cannot simply be attributed to a sour political mood or machinations gone wrong in Washington, DC.

There was practically little constituency—not among social movements, unions, consumers, executives, or even the Democratic Party—for such an antiseptic, technocratic solution to what was a major political issue. For investors and public interest activists, however, the idea that better accounting and more efficient allocation of investment capital could usher in a new era of corporate social responsibility remained a convenient and alluring idea.

—

A BOOKEND FOR the corporate protests came in 1980 with Big Business Day and the Corporate Democracy Act. Both were Ralph Nader projects, and both built on more than a decade of activism. Big Business Day brought attention to the bad behavior of big corporations such as Exxon and Citicorp and drummed up support for legislative reform. The protest took place in about 150 cities across the country, included labor, consumer, and environmental activists, and consisted of teach-ins, rallies, and in Washington, DC, a "Corporate Hall of Shame." The recklessness and power of big corporations, from specific instances such as the poisoning of Love Canal in New York to more general claims about how business interests influenced politics, were presented as evidence that private institutions had subverted the democratic public good.[63]

The message of Big Business Day, however, did not just consist in opposing business. Organizers also had a vision for what corporations could do better. Speakers made the case that corporations should be committed to and accountable for benchmarks that extended beyond shareholder profit to include the interests of other stakeholders such as consumers, workers, and local communities. Among those delivering the stakeholder idea were Nader, liberal economist John Kenneth Galbraith, democratic socialist Michael Harrington, public and private sector union leaders such as United Farm Workers organizer Cesar Chavez, and the president of the United Auto Workers, Douglas Fraser, as well as a few Democratic politicians.[64]

But the event was most successful at stirring up the ire of conservative business interests. "Kick-a-businessman day," *BusinessWeek* said, was a cynical attempt to revive interest in a consumer movement that had waned in strength since Nader faced off against the auto industry. Likewise, in the pages of the *Wall Street Journal*, the conservative economist Herbert Stein dismissed criticisms of the big American corporation. "Who do they think created the unparalleled affluence enjoyed by the American people? Ralph Nader?" Such questions needed no answers.[65]

Far from signaling a decade of corporate reform efforts, Big Business Day elicited one of the most coordinated and sophisticated business counterattacks of the new conservative era. The Business Roundtable and the US Chamber of Commerce began organizing a response almost immediately after the event was announced. They reacted to left-liberal activists by going on the offensive, calling it "Anti-Business Day," and presenting their own version of events that highlighted the efficiency and productivity of the American economy. The chamber unfurled a seventy-foot-long banner that could be seen from the Washington Mall: "It's Your Business, America. The US Chamber Salutes America's 15 Million Businesses." Newly influential right-wing think-tanks such as the American Enterprise Institute, the Cato Institute, and the Heritage Foundation sponsored opposition programs such as "Growth Day," which sought to highlight the "positive achievements of the private-enterprise system." At a breakfast well attended by lawmakers and the press, they attacked government regulation and praised the capitalist system as the "finest wealth-generating tool in the world."[66]

At a US Senate Subcommittee on Securities hearing, Senator Howard Metzenbaum, a Democrat from Ohio, noted a collapse in public support of big business, a decline in the relative number of people who invested in corporations, and the widespread failure of corporate boards to provide institutional supervision. "There is no doubt that we face major problems in the governance of our major corporations," he said. The Corporate Democracy Act of 1980, which Metzenbaum had introduced and which was attacked by ascendant conservatives who called it antibusiness, would have transformed corporate capitalism in profound ways.[67]

The bill built on ideas that had percolated during a decade and a half of activism and had sought to change the governance of big business. The boards of directors, for example, would be restored to their original status as auditing institutions. Directors would come from outside the corporation and be given a mandate and the resources to oversee managers and to keep track of business decisions that affected important social issues. It would have empowered shareholders and other stakeholders to vote on new kinds of questions and would have given them authority to supervise managers. The act envisioned the corporation as a publicly accountable institution that would be required to provide accessible information to the general public and to give advanced notice of business decisions that might significantly affect unemployment. "The fundamental premise of Big Business Day is that shareholders are just one of many 'stakeholders' of a corporation," wrote Mark Green, a Nader associate and public interest progressive. "Yet other than shareholders, these other stakeholders, like workers, consumers and local communities, are denied access to a voice in these giant private governments." The arguments were sophisticated. The rhetoric was powerful. But few were listening.[68]

It was not just the election of Ronald Reagan in 1980 that made Big Business Day and the Corporate Democracy Act seem quixotic. As Metzenbaum put it that November, "I do not delude myself into thinking that this bill will be promptly enacted, especially after the results of the recent election." It was also that these corporate reform efforts provoked an unprecedented opposition from right-wing think-tanks and large business groups. Big business had come a long way since Saul Alinsky had marched into the shareholders' meeting of Eastman Kodak in 1967. It was now more organized, experienced, and poised to preside over more than a decade of bull markets and shareholder value—a far cry from the vision of corporate democracy that activists had nurtured and fought for.

"Corporation without boundaries" became a phrase du jour in 1980s and 1990s management speak.[69] If the corporation of previous decades had been understood by both liberals and leftists as a kind of social as well as economic institution, the corporation, in the new imagination, was an institutional container for markets—or perhaps a node of a larger market network.[70] Established firms were gutted for their cash and assets, which were diverted to more profitable investments, as a new generation of corporate raiders laid waste to diversified conglomerates (once a cutting-edge way to structure a corporation, now derided as lumbering giants).[71] The large corporation became as fungible as the financial markets would allow through facilitating the selling off of jobs, assets, and divisions of the firm, or their absorption and reconfiguration into new firms, or their replacement by sophisticated contracts and subcontracts. What the corporation was good for would be answered through measurements of shareholder value and return on investment.[72]

The Cold War had kept business and Washington committed to safeguarding a large middle class, keeping deflation at bay, providing social welfare relief, and spurring innovation by big investments. But the Cold War was fading in significance, and the problem of inflation could hardly be solved by ramping up social welfare or new capital expenditures—both of which would, after all, only spur inflation further. The federal government simply no longer possessed the policy-making mechanisms and the political will that had sustained industrial capitalism and made it into a force for middle-class growth and social stability.[73]

In its place came a chaotic economic order, one in which capital was more liquid and global. Historian Jonathan Levy calls this the capitalism of asset price appreciation. This form of capitalism, instead of prioritizing a broad and stable middle-class income, focused almost solely on the appreciation of capital. At the same time, it directed the majority of new income gains away from labor earnings or pay and to the owners of capital. An economy centered on the appreciation of asset prices transformed the way most of us generate wealth. It's one reason that housing prices have become so important to the American economy. Many households whose labor earnings remained static or declined nevertheless used debt to purchase and refinance homes. The increasing importance of this source of wealth for the economic well-being of Americans only made the values of homes go up. "Debt thus replaced income growth through pay. So long as home prices went up," Levy writes.[74]

The so-called Volcker Shock, so named for Federal Reserve

chairman Paul Volcker's raising of interest rates beginning in the fall of 1979, also contributed to deindustrialization, a process that had begun a decade or more before, by making short-term investment more valuable than long-term capital outlays. Of particular importance was the precipitous rise in short-term interest rates, which surpassed 19 percent in 1981. One result was that a wave of speculative hot money flooded into the United States, all but guaranteeing the dollar's role as the hegemonic global currency of transaction and reserve. Big business looked away from productive capital and toward more liquid, money-like assets. And herein lies a great divergence: every dollar that sat in high-interest bank accounts was not available to finance economic activity that would expand employment or industrial output. And because the Federal Reserve made its ascent upon and continued its dominance at the summit of a global economic policy that was dependent on the success of short-term investments, asset bubbles proliferated in the late twentieth and early twenty-first centuries. It didn't necessarily matter what they were—tech stocks, oil and gas, savings-and-loan banks, home mortgages. What mattered was short-term asset appreciation and a liquid market to facilitate the exchange of financial products.

Some have said that the American corporation vanished during those decades.[75] Others have said that the corporation was "deinstitutionalized" or became "hollowed out."[76] But the corporation did not so much vanish or deconstruct as it was reorganized and its governance made to fit the goals of a new mode of political economic logic. This new regime of corporate capitalism was set in motion by a constellation of social, political, and economic transformations that were the final putting to rest of the old New Deal settlement.

The conventional wisdom of the era was evident on the front cover of the Coca-Cola Company's 1984 annual report, which showed above a photo of a fizzing glass of iced soda the words: "To increase shareholder value over time is the objective driving this enterprise."[77] Much like their predecessors Louis Wolfson and

James Ling but now on a much larger scale, corporate raiders such as Carl Icahn and T. Boone Pickens kept executives faithful to this objective as they hunted for companies that were financially inefficient or possessed assets that could be sold off or managed differently.[78] High-profile hostile takeovers rocked Wall Street, such as the leveraged buyout of RJR Nabisco, which was dramatized for popular readers and HBO viewers in the book and made-for-TV movie *Barbarians at the Gate*.[79] Icahn, for his part, thought of his work in patriotic terms. "I believe I'm doing something that must be done. Productivity in the US continues to decline," he told *Fortune*. "I get really angry at the managements of many US corporations. Outrage is probably what drives me the most."[80] A total of $1.3 trillion changed hands in the 1980s as 143 companies in the Fortune 500 (or 28 percent) disappeared in mergers and hostile takeovers.[81]

In an article for the *Atlanta Journal-Constitution*, Henry Manne lauded these recent trends in corporate management. "Mergers and takeovers represent our most important devices for moving productive assets into the hands of more efficient managers," he wrote.[82] The governance and practices of big business in those years came to reflect more closely the world that Manne had described and envisioned in his law and economics work in the early 1960s—a world where deregulation enabled mergers and takeovers, where management was responsive to active financial markets, and where shareholder value reflected the efficiency of management.[83]

Under the direction of financializing CEOs such as General Electric's Jack Welch, who "managed by stress," large and lumbering conglomerates traded-in the stability and structure of the maze-like organizational chart for something much more like an internal market. Upon taking the reins of General Electric (GE), Welch immediately fired 100,000 people, graded each professional with efficiency statistics, and made his employees compete with each other annually in order to keep their jobs.[84] In an interview with the *Harvard Business Review* in 1989, Welch used market language to describe how corporate employees needed to be motivated by "adding value" instead of by "control": "[E]ach staff person has to ask, How do I add value? How do I help make people on the line more effective and more competitive?"[85]

Dubbed "Neutron Jack" by labor unions for how he emptied out factories and office buildings, Welch laid off many thousands of workers more during his multidecade tenure at General Electric. Wall Street loved it, sending stock prices soaring in the 1980s and 1990s. Workers? Not so much. The GE workforce of Schenectady, New York, shrank from 24,000 to about 7,000 over the course of twenty years. Bernie Witkowski, who started out as a stock boy right after high school and ended up a master electrician, worked at GE for most of his career, as did most of his family. "GE was the thing. Almost all my uncles worked for General Electric in Schenectady, everybody worked for GE. And when I was brought up, that's what we heard all the time. 'Oh, when you get out of high school, you go to GE, you go to GE,'" he said. "My cousins went to GE. I went."[86]

When Witkowski started at the company, he remembered it constructing new buildings in Schenectady, but he stayed on long enough to see a lot of them torn down and most of the workers get laid off.[87] Welch pioneered a system that came to be called "rank and yank," which forced managers to rank, on an annual basis, the productivity of workers and lay off the bottom ten.[88] "I loved GE," said one veteran employee. "It put a roof on all of our houses. . . . Then you look at the stock dividends and bonuses the big shots are getting, and they turned around and tell us how they had to lay off people."[89] As far as worker sentiments toward Jack Welch went, Witkowski said, "There was nothing good to be said about him."[90]

Cost-cutting layoffs and liquidations, debt-leveraged mergers and acquisitions, and massive corporate reorganizations—practices that were at one time criticized, regulated, and sometimes prosecuted—went from the margins to the mainstream. "We're going to turn the bull loose!" Ronald Reagan told traders in 1985. His visit to the

Total Value of Stock Exchange Shares as Percentage of US GDP & the Number of Publicly Traded Corporations per Million People, 1975–2000

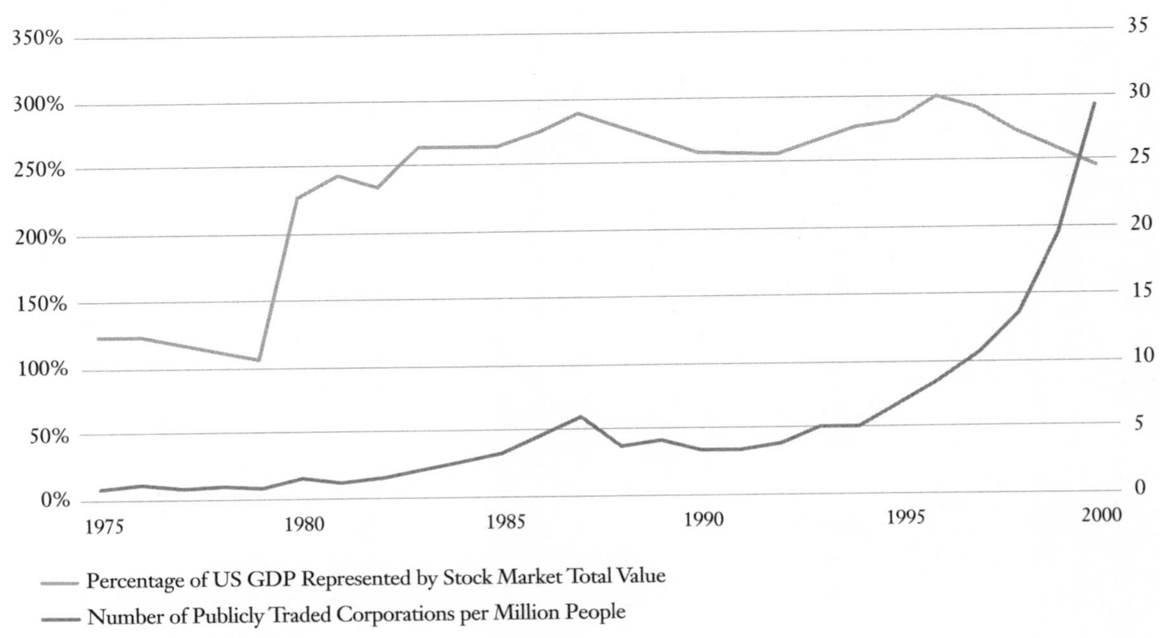

New York Stock Exchange, the first visit of a sitting president, only confirmed a remarkable shift in what American elites expected from big business: not social leadership, long-term stability, or industrial production but rather growth built on the thin air of financial assets increasingly divorced from anything in the real economy, including production, services—and workers. From 1982 to 1999, the Dow Jones Industrial Average experienced on average 15 percent total return each year—amounting to one of the longest bull markets in American history.[91] The roaring nineties saw money flow into the United States at a previously unseen pace—a 90 percent increase in ten years. The transition to the knowledge economy was complete as manufacturing shrunk to only 14 percent of total output and employment to an even lower percentage of total output.[92]

Even as the American economy became more tethered to the ups and downs of asset prices, the institutionalization of corporate social responsibility continued apace in business schools. Many of the most prestigious institutions such as Harvard, Wharton, and Columbia had for decades sought to impress on the American executive class a stamp of distinction: they would be social leaders, not mere technicians of management. In the 1970s and the 1980s, something unusual happened in business schools in the United States. They started hiring philosophers.[93]

This intersection between business and philosophy accelerated the development of courses focused on social issues and what many academics called the *business environment*. But the new courses on business ethics focused less on providing executives with an understanding of the larger social and political landscape of business. This new academic perspective suggested, instead, a rather novel idea: that the social problems of business might be solved by the individualistic ethics of executives. Cultivate the right executive soul and the seemingly intractable problems of governance might simply fade to the background.

The birth of the modern field of business ethics might be pinpointed to November 1974. That was when a conference on the subject was hosted by the philosophy department and the business college of the University of Kansas.[94] Shortly after, a philosophy professor named Norman Bowie procured support from the National Endowment for the Humanities for a three-year grant for philosophy professors, business school professors, and business leaders to develop courses in business ethics.[95] New volumes in business ethics went to print over the next several years and so did new journals, edited by philosophers but read by business school professors and students. [96] By the middle of the 1980s, there were about 500 courses in business ethics taught across the country to 40,000 students annually.[97]

But it was financial scandals, ironically, that were an important engine for this expanding curriculum. In 1986, Ivan Boesky, a stock trader who bet on corporate takeovers and real estate investments, made the cover of *Time* magazine (which dubbed him "Ivan the Terrible") for his financial misdealings, for which he pleaded guilty to insider-trading charges among other things.[98] As a part of his plea deal, Boesky implicated financier Michael Milken, a major figure in private equity, as well as the investment bank Drexel Burnham Lambert.[99] The next year at a US Senate oversight hearing, the Republican senator from New York, Al D'Amato, said that because of recent scandals "the public cannot help but think that the dice are loaded" in the markets.[100] That year, Securities and Exchange Commission chairman John Shad led a fund-raising campaign for a business ethics program at Harvard.[101] That wouldn't be the last time a financial scandal became the proximate cause of a new, flashy business ethics center.

THE FOUNDER AND HEAD of Nike came to the National Press Club in May 1998 with the intention of challenging the reputation of human rights negligence that had dogged the shoe and apparel company for the past several years. Speaking to a group of executives, members of the press, and the national C-SPAN audience, Philip Knight gave the impression that Nike was committed to substantive changes to its labor practices even as he struggled to shake the defensive posture that the company had been maintaining for months. "I figured that I'd just come out," he said, "and let you journalists have a look at the great Satan up close and personal."[102] Muffled laughter can be heard on the video recording.

This was probably the most trying test of Phil Knight's storied career. He started what eventually became the dominant athletic brand, as the oft-repeated story went, by selling imported Japanese shoes out of the back of his Plymouth Valiant automobile in the 1960s. Nike went public in 1980 and became the consumer icon of Michael Jordan and Tiger Woods in the 1990s. The company rode a wave of transformation in the textile industry by manufacturing its innovative product designs with more innovative global supply chains. Although Nike found success in no small part because of its exceptional ability to use advertising and celebrity to establish a powerful brand, it was this agile entrepreneurialism, which traded-in old-school commitments to domestic manufacturing for short-term international subcontractors, that made the company.

Nike was the model of a new kind of corporation. Unlike postwar giants such as General Electric or General Motors that established market power by means of vertical integration and conglomeration, a new generation of firms resembled something less tangible and permanent. A core team of talent worked on design in-house; the rest of the company's needs, from marketing to production to distribution, were met by either consultants or contractors.[103] This flexible and contractual structure of production saddled Nike with few entrenched commitments to various social and legal groups. That was particularly true when it came to labor, in which case subcontractors operated in developing countries where third-party monitoring was as scarce as regulation and labor unions. The social responsibilities that the company maintained were those stated explicitly in its contracts with buyers, suppliers, customers, or shareholders.[104] Because the organization's structure was global and its relationships with the public less visible, its corporate social responsibilities were less burdensome than those of traditional companies. Or so Nike had assumed.

In the 1990s, the shoe company became an object of criticism for activists, journalists, and NGOs. Highly publicized investigations found human rights abuses at its plants in Indonesia, Vietnam, and Thailand. Underage workers, primarily young girls, suffered through long work days, low wages, and socially degrading conditions.[105] The accounting firm Ernst & Young found dangerously polluted working conditions in factories in Vietnam.[106] The company initially showed little willingness to address these conditions, beginning first of all with Phil Knight. "There is no value in making things anymore," he told a journalist in the midst of this public relations storm. "There's no reward for those who make shoes in Vietnam or Indonesia. The reward goes to those who can think of clever ways to make people think those shoes are worth a lot more than they really are."[107] Knight made the mistake of telling the truth on the record when he explained to documentary filmmaker Michael Moore that it didn't bother him that fourteen-year-old girls were working in Nike factories in Indonesia.[108]

Knight's address at the National Press Club, however, was heralded as a turning point in the company's approach to human rights issues.[109] He told the public that the company would improve air-quality conditions at its 350 overseas plants and raise its minimum hiring age to eighteen at its footwear plants and sixteen at its apparel plants.[110] Nike retained the larger contractual nexus of manufacturing even as it sought to mitigate the most egregious abuses of the system that had been the foundation of the firm's market dominance. Knight promised voluntary reform, not structural transformation.

Nike's pivot on production standards, although criticized at the time by activists and journalists as not robust enough, ushered in a new era in the history of corporate social responsibility.[111] Knight's collection of proposals, which included health and social auditing by NGOs, expanded education programs for workers, microloans in host countries, support for university research on responsible business practices, and women's and girl's empowerment programs—all of these became standard features of multinational corporations' public relations strategies in the late 1990s and early 2000s. "I truly believe that the American consumer does not want to buy products made in abusive conditions," Knight said. "The challenge is to give them assurances."[112]

Although Nike's pivot came in response to a public relations crisis, it was a part of a broader international movement toward corporate social responsibility (or CSR, as it became widely known in acronym by the 1990s) that was understood by many to be something more than ad hoc. Its strongest supporters believed that it was the beginning of a new kind of capitalism—one that eschewed the reckless pursuit of profit and took into account what was good for society. The Clinton administration, in response to the crisis over sweatshops, formed the Apparel Industry Partnership, which included labor, industry, and public interest groups and eventually led to the creation of the Fair Labor Association in 1999. The organization produced a code of conduct for multinationals, which included minimum wages, compliance monitoring, and minimum age requirements for workers.[113] But the Fair Labor Association was just the beginning.

At the World Economic Forum at Davos that same year, UN secretary-general Kofi Annan expressed the hope that global capitalism could balance the needs of society and the economy. "You can uphold human rights and decent labor and environmental standards directly, by your own conduct of your own business," he told business leaders. "We have to choose between a global market driven only by calculations of short-term profit, and one which has a human face."[114] With support from multinationals, Annan helped to form the United Nations Global Compact, a voluntary CSR initiative explicitly sold as an alternative to national and international government regulation, which sought to make standards of responsibility a feature of multinationals' production in developing countries.

"Many people," wrote a pair of business consultants in 2002, "would be amazed if they lifted the stone of contemporary business activity and saw the army of consultants, experts, charlatans and do-gooders scurrying around inside and outside companies trying to help them be more socially responsible."[115] The number of NGOs, business school professors, and CEOs who promoted the language of CSR grew rapidly in the 2000s. The idea that multinationals should embrace social responsibilities, particularly in the developing world, was eventually embraced by antipoverty agencies and policy makers at institutions ranging from UNICEF, USAID, and the World Bank to the World Economic Forum, the Bill and Melinda Gates Foundation, and the Clinton Global Initiative.[116] Even Pope Benedict XVI wrote about the "need for greater *social responsibility* on the part of business" in his 2009 encyclical, *Caritas in veritate*.[117] Yet, as religious leaders, scholars, and business executives discussed the concept at length, CSR remained an abstract concept. *The Economist* defined it in terms of a partisan spectrum. "The left demands that more rules be applied to companies, to make them more responsible," the magazine explained, using the language of globalization. "The right fires back that governments already subcontract far too much of their social policy to companies."[118] Many business leaders on both sides of the political spectrum employed strategies of CSR as a part of an attempt to preserve their own autonomy, shore up the legitimacy of global capitalism, and resist the development of a patchwork of costly regulatory regimes.

In the wake of a new torrent of scandals from Enron, WorldCom, and Tyco International, in 2004 the Business Roundtable funded the Business Roundtable Institute for Corporate Ethics at the University of Virginia's Darden School of Business.[119] The chairman of that corporate ethics institute was R. Edward Freeman, a longtime business professor and member of that cohort of academics trained in philosophy (particularly the study of deontology; that is, ethics and duties) who joined business schools in the 1970s and 1980s. Freeman has been the dean of the stakeholder school, which was an approach to organizational management and business ethics that gained popularity among academics in the 1980s and has had a powerful influence on the way that business leaders imagine their role in business and society.

The concept didn't originate with Freeman: he credits academics at the Stanford Research Institute, a private research group founded by Stanford University in 1946, for coining the phrase "stakeholder theory" and developing the idea.[120] Those researchers defined stakeholders as "those groups without whose support the organization would cease to exist."[121] In a 1979 article for *Management Review*, Freeman wrote that "senior business executives must now negotiate increasingly with a growing number of external groups." He defined these as stakeholders: government agencies, environmentalists, consumer advocates, as well as shareholders, competitors, and regulators.[122] His 1984 book, *Strategic Management: A Stakeholder Approach*, has become a classic of management literature and, according to Google Scholar, has been cited more than 51,000 times.

Throughout his career, Freeman talked about what he calls the "old story of business"; that is, engaging in business strategy without regard for ethical reasoning and focusing narrowly on profit. He contended that business leaders ought to see their organizations in terms of collaboration among an intersecting cast of stakeholders.[123] *The Power of And*, a book that tells laudable stories of companies such as Salesforce, Whole Foods, and Patagonia engaging in socially enlightened behavior, is a popular presentation of a concept that Freeman has worked out (usually with coauthors and collaborators) in a number of prominent books published over the past few decades. First there was *Strategic Management*, which has continued to stay in print through multiple printings and a reissue, followed in 1988 by *Corporate Strategy and the Search for Ethics*, which describes a "revolution that is going on in management" and argues that "the search for excellence and the search for ethics amount to the same thing."[124] His 2007 book, *Managing for Stakeholders*, again asserted the need for a "new way" of thinking about business. "Business can be understood as a set of relationships among groups that have a stake in the activities that make up the business," Freeman and his coauthors write. "The executive's or entrepreneur's job is to manage and shape these relationships, hence the term 'managing for stakeholders.' "[125] In the long run (though it's hard sometimes to say how long), the success of the CEO and fellow executives consists, according to Freeman, in getting stakeholder interests aligned in such a way that trade-offs disappear.

There is a pervasive sense not just in Freeman's work but also in the work of many promoters of stakeholder theory that the deleterious and unattractive dynamics of business, of greed and conflict and environmental pollution, are on the verge of becoming obsolete. As a theory of ethics, stakeholder theory is dubious at best.[126] Not only does it rely on a misbegotten conception that, with just the right imagination and ingenuity, a reliable "harmonization" between profit-seeking and ethical conduct can be achieved, but also it provides no coherent explanation of what ethical conduct means. In the end, what is ethical is what "creates value" for stakeholders and what contributes to the ongoing viability of the business. Freeman's friendship with John Mackey, founder and CEO of Whole Foods, put Freeman's name on the map as the theorist behind what Mackey has promoted for years as "conscious capitalism." Freeman's accessible and attractive road map to restoring the ethical credibility of big business has proved useful to the most powerful chief executives in the country.

Consider the changing rhetoric of the Business Roundtable, a CEO lobbying organization that has had a long relationship with Freeman. Back in 1981, the lobbyist group put out a statement saying that social responsibility and long-term business growth were two sides of the same coin. "More than ever, managers of corporations are expected to serve the public interests as well as private profit," it read. Fast forward sixteen years to 1997, and the Business Roundtable put out a much different statement that strongly favored shareholder value and repudiated the notion that "the board must somehow balance the interests of stockholders against the interests of other stakeholders." And again, in 2019, the group put out a statement that seems to have come full circle, declaring its commitment to all stakeholders: customers, employees, suppliers, communities, and shareholders.

Intergenerational waffling? Perhaps. But it also shows the degree to which high-profile CEOs have sought to position themselves in response to changing public perceptions of the large business corporation. In recent years, the Business Roundtable found itself the subject of popular historical narratives that cast the group's 1997 statement in support of shareholder value as a capitulation to the short-term interests of finance capital that led, among other things, to the ruin of long-term growth and stable jobs.[127]

Jamie Dimon, CEO of JPMorgan Chase, spearheaded an effort as the chairman of the Business Roundtable to blunt these criticisms. He hosted a private get-together of a handful of the group's most high-profile critics and a few CEOs at a dinner in Manhattan. Along with industry leaders such as Vanguard Group chairman William McNabb and BlackRock chairman and CEO Larry Fink, Dimon put together the new "Statement on the Purpose of a Corporation," which was released in August 2019. Signed by more than 180 CEOs, the one-page document indicates that the language of responsibility and stakeholder value has become indispensable for the way contemporary business leaders explain and justify their powerful role in the American economy.

Measured in terms of public relations, the statement was remarkably successful. The popular business press outdid itself with breathless encomia to the new business enlightenment. The *New York Times* called it an "explicit rebuke" to the Friedman Doctrine, the notion that the sole responsibility of business is to generate profits for shareholders, the "mind-set" that made the 1980s and 1990s an era of shareholder value.[128] Never mind the fact that the statement never actually rejects the shareholder value or Milton Friedman's ideas.

Joshua Bolten, the president and CEO of the Business Roundtable, said it wasn't intended as a rejection of Friedman. "It was not a demotion of the long-term shareholders, because, in our view, the interests of all the stakeholders align in the long-run success of the enterprise," he told the *New York Times.* As many defenders of stakeholder value maintain, the Friedman Doctrine can and should be reconciled with the ideals of ethics and responsibility. "I actually think if Milton Friedman were alive today—I think he'd be a stakeholder theorist," R. Edward Freeman said in a video for the Business Roundtable Institute for Corporate Ethics in 2009. "I think he would understand that the only way to create value for shareholders in today's world is to pay attention to customers, suppliers, employees, communities, and shareholders at the same time."[129]

One important detail about the Business Roundtable's 2019 statement that the initial reporting missed was that the many dozens of CEOs who initially signed the statement never bothered to ask their boards of directors for support (or for permission). That fact alone demonstrated the limited ambitions of the statement itself: that it was not an expression of a new purpose for America's major corporations. It was, instead, a representation of the ideals of the executive class—or at least of the ideals the executives wish to be attributed to them.

CONCLUSION

Larry Fink, President of the World

What if doing well by doing good was not just a theory? What if it could be proved that profit-seeking and responsible behavior were compatible? And what if it could be established, furthermore, that socially responsible firms were consistently more profitable or productive than other, less socially responsible firms? These seem to be the fundamental questions at stake in the viability of both the movement for socially responsible management and the movement for socially responsible investing. Over the past fifty years, researchers have tried to answer these questions using a variety of sophisticated models.

Given the continued viability of socially interested entities such as Dreyfus's Third Century Fund, the Pax World Fund, or the more recent Generation Investment Management (cofounded by Al Gore in 2004), one might guess that the profitability of social responsibility was an established fact. An early study in 1972 made a rather crude case, showing how the shares of fourteen companies selected for being particularly socially responsible outperformed the Dow Jones Industrial Average that year.[1] But just a few years later, another study made the exact opposite argument: that there was a negative correlation between the social responsibility of a publicly traded firm and its share price.[2]

For many years, the profitability debate continued in a similarly unsatisfying manner as some economists and management experts made the case that higher ethics led to higher returns, and critics questioned both the motives and the findings of that research. A literature review in the 1980s concluded not only that there was no positive correlation between responsibility and profitability, but also that the researchers had lacked the necessary data and categories to address the question.[3] Another review of empirical studies ten years later made an opposite conclusion—there was a positive correlation at least between financial performance and the *perception* of social responsibility.[4]

The inability of experts to settle the profitability debate in the late twentieth century resulted from the same dynamics that made corporate social responsibility itself a persistent debate in America over the past century. What did social responsibility mean? And who decides? Who gets to benefit from it?

But in the early twenty-first century, the mirage of no tradeoffs hovered on the horizon of big business again. It was conjured by a growing interest in the use of investment capital to meet the challenge of climate change. The impetus for this change came from the world of finance and from the UN Global Compact, which produced a report in 2004 endorsed by more than twenty prominent institutions including the World Bank Group, Morgan Stanley, HSBC, Deutsche Bank, Goldman Sachs, Credit Suisse, and UBS—together holding more than $6 trillion in assets.

The report was called, regrettably, *Who Cares Wins*, and it developed an idea that would change the way people around the world conducted business, invested in companies, and talked about capitalism.[5] Instead of christening this idea with a snappy name, the Financial Sector Initiative of the UN Global Compact represented it by a list: environmental, social, and governance—giving birth to yet another acronym, ESG. The report recommended, simply, that analysts, financial institutions, companies, investors, pension funds, consultants, and regulators make categories of environment, social, and governance a key part of their work.

Anticipating critics who might suppose that profitability would be at odds with social responsibility, the Financial Sector Initiative explained in its official prose that ESG "can increase shareholder value by better managing risks related to emerging ESG issues, by anticipating regulatory changes or consumer trends, and by accessing new markets or reducing costs."[6] ESG, in other words, was precisely the set of indicators that business needed to attend to in order to remain competitive in the fast-changing world of the twenty-first century. Despite significant international support in the financial sector for the statement, however, the UN Global Compact's promotion of ESG came and went with little fanfare.

ESG never would have taken off if it hadn't been for the 2008 financial crisis and for the rise of a company called BlackRock. In 2008, the company and its founder, Larry Fink, were almost entirely unknown outside of Wall Street circles, but Fink, who made a name for himself in the 1970s developing and trading mortgage-backed securities, was at the center of the federal government's emergency response to the crisis. He helped structure the billion-dollar deals that sold Bear Stearns to JP Morgan and that bailed out AIG, Citigroup, and Fannie Mae and Freddie Mac. The Federal Reserve then hired BlackRock to manage those toxic assets that the government had taken on.[7]

In the wake of the 2008 crisis, BlackRock snatched up $1.5 billion in assets with its acquisition of a firm called R3 Capital Management, and it also acquired Barclays Global Investors for $15.2 billion.[8] With these acquisitions, BlackRock's assets more than doubled in 2009 to $3.29 trillion, making it the world's largest money manager.[9] In 2010, *Vanity Fair* magazine quoted a senior bank executive who said, "A risk that needs to be considered is the impact of having so much of the global market influenced by one firm, by the perspective of one man."[10]

One key factor driving Fink's rise has been a larger structural change in the way investments are managed: in recent decades, many investors have turned away from expensive and actively managed funds (think high-yield, high-risk mutual funds) to cheaper and passively managed index funds. Instead of relying on the research and ingenuity of money managers to sniff out promising investments, passively managed funds simply replicate the benchmarks of an already established index such as the Dow Jones Industrial Average or the S&P 500. As Wall Street in general grows, so do the funds. And those funds have begun to dwarf other kinds of investments.

Most of the largest index funds are managed by just three firms: BlackRock, with about $10 trillion in assets; Vanguard Group, with $8 trillion; and State Street Corporation, with $4 trillion.[11] Those assets don't simply represent financial value, but also potentially significant influence over the way corporate America does its business. Two Harvard law professors recently estimated that within twenty years, the so-called Big Three could control as much as 40 percent of the shareholder votes of companies listed on the S&P 500.[12]

Over the past ten years, these mega investment-management firms have all taken an interest in ESG, but perhaps none has been more vocal and aggressive about it than Larry Fink. In 2012, he began publishing an annual letter to CEOs explaining BlackRock's expectations and priorities, a key part of which has consistently been environmental issues. "BlackRock's approach to corporate governance can be described as value-focused engagement," he wrote in 2012. "We reach our voting decisions independently of proxy advisory firms on the basis of guidelines that reflect our perspective as a fiduciary investor with responsibilities to protect the economic interests of our clients."[13]

In his 2022 letter to CEOs, Fink expressed his support for stakeholder capitalism, which he defined, much like R. Edward Freeman, as *creating value* for those who have relationships with the firm. "Stakeholder capitalism is not about politics," he wrote. "It is not a social or ideological agenda. It is not 'woke.' *It is cap-*

italism, driven by mutually beneficial relationships between you and the employees, customers, suppliers, and communities your company relies on to *prosper*."[14]

When such an important figure in finance talks about ideas like this, those ideas become a de facto part of the mainstream. One study showed that in firms where BlackRock owned at least 5 percent of the outstanding shares, the companies were 22 percent more likely to use language about such things as environmental issues or social risks in their disclosures to the Securities and Exchange Commission—reflecting the language of Fink's letters.[15]

But the significance of Larry Fink's advocacy for ESG is not simply about influence. He has a big bully pulpit, sure, and maybe the biggest bully pulpit Wall Street can afford, but he has other, more tangible forms of power. What is remarkable about the financial industry's embrace of ESG is that it turns on its head almost all of the power dynamics that had for decades plagued the corporate social responsibility movement. Before, it was activists jockeying with profit-seeking shareholders for influence over management. Or, it was business leaders keeping profit-seeking shareholders and social movement activists at bay in order to exercise a paternalistic form of social statesmanship.

But now, we see something quite novel: investors with unprecedented power demanding that management adopt socially responsible practices such as reduction of carbon emissions. If it is true, as conventional wisdom holds, that shareholders are in some sense *owners* of the company, then only a few large institutional investors own most of the publicly traded companies. One might reasonably ask, as Bloomberg's Matt Levine somewhat facetiously asked recently, "Is Larry Fink president of the world?"[16]

And what about profitability? Well, what about it? When mega institutional investors direct management policy and plan financial strategies according to ESG priorities, their outsized influence shapes (or distorts, if you like) markets. In short, financial assets deemed ESG compliant might become prima facie more valuable. Under these market-bending conditions, the profitability versus social responsibility debate might seem like it is being rendered obsolete—and not because there exists some natural harmony between the two but because big finance made it so.[17]

As top firms were transforming financial markets and seemingly leading a cultural shift on Wall Street in favor of more environmentally sustainable investments, ESG became the subject of growing opposition in 2023. Republican lawmakers in 37 states introduced more than 150 pieces of legislation aimed at banning or limiting such investments, and 14 states, including West Virginia and Texas, adopted some kind of anti-ESG proposal.[18] A drumbeat of hostility made ESG the object of intensifying cultural politics, in part causing Vanguard to renege on its commitment to ending greenhouse gas emissions and even BlackRock to remove some sustainability investments from its portfolios.[19] It was the first time that a major social responsibility movement experienced such massive opposition, a backlash expressed in the free market language that echoed the ideas of Henry Manne and Milton Friedman—that big business leaders were using for-profit market mechanisms to serve political interests. Even Larry Fink was forced to admit that ESG had become such a toxic brand that the term was no longer worth using.[20]

Like Fink's BlackRock, many companies started to downplay their environmental efforts in public—what some journalists started to call "greenhushing"—even as they remained committed to such causes behind the scenes.[21] For many business leaders, it seemed there was no other choice. The climate crisis was making business support for environmental causes into a necessary part of risk management and long-term strategy. ESG may very well, then, join a long list of terms, some of which have been discussed in this book, that have fallen out of favor, such as social trusteeship, business statesmanship, or even corporate social responsibility. But the concerns driving ESG, or whatever business leaders decide to call it next, is not going to disappear. Already businesses are developing new terms to brand investments and causes aimed at social and environmental issues.[22] Both in the distant past and in more recent history, however, this near constant churn of new terms and strategies aimed at reconciling corporate power and social responsibility suggests a deep confusion about what the corporate is—and how it should be controlled.[23]

Without special advantages granted by the state, corporate capitalism never would have succeeded. Legal tools such as limited liability, the shield of corporate personhood, and asset lock-in (which ensures that shares can be kept or traded but never cashed out) allowed large corporations to pool unprecedented amounts of capital and slip the nets of mutual obligation and bonds of accountability. State charters grant a wide range of special privileges that no individual or group of individuals could achieve on their own. This legal arrangement effectively makes corporations a sort of concession of state power that is far more strategically advantageous than many other forms of business (and often far more powerful). Neither entirely public nor completely private, business corporations are created by governmental institutions, which grant them powers and protections that only a sovereign state can confer and enforce.[24]

But it was the form of the large publicly traded firm that obscured the political and social origins of the corporation. Rather than a person or a small group of people owning and operating a local firm, many hundreds or thousands of people own shares in large businesses that are operated across the nation or the globe by a class of professional managers. This separation of ownership from control sparked recurring conflicts among shareholders and other investors, managers, executives, directors, and workers—all of them stakeholders who often have differing or sometimes opposed interests.[25] And it all but guaranteed that those who know the most about the day-to-day operations of a business and who make practical decisions are not those who have a controlling financial stake in the firm—and who do not enjoy the privileges and power of ownership. Perhaps more important, it is extremely difficult (arguably impossible) for any single stakeholder to possess the ability, knowledge, or the will to accept and fulfill nonmarket responsibilities.

The revelation, then, that financial instruments might be wielded not just by marginalized activists such as James Peck or Franklin Florence or Alice Tepper (now Alice Tepper Marlin) but also by institutions with the capital (and votes) to force management's hand on climate change, among other issues, has come as something of a surprise to many on the political right, such as Ron DeSantis. But this turn of events by which those who long thought of themselves as defenders of shareholder interests were forced to reconsider their support for financial markets was also distracting, in part, because it was too easy for pundits and politicians to construe the situation of those defenders simply as a story of hypocrisy or flip-flopping.

The corporate culture war of the early twenty-first century was, rather, built atop long-standing disagreements and misunderstandings about what corporations are and what they are good for—and strikes at the problem that this book tries to understand and explain. An institution bound by financial abstractions that have only become more abstract over the decades, the large publicly traded corporation tended to direct its mighty and unequaled resources toward goals that were often severely restricted by fiduciary duties to shareholders and other investors.

With some notable exceptions, almost all of the characters in this history were driven by deep moral commitments and beliefs about democracy and justice—and, ultimately, by what they perceived as good for the world and for people. Whether they worked in a corner office or protested on the streets outside, they sought through flawed if sometimes self-serving or confused ways to make the big-business corporation serve the good of society and, indeed, as an expression of a just and socially responsible organization of human beings acting together. But in each case, unless they could be translated into financial metrics or aligned to the interests of investors, such intentions have resulted in bitter frustrations or halting victories.

—

THE WAY THAT Wall Street has influenced corporate America in these past few decades is only part of the problem. Ultimately, corporate social responsibility cannot be separated from fundamental conditions of corporate governance that predate the bull market of the late twentieth century. Business power as it has conventionally been structured has not encouraged, empowered, or often allowed directors, executives, managers, or shareholders to assess what is good or bad in the deepest ethical senses—or to do anything meaningful and lasting about those assessments. This history shows how our most prominent economic institutions have separated noneconomic considerations from the ability to act on them. This is nothing less than a moral fracture at the heart of the corporation—a fatal and rarely understood flaw that makes its history over the past century a regrettable tragedy.

Among other things, it suggests that the corporate octopus is an institution incapable of being tamed.

And yet the search for a corporate soul continues. In movements for CSR and ESG and in activism to pressure corporations to align themselves with political values and cultural ideals, we can trace the outlines of a profound recognition that economic success—or at least the kind that can be rendered into measures of GDP, quarterly earnings, return on investment, and so forth—is not enough. And it has never been enough. Hidden beneath the surface of this history is a longing for an economy that puts the human person at the center and heeds weightier matters of justice and human flourishing.

It may be tempting to imagine that what we need is more

data about corporate conduct collected in a more systematic and rigorous manner—like financial measurements computed on a spreadsheet. Indeed, it seems that many activists and consultants believe that well-branded and publicized lists of corporations ranked according to new criteria of sustainability or equity of various kinds—along with associated boycotts, investment funds, or asset categories—are just the tools we have been looking for. Such projects of information gathering (much like the publicity efforts of the Progressive Era) may seem attractive because they appear rational and objective. It is a way to fight fire with fire—or, in this case, a way to face off against investors and chief financial officers by use of a different form of accounting.

But these appeals to scores and rankings, some of which claim to put a dollar figure on ethical misconduct, tend to dissolve into yet another form of corporate risk management. More significant, they elude and obscure the reality of the human person and the obligation each of us has to act responsibly and not defer to bureaucratic rule by no one.[26] The large publicly traded corporation, admittedly, is an abstract bureaucracy, but the conflicts discussed in this book are primarily moral and political in nature. How should we understand the relationship that our lives and our communities have to this institution? These conflicts suggest a more challenging, perhaps costlier way: bring moral judgment back into business life. The very possibility of making such judgments, however, rests on the willingness and the institutional empowerment of human beings to consider the humane purposes of the economy, to deliberate together about how to use proper means to achieve those ends, and maybe even to limit the scope and scale of the corporation. Such tasks will inevitably lead us back to the question posed at the beginning of this book, "What is the corporation good for?"

ACKNOWLEDGMENTS

The conflicts over corporate power described in this book were partly fueled by an ethical imagination and a culture that sees the economy through the lens of scarcity, competition, and profit seeking. This is an impoverished way of thinking about life in general, of which the economy is merely a part. It requires a suspension of disbelief because life is an abundant gift, whose gratuitousness is made clear in a million simple, everyday ways, though perhaps most rewardingly through friendships. I have had the good fortune of writing this book in the company of many generous friends.

The Institute for Advanced Studies in Culture at the University of Virginia has been a home for me in more ways than one. Many thanks to James Davison Hunter and Ryan Olson for their support for and confidence in my work. Much of the research and the writing that went into this project was shaped and colored in large and small ways by the community here, which includes Kelly Blumberg, Carl Bowman, Simon Brauer, Tal Brewer, Ty Buckman, Garnette Cadogan, Elizabeth Clark, Bob Cochran, Matt Crawford, Joseph Davis, Leigh Martin Harrison, Mark Hoipkemier, Christopher Jacobi, Alan Jacobs, Elisabeth Lasch-Quinn, Jackson Lears, Andrew Lynn, James Mumford, Paul Nedelisky, John Owen, Malloy Owen, Angel Adams Parham, Kyle Peutz, Ohad Reiss-Sorokin, Isaac Ariail Reed, Paul Scherz, Jonathan Teubner, Tonya Tyree, Victoria Van Dixhoorn, Michael Weinman, Stephen White, Chris Yates, and Olivier Zunz. Thanks to you all for your generosity, conversations, and conviviality.

My intellectual horizons widened quickly and considerably after Jay Tolson asked me to join the staff of the *Hedgehog Review* as an editor. He has pushed me to think more deeply about the cultural meaning of our deepest conflicts and to be more careful than I had previously thought possible about grammar and style. Thanks to Leann Davis Alspaugh and Samantha Jordan for your camaraderie and kindness in our pursuit of that "one big thing." To be able to edit and publish a little magazine in the company of such fine people is a gift, for which I am thankful every day.

The Department of History at Rutgers University was a remarkable and enlivening place for me to go to graduate school and to begin work on a dissertation project that, very slowly, grew into this book. From the beginning, Jackson Lears was a generous mentor who taught me to see the complexities of history in the sources of unintended outcomes, roads not taken, and tragedy and to not get lost in abstraction and theory but to "bring on the people." Thanks to him and Karen Parker Lears for their friendship and for the hospitality of giving me a place to spend some long nights during the coronavirus pandemic to pound out early drafts of these chapters. Jennifer Mittelstadt was just the guide I needed for many things but especially for asking big questions about public policy and the political economy of the United States. David Greenberg was a reliable source of encouragement who helped set me on the right path early on when I didn't know where I was going with this project. Thanks to my dear friend Charlie Riggs for the company and conversations in mirth and in dark hours. At Rutgers, the list of friends, guides, and fellow travelers grows long: Zach Bennett, Chris Blakely, Julia Bowes, Rachel Bunker, Dorothy Sue Cobble, Eli Cook, Maco Faniel, Marlene Gaynair, Billy Kelly, James Livingston, Pat McGrath, Jessica Nelson, Jaime Pietruska, Mars Plater, Melissa Reynolds, Dawn Ruskai, Paul Sampson, Judith Serkis, Peter Sorenson, Dustin Stalnaker, Ryan Tate, Amy Zanoni, and many others.

My time in the History and the Classics and Letters Departments at the University of Oklahoma made me fall in love with scholarship—and want to contribute to it. Special thanks to Kyle Harper and David Chappell for their guidance, encouragement, and friendship.

Many thanks to the librarians, archivists, and staff members at the University of Oklahoma–Tulsa, University of Tulsa, Rutgers University, University of Virginia, and at the Franklin Delano Roosevelt Presidential Library; Kansas Historical Society; Wisconsin Historical Society; Special Collections at the University of Tennessee, Knoxville; Rare Book and Manuscript Library at Columbia University; Hoover Institution Library and Archives; Special Collections the University of Chicago Library; Mudd Manuscript Library at Princeton University; John F. Kennedy Presidential Library; and Securities and Exchange Commission Historical Society.

I was aided in the research and writing of this book by workshops and conferences, including the Business History Conference; American Historical Association; Society for US Intellectual History; Workshop on the History of Environment, Agriculture, Technology, and Science; Movements and Directions in Capitalism at the University of Virginia; Newberry Library's History of Capitalism Seminar; Hoover Institution Political Economy Workshop; Rutgers Center for Historical Analysis; Institute for Advanced Studies in Culture's Emerging Ideas Workshop; and Cornell University's History of Capitalism Summer Camp.

Special thanks to Joseph Davis for leading and participating in the manuscript workshop hosted by the Institute for Advanced Studies in Culture in November 2022, and many thanks to all participants: Matthew Caulfield, David Ciepley, Jennifer Delton, Allison Elias, Jackson Lears, Andrew Lynn (for this, many other CSR-related things, and many long conversations), Ohad Reiss-Sorokin, Jesse Schupack, and Jay Tolson. I was aided along the way by corrections, assistance, and ideas from Jennifer Baier, Gavin Bencke, Leah Benque, Kevin Boyle, Angus Burgin, Jennifer Burns, Larry Glickman, Louis Hyman, Richard John, Robert Johnston, Jessica Levy, Kenneth Lipartito, Sarah Milov, Charlie Riggs, David Singerman, Harwell Wells, and Olivier Zunz.

Special thanks go to Justin Cahill. For his detailed attention to drafts and editing wisdom and for his shepherding this project from proposal to proofs, I am immensely grateful. Thanks also to everyone at W. W. Norton & Company, especially to Angie Merila, Caroline Adams, Christopher Curioli, Rebecca Munro, Louise Mattarelliano, Rachel Salzman, and Steve Colca.

For the conversation, occasional feedback, and friendship, thanks to Justin Aldrich, Sam Beer, Thomas Brewer, Greg and Gretchen Davis, Thomas and Natalie Fickley, John and Hannah Fitzhugh, Jack Gallemore, Bobby Griffith, Mike Haggerty, Brad and Rita Knol (for the writing retreat and so much more), Fr. John Mason and Bonnie Lock, Fr. Sean McDermott, Ken Myers, Fr. Glenn Spencer, Asher Spruill, and Tyler Syck. Much love to Dore, Karen, and all the Schupacks. My family, from whom this project and my career have for so long taken away my time and attention, is always on my heart and mind: Elon and Mark Jacobs, Emily and Wilson Wise, Donald Williams, my dear mother, Debbie Williams, and many others. This book is dedicated to the memory of my father, Don Williams, who would have taken no small delight in seeing this in print—a dream we dreamed and talked about, now so many years ago.

Without Sally, not a page would be possible—nor countless other good things I have come to know and to do. She taught me to say what I mean, sustained me through drafts and doubts, and celebrated with me every step of the way. Our friendship has created a little economy of love, the gift of a good life, and the voices of Abraham and Dominic on our porch and down our halls—and who knows what else to come. To you and the boys, I offer this humble token of thanks.

NOTES

Epigraphs

1. *Southern Mercury*, April 17, 1890.
2. Quoted in Friedrich A. Hayek, "The Corporation in a Democratic Society," in *Management and Corporations, 1985*, ed. Melvin Anshen and George Bach (New York: McGraw-Hill, 1960), 117.
3. "Larry Fink's 2022 Letter to CEOs," BlackRock, accessed October 4, 2022.

Introduction: What Is the Corporation Good For?

1. Joseph Bucklin Bishop, *Our Political Drama: Conventions, Campaigns, Candidates* (New York: Scott-Thaw Co, 1904), 156; Stephen Hess and Sandy Northrop, *Drawn and Quartered: The History of American Political Cartoons* (Montgomery, AL: Elliott & Clark, 1996), 60, 65. On antimonopoly politics and cartoons, see Richard R. John, "Robber Barons Redux: Antimonopoly Reconsidered," *Enterprise & Society* 13, no. 1 (March 2012): 1–38.
2. Frank Norris, *The Octopus: A Story of California* (New York: Doubleday, Page & Co., 1901).
3. Ida M. Tarbell, *The History of the Standard Oil Company*, vol. 1 (New York: Macmillan, 1925), 182.
4. Robert Anthony Fredona and Sophus A. Reinert, "Leviathan and Kraken: States, Corporations, and Political Economy," *History and Theory*, June 9, 2020, 167–87.
5. James Madison, *The Writings of James Madison: 1819–1836*, vol. 9 (New York: G. P. Putnam's Sons, 1910), 281.
6. Santa Clara County v. Southern Pacific Railroad Company, 118 US 394 (1886). On the development of corporate constitutional rights, see Adam Winkler, *We the Corporations: How American Businesses Won Their Civil Rights* (New York: Liveright, 2018).
7. "Can a Corporation Be Libeled?" *New York Times*, June 24, 1885.

8. John R. Commons, *Legal Foundations of Capitalism* (New York: Routledge, 2017), 371.
9. Kyle Edward Williams, "'Roosevelt's Populism': The Kansas Oil War of 1905 and the Making of Corporate Capitalism," *Journal of the Gilded Age and Progressive Era* 19, no. 1 (January 2020): 96–121.
10. Philip Eastman, "Going Against the Octopus," *Saturday Evening Post*, April 8, 1905.
11. Matt Taibbi, "The Great American Bubble Machine," *Rolling Stone*, July 9, 2009.
12. "Stephen Schwarzman Defended Donald Trump at CEO Meeting on Election Results," *Financial Times*, November 14, 2020.
13. "State of Corporate Citizenship," Boston College Center for Corporate Citizenship, accessed April 28, 2023, https://ccc.bc.edu/content/ccc/research/reports/state-of-corporate-citizenship.html.
14. "Sherrilyn Ifill on the Moral Responsibility of Business in Politics," *The Economist*, April 16, 2022.
15. Andrew Ross Sorkin et al., "DeSantis Claims Win in Campaign Against E.S.G.," *New York Times*, August 24, 2022, Business & Policy.
16. Ross Douthat, "The Rise of Woke Capital," *New York Times*, February 28, 2018, Opinion.

Chapter One: The New Princes of Industry

1. Richard Hofstadter, *The American Political Tradition and the Men Who Made It* (New York: Vintage, 1989), 298; *Topeka Daily Capital*, March 10, 1904.
2. Robert H. Wiebe, *Businessmen and Reform: A Study of the Progressive Movement* (Cambridge, MA: Harvard University Press, 1962), 45–47, 79–81; Gabriel Kolko, *The Triumph of Conservatism: A Re-Interpretation of American History, 1900-1916* (New York: Free Press, 1977), 65–89; Arthur M. Johnson, "Antitrust Policy in Transition, 1908: Ideal and Reality," *Mississippi Valley Historical Review* 48, no. 3 (1961): 415–34.
3. Theodore Roosevelt, Remarks at the Music Hall in Cincinnati, Ohio, September 20, 1902, in *A Compilation of the Messages and Speeches of Theodore Roosevelt, 1901-1905*, ed. Alfred Henry Lewis (Washington, DC: Bureau of National Literature and Art, 1906), 153.
4. Martin J. Sklar, *The Corporate Reconstruction of American Capitalism, 1890–1916: The Market, the Law, and Politics* (Cambridge: Cambridge University Press, 1988), 346. Actually, Sklar called him a "trust-muster," but that strikes me as a malformed noun.
5. Ron Chernow, *The House of Morgan: An American Banking Dynasty and the Rise of Modern Finance* (New York: Simon & Schuster, 1991), 122–28; Robert F. Bruner and Sean D. Carr, *The Panic of 1907: Lessons Learned from the Market's Perfect Storm* (Hoboken, NJ: Wiley, 2009).
6. Bruner and Carr, *The Panic of 1907*, 97–103. The idea of corporate licensing

was supported by the Populist William Jennings Bryan and, later, by William Howard Taft. For a further discussion of the idea of federal incorporation during this period, see Melvin I. Urofsky, "Proposed Federal Incorporation in the Progressive Era," *American Journal of Legal History* 26, no. 2 (1982): 160–83.

7. *Proceedings of the National Conference on Trusts and Combinations Under the Auspices of the National Civic Federation, Chicago, October 22–25, 1907* (New York: National Civic Federation, 1908), 156, 453–65.
8. Theodore Roosevelt, "Seventh Annual Message, December 3, 1907," in *A Compilation of the Messages and Papers of the Presidents*, vol. 16 (New York: Bureau of National Literature, 1917), 7458.
9. I rely here on the work of Martin J. Sklar in *The Corporate Reconstruction*, 228–85.
10. Sklar, *The Corporate Reconstruction*, 245.
11. "Amending the Anti-Trust Act," *New York Times*, March 24, 1908.
12. Jonathan Barron Baskin and Paul J. Miranti, Jr., *A History of Corporate Finance* (New York: Cambridge University Press, 1997), 174, 196. The social, political, and cultural transformations brought about by the rise of the large corporation are of remarkable historical significance. The literature on this, however, is aging quickly, but here is a mixed and representative sample: Kolko, *The Triumph of Conservatism*; David Montgomery, *The Fall of the House of Labor: The Workplace, the State, and American Labor Activism, 1865-1925* (Cambridge: Cambridge University Press, 1987); Sklar, *The Corporate Reconstruction*; James Weinstein, *The Corporate Ideal in the Liberal State, 1900-1918* (Boston: Beacon Press, 1968); Meg Jacobs, *Pocketbook Politics: Economic Citizenship in Twentieth-Century America* (Princeton, NJ: Princeton University Press, 2007); Olivier Zunz, *Making America Corporate, 1870-1920* (Chicago: University of Chicago Press, 1990); William Leach, *Land of Desire: Merchants, Power, and the Rise of a New American Culture* (New York: Pantheon, 1993); Charles Postel, *The Populist Vision* (New York: Oxford University Press, 2009).
13. E. J. Kahn, *The World of Swope* (New York: Simon & Schuster, 1965), 84; David G. Loth, *Swope of G.E.: The Story of Gerard Swope and General Electric in American Business* (New York: Simon & Schuster, 1958), 9.
14. Gerard Swope, "Reminiscences of Gerard Swope," interview by Harlan B. Phillips, 1955, Oral History Research Office, Columbia University, New York, 30.
15. Loth, *Swope of GE*, 117–23.
16. See Kim McQuaid, "Young, Swope and General Electric's 'New Capitalism': A Study in Corporate Liberalism, 1920–33," *American Journal of Economics and Sociology* 36, no. 3 (1977): 323–34.
17. Ida M. Tarbell, *Owen D. Young: A New Type of Industrial Leader* (New York: Macmillan, 1932), vii, 232.
18. Owen D. Young, "What Is Right in Business," Speech at Park Avenue Baptist

Church, New York, January 20, 1929, in *Selected Addresses of Owen D. Young and Gerard Swope* (New York: General Electric Company, 1930), 262.

19. Tarbell, *Owen D. Young*, 233; "Young Bars Profit as Trade's Sole Aim," *New York Times*, May 13, 1932.
20. Owen D. Young, *Selected Addresses*, 263.
21. "Ford's Plans Halted," *Washington Post*, November 1, 1917.
22. *Dodge v. Ford Motor Company*, 204 Mich. 459, 170 N.W. 668 (Mich. 1919). For a discussion on the relationship between *Dodge* and the principle of shareholder value, see Lynn A Stout, *The Shareholder Value Myth: How Putting Shareholders First Harms Investors, Corporations, and the Public* (San Francisco: Berrett-Koehler Publishers, 2012), 25–29.
23. Owen D. Young, *Selected Addresses*, 43, 35–43.
24. See Ellis W. Hawley, "Herbert Hoover, the Commerce Secretariat, and the Vision of an 'Associative State,' 1921–1928," *Journal of American History* 61, no. 1 (1974): 116–40; Guy Alchon, *The Invisible Hand of Planning: Capitalism, Social Science, and the State in the 1920s* (Princeton, NJ: Princeton University Press, 1985).
25. Herbert Hoover, *American Individualism* (New York: Doubleday, Page & Co., 1922), 40.
26. See Thomas G. Andrews, *Killing for Coal: America's Deadliest Labor War* (Cambridge, MA: Harvard University Press, 2008); Nigel Sellars, "Wobblies in the Oilfields: The Suppression of the Industrial Workers of the World in Oklahoma," in *An Oklahoma I Had Never Seen Before: Alternative Views of Oklahoma History*, ed. Davis D. Joyce (Norman: University of Oklahoma Press, 1998), 129–44.
27. National Bureau of Economic Research, Dow-Jones Industrial Stock Price Index for United States [M1109BUSM293NNBR], FRED, Federal Reserve Bank of St. Louis, accessed September 20, 2020, https://fred.stlouisfed.org/series/M1109BUSM293NNBR; John Kenneth Galbraith, *The Great Crash, 1929* (New York: Mariner Books, 2009), 22; Republican Party, *Republican Campaign Textbook* (Chicago: Republican National Committee, 1928), 21; John Dewey, *Individualism, Old and New* (New York: Minton, Balch & Company, 1930), 29.
28. "Bankers v. Panic," *Time*, November 4, 1929; William Leuchtenburg, *Franklin D. Roosevelt and the New Deal, 1932–1940* (New York: Harper & Row, 1963), 1; Table Ba470–477—Labor Force, Employment, and Unemployment: 1890–1990, in *Historical Statistics of the United States Millennium Edition* (New York: Cambridge University Press, 2006); Table Ca9–19—Gross Domestic Product: 1790–2002, in *Historical Statistics of the United States Millennium Edition* (New York: Cambridge University Press, 2006); Table Cb28–31—Indexes of Industrial Production: 1884–2003, in *Historical Statistics of the United States Millennium Edition* (New York: Cambridge University Press, 2006); Calvin Fisher Schmid, "Appendix A: Hooverville: A Social Document," in *Social Trends in Seattle* (Seattle: University of Washington Press, 1944), 289.

29. Herbert Hoover, Radio Address to the Nation from Elko, Nevada, November 7, 1932, in Gerhard Peters and John T. Woolley, The American Presidency Project, accessed September 15, 2020, https://www.presidency.ucsb.edu/node/207527; Franklin D. Roosevelt, Radio Address re a National Program of Restoration, April 7, 1932, Speech File 469, The Master Speech Files, 1898, 1910–1945, FDR Presidential Library; Franklin D. Roosevelt, Commonwealth Club Speech, September 23, 1932, Speech File 522, The Master Speech Files, 1898, 1910–1945, FDR Presidential Library. On the question of the New Deal's substance, see Eric Rauchway, *Winter War: Hoover, Roosevelt, and the First Clash Over the New Deal* (New York: Basic Books, 2018), 14–18. On the progressive origins of New Deal politics, see Daniel T. Rodgers, *Atlantic Crossings: Social Politics in a Progressive Age* (Cambridge, MA: Harvard University Press, 1998).
30. Ferdinand Pecora, "Reminiscences of Ferdinand Pecora," interview by Donald Shaugnessy, 1962, Oral History Research Office, Columbia University, New York, interview no. 3. Quoted in Michael Perino, *The Hellhound of Wall Street: How Ferdinand Pecora's Investigation of the Great Crash Forever Changed American Finance* (New York: Penguin, 2010), 33.
31. Perino, *The Hellhound of Wall Street*, 60–61.
32. "5 Bankers Called in Market Inquiry," *New York Times*, February 8, 1933; "National City Bank Accedes to Inquiry," *New York Times*, February 9, 1933; "Pecora Subpoenas 3 in Stock Inquiry," *New York Times*, January 31, 1933; Perino, *The Hellhound of Wall Street*, 71; "Mitchell Avoid Income Tax in 1929 by '$2,800,000 Loss,'" *New York Times*, February 22, 1933; "National City Lent $2,400,000 to Save Stock of Officers," *New York Times*, February 23, 1933; "National City Sold Bank Stock Short During 1929 Boom," *New York Times*, February 24, 1933; "National City Sold Peru Bond Issues in 'Honest Mistake,'" *New York Times*, February 28, 1933; Raymond Moley, *The First New Deal* (New York: Harcourt, 1966), 308–10.
33. "Bedroom, Jail, Death," *Time*, March 27, 1933.
34. Martin Horn, *J.P. Morgan & Co. and the Crisis of Capitalism: From the Wall Street Crash to World War II* (Cambridge: Cambridge University Press, 2022), 229n54; Ron Chernow, *The House of Morgan: An American Banking Dynasty and the Rise of Modern Finance* (New York: Atlantic Monthly Press, 1990), 361.
35. Jordan A. Schwarz, *Liberal: Adolf A. Berle and the Vision of an American Era* (New York: Free Press, 1987), 70–72; William E. Leuchtenburg, *Franklin D. Roosevelt and the New Deal, 1932–1940* (New York: Harper & Row, 1963), 32; Adolf A. Berle, Jr., "The Reminiscences of Adolf A. Berle, Jr.," interview by Douglas Scott, 1974, Oral History Research Office, Columbia University, New York, 167. The title was originally coined by James Kieran of the *New York Times*: "The 'Cabinet' Mr. Roosevelt Already Has," *New York Times*, November 20, 1932.
36. Schwarz, *Liberal*, 78.
37. Franklin Roosevelt, "Commonwealth Club Speech."

38. Schwarz, *Liberal*, 62.
39. See A. A. Berle, "Corporate Powers as Powers in Trust," *Harvard Law Review* 44, no. 7 (1931): 1049–74; A. A. Berle, "For Whom Corporate Managers Are Trustees: A Note," *Harvard Law Review* 45, no. 8 (1932): 1365–72; Adolf A. Berle, "A High Road for Business," *Scribner's*, June 1933; Adolf A. Berle and Gardiner C. Means, *The Modern Corporation and Private Property* (New York: Harcourt, Brace & World, 1932); Adolf A. Berle, "High Finance: Master or Servant," *Yale Review* 23, no. 1 (September 1933); A. A. Berle, Jr., "How Labor Could Control," *New Republic*, September 7, 1921.
40. Social Science Research Council, *1927 Annual Report*, 25. For a careful study of Berle and his work on the corporation, see Nicholas Lemann, *Transaction Man: The Rise of the Deal and the Decline of the American Dream* (New York: Farrar, Straus and Giroux, 2019), 23–69.
41. Leuchtenburg, *Franklin D. Roosevelt and the New Deal*, 34.
42. Berle and Means, *The Modern Corporation and Private Property*, 19–30.
43. Berle and Means, *The Modern Corporation and Private Property*, 48.
44. Berle and Means, *The Modern Corporation and Private Property*, 63–64.
45. Berle and Means, *The Modern Corporation and Private Property*, 303.
46. The notion of the separation of ownership and control had been described earlier, notably by Walter Lippmann, Louis D. Brandeis, and Thorstein Veblen, but the Berle and Means thesis moved beyond the principal-agent legal problematic into the realm of empirical observation and social criticism. See Harwell Wells, "The Birth of Corporate Governance," *Seattle University Law Review* 33, no. 4 (January 1, 2010): 1247–92.
47. Berle and Means, *The Modern Corporation and Private Property*, 116.
48. Adolf A. Berle, "High Finance: Master or Servant," *Yale Review* 23, no. 1 (September 1933), 24.
49. Adolf A. Berle, "High Finance: Master or Servant," 22, 27.
50. Berle and Means, *The Modern Corporation and Private Property*, 65.
51. See Howard Brick, *Transcending Capitalism: Visions of a New Society in Modern American Thought* (Ithaca, NY: Cornell University Press, 2015).
52. Brick, *Transcending Capitalism*, 43
53. Berle and Scott, "The Reminiscences of Adolf A. Berle, Jr.": 121.
54. *Congressional Record*, 73rd Cong., 1st Sess., 88, 937; Michael E. Parrish, *Securities Regulation and the New Deal* (New Haven, CT: Yale University Press, 1970), 47–48.
55. "Morgan Party's Bill Placed at $2000 Daily," *Los Angeles Times*, June 3, 1933.
56. James M. Landis, "The Reminiscences of James M. Landis," interview by Neil Newton Gold, 1975, Oral History Research Office, Columbia University, New York, 204.
57. James M. Landis, "Legislative History of the Securities Act of 1933," *George Washington Law Review* 28 (1960–1959): 33.
58. Parrish, *Securities Regulation and the New Deal*, 57–61. It is impossible to convey the depth and complexity of these processes here. For fuller context

and background, see Thomas McCraw's indispensable *Prophets of Regulation* (Cambridge, MA: Harvard University Press, 1984), and Ellis W. Hawley's unsuperseded *The New Deal and the Problem of Monopoly* (New Haven, CT: Princeton University Press, 1966).

59. Nelson Lichtenstein, *State of the Union: A Century of American Labor* (Princeton, NJ: Princeton University Press, 2002), 52; Christopher L. Tomlins, "AFL Unions in the 1930s: Their Performance in Historical Perspective," *Journal of American History* 65, no. 4 (1979): 1023.
60. McCraw, *Prophets of Regulation*, 173.
61. On the growth of the volume of traded stocks in the late nineteenth and early twentieth centuries, see Mary O'Sullivan, "The Expansion of the U.S. Stock Market, 1885–1930: Historical Facts and Theoretical Fashions," *Enterprise & Society* 8, no. 3 (2007): 489–542.
62. William O. Douglas and George Bates, "The Federal Securities Act of 1933," *Yale Law Journal* 43, no. 2 (January 1, 1933): 171, 216–17.
63. "Uncertainty Given Blame for Slow Capital Market," *Los Angeles Times*, December 7, 1933.
64. Quoted in Thomas K. McCraw, *Prophets of Regulation: Charles Francis Adams, Louis D. Brandeis, James M. Landis, Alfred E. Kahn* (Cambridge, MA: Belknap Press of Harvard University Press, 1984), 178.
65. On Whitney's opposition to the Securities and Exchange Act of 1934, see Seligman, *The Transformation of Wall Street*, 75–76; Parrish, *Securities Regulation and the New Deal*, 123–24.
66. Adolf Berle to James Landis, February 28, 1934, Securities and Exchange Historical Society.
67. Box 22, Stock Market Investigation, 1933–34. Folder: Draft: Memorandum with Corrections in Berle's Hand [Re: Modifications in Securities Act of 1933], Berle Papers, FDR Presidential Library.
68. US Department of Commerce and US Bureau of Economic Analysis, "1932," *Survey of Current Business. Business Statistics (Biennial Supplement)* (1932), 93; US Department of Commerce and US Bureau of Economic Analysis, "1955," *Survey of Current Business. Business Statistics (Biennial Supplement)* (1955), 94; Robert Sobel, *The Big Board: A History of the New York Stock Market* (New York: Free Press, 1965), 302–3.
69. "Memorandum to the Secretary of Commerce for Transmission to the President," January 27, 1934, Box 22, Adolf Berle Papers, FDR Presidential Library.
70. William Lasser, *Benjamin V. Cohen: Architect of the New Deal* (New Haven, CT: Yale University Press, 2008), 88–89; Parrish, *Securities Regulation and the New Deal*, 116–20; Seligman, *The Transformation of Wall Street*, 85–87, 98–100.
71. Joseph P. Kennedy, Address at the National Press Club, July 25, 1934, SEC Historical Society.
72. Ralph F. de Bedts, "The First Chairmen of the Securities and Exchange

Commission: Successful Ambassadors of the New Deal to Wall Street," *American Journal of Economics and Sociology* 23, no. 2 (1964), 168.

73. Kennedy, Address at the National Press Club, July 25, 1934.
74. de Bedts, "The First Chairmen of the Securities and Exchange Commission," 173.
75. James M. Landis, *The Administrative Process* (New Haven, CT: Yale University Press, 1938), 9.
76. McCraw, *Prophets of Regulation*, 185.
77. Landis, *The Administrative Process*, 1.
78. Landis, *The Administrative Process*, 15.
79. Landis, *The Administrative Process*, 34–36; see also Morton J. Horwitz, *The Transformation of American Law, 1870-1960* (New York: Oxford University Press, 1992), 213–25.
80. Landis, *The Administrative Process*, 70, 171.
81. Justin O'Brien, *The Triumph, Tragedy and Lost Legacy of James M. Landis* (Oxford: Hart, 2014), 77.
82. For a discussion of this pivot toward a technocratic "managerial approach," see K. Sabeel Rahman, *Democracy Against Domination* (New York: Oxford University Press, 2016), 6–7.
83. "SEC," *Fortune*, June 1940, 91.
84. "Federal Incorporation," Box 3, Series 1, Gardiner C. Means Papers, FDR Presidential Library; Adolf Berle to William O. Douglas, December 30, 1933, Box 2, Folder 5, General Correspondence, William O. Douglas Papers, Library of Congress; Douglas to Berle, January 3, 1934, Box 2, Folder 5, General Correspondence, William O. Douglas Papers, Library of Congress.
85. Schwarz, *Liberal*, 82–83.
86. "Text of Committee Report to Roosevelt on Federal Regulation of the Stock Exchanges," *New York Times*, January 28, 1934.
87. US Congress, Senate, Committee on Banking and Currency, *Stock Exchange Practices: Hearings Before the Committee on Banking and Currency, Part 15*, 73rd Cong., 1st Sess., 1934.
88. US Congress, Senate, Committee, *Stock Exchange Practices*, 6536.
89. Frankfurter to Roosevelt, March 6, 1934, Reel 60, Felix Frankfurter Collection, Manuscript Division, Library of Congress.
90. Felix Frankfurter to William O. Douglas, January 16, 1934, Box 6, Folder 6, General Correspondence, William O. Douglas Papers, Library of Congress.
91. Frankfurter to Douglas, March 16, 1934, Box 6, Folder 6, General Correspondence, William O. Douglas Papers, Library of Congress.
92. "Federal Incorporation Waits," *New York Times*, March 1, 1934.
93. "Some New Deal Quarters Hatching Plan for a Federal Incorporation Law," *Wall Street Journal*, August 10, 1935; Hawley, *The New Deal and the Problem of Monopoly*, 371–72. Federal incorporation was discussed at length in the Temporary National Economic Committee, a joint congressional–executive branch committee that worked from 1938 to 1941.

94. Joseph O'Mahoney, "Federal Incorporation of Interstate Business," *Vital Speeches of the Day*, January 1, 1937, 175.
95. Alan Brinkley, *The End of Reform: New Deal Liberalism in Recession and War* (New York: Vintage, 1996), 93, 310n23.
96. I borrow this helpful concept from John J. Flynn, "Corporate Democracy: Nice Work if You Can Get It," in *Corporate Power in America*, ed. Ralph Nader and Mark J. Green (New York: Grossman, 1973), 94–110.

Chapter Two: The Single and Most Serious Danger

1. Elmo Roper, "The Public Looks at Business," *Harvard Business Review* 27, no. 2 (March 1949): 166. In 1954, 80 percent of Americans gave a favorable opinion of big business. See Opinion Research Corporation, ORC Public Opinion Index, August 1954 [survey question], USORC.55JAN.R01 (Ithaca, NY: Cornell University, Roper Center for Public Opinion Research, iPOLL).
2. Mark R. Wilson, *Destructive Creation: American Business and the Winning of World War II* (Philadelphia: University of Pennsylvania Press, 2016), 137.
3. Alan Brinkley, *The End of Reform: New Deal Liberalism in Recession and War* (New York: Vintage, 1996), 139; James T. Sparrow, *Warfare State: World War II Americans and the Age of Big Government* (New York: Oxford University Press, 2011), 6.
4. Wilson, *Destructive Creation*, 92–93.
5. Quoted in Wilson, *Destructive Creation*, 92.
6. Nelson Lichtenstein, *Walter Reuther: The Most Dangerous Man in Detroit* (New York: Basic Books, 1995), 280.
7. Adolf A. Berle, Jr., *Economic Power and the Free Society* (New York: Fund for the Republic, 1957), 7.
8. Peter F. Drucker, *Concept of the Corporation* (New Brunswick, NJ: Transaction Publishers, 2009), 140.
9. I rely for this narrative on Harwell Wells, "Shareholder Meetings and Freedom Rides: The Story of Peck v. Greyhound," *Seattle University Law Review* 45 (2021).
10. "Bus Firm to Be Urged to End Segregation," *Morning News* (Wilmington, DE), May 18, 1948; "Racial Discrimination Issue Up at Greyhound Meeting," *Wall Street Journal*, May 19, 1948; Richard Marens, "Inventing Corporate Governance: The Mid-Century Emergence of Shareholder Activism," *Journal of Business and Management* 8, no. 4 (Fall 2002): 365–89.
11. Securities and Exchange Bill of 1934, H.R. 9323, H.Rept. No. 1383, 73rd Cong., 2nd Sess., *Congressional Record* 78 (April 30, 1934), 7705; Donald E. Schwartz and Elliott J. Weiss, "An Assessment of the SEC Shareholder Proposal Rule," *Georgetown Law Journal* 65 (1977): 635, 636–37; Marc I. Steinberg, *The Federalization of Corporate Governance* (New York: Oxford University Press, 2018), 168–69; Milton V. Freeman, "An Estimate of the Practical Consequences of the Stockholder's Proposal Rule: The Seamless

Symposium," *University of Detroit Law Journal* 34 (1956–57): 555; Edward T. McCormick, "The Corporate Secretary and the Proxy Rules," presented at American Society of Corporate Secretaries, Atlantic City, NJ, May 13, 1950, 2; "Purcell Calls for Proxy Rule Changers to Prevent Corporate Mismanagement," *Commercial and Financial Chronicle*, September 10, 1942.

12. James Peck, "Minority Stockholders v. Jim Crow," *The Crisis*, June/July 1951, 375.
13. "Greyhound Co. Asked to End Jim Crow Seats," Associated Press, May 18, 1948.
14. "Bus Firm to Be Urged to End Segregation," *Morning News*.
15. Peck, "Minority Stockholders v. Jim Crow," 375.
16. Peck, "Minority Stockholders v. Jim Crow," 376.
17. "Greyhound Meeting Picketed by Two Men," *News Journal* (Wilmington, DE), May 16, 1950.
18. "Law Requires Segregation," *Atlanta Constitution*, May 17, 1950; Peck, *The Crisis*, 376.
19. Peck, "Minority Stockholders v. Jim Crow," 376.
20. Peck, "Minority Stockholders v. Jim Crow," 376–77.
21. "SEC Oks Refusal to Stop Bus Bias," *Chicago Defender*, April 5, 1951.
22. Harry Heller, "Stockholder Proposals Part IV: The Role of the Securities Exchange Commission," in *Corporate Democracy: A Compilation of the Original Dicta Published by the Virginia Law Weekly, 1952–1953* (Charlottesville: Virginia Law Weekly), 74.
23. Peck v. Greyhound, 97 F.Supp. 679, 680 (SDNY 1951); Derek Charles Catsam, *Freedom's Main Line: The Journey of Reconciliation and the Freedom Rides* (Lexington: University Press of Kentucky, 2009), 58.
24. "Stockholder Files Against Bus Company," *New York Amsterdam News*, April 7, 1951.
25. "Judge Drops Stockholder's Agenda Case," *New York Amsterdam News*, April 14, 1951.
26. Peck, *The Crisis*, 377.
27. Peck, *The Crisis*, 378.
28. SEC Release No. 34–4668, January 31, 1952, quoted in Wells, "Shareholder Meetings and Freedom Rides," 37.
29. James Peck, "Minority Stockholders vs. Jim Crow—Continued," *The Crisis*, June/July 1952, 368.
30. Harold H. Martin, "Florida's Fabulous Junkman," *Saturday Evening Post*, July 24, 1954.
31. Diana B. Henriques, *The White Sharks of Wall Street: Thomas Mellon Evans and the Original Corporate Raiders* (New York: Scribner, 2000), 75–79, 170–77.
32. Robert Sobel, *Dangerous Dreamers: The Financial Innovators from Charles Merrill to Michael Milken* (New York: Wiley, 1993), 14–15.
33. Louis E. Wolfson, "How American Business Can Recapture Its Pioneering Spirit," *Vital Speeches of the Day*, December 1, 1959, 109.

34. Henriques, *The White Sharks of Wall Street*, 150; Sobel, *Dangerous Dreamers*, 16–17.
35. David Karr, *Fight for Control* (New York: Ballantine, 1956),152.
36. Karr, *Fight for Control*, 156.
37. Montgomery Ward & Co. Incorporated, *1955 Annual Report*, 3.
38. Henriques, *The White Sharks of Wall Street*, 156–57.
39. Karr, *Fight for Control*, 167–68.
40. Ed Reid and Ovid Demaris, *The Green Felt Jungle* (New York: Pocket Books, 1964), 94.
41. Wolfson, "How American Business Can Recapture Its Pioneering Spirit," *Vital Speeches of the Day*, 113.
42. John Armour and Brian Cheffins, "The Origins of the Market for Corporate Control," *University of Illinois Law Review* 2014, no. 5 (2014): 1835–66.
43. Data culled from annual reports from the Securities and Exchange Commission; see also Frank D. Emerson and Franklin C. Latcham, "Proxy Contests: A Study in Shareholder Sovereignty," *California Law Review* 41, no. 3 (1953): 393–438; John H. Armour and Brian R. Cheffins, "Origins of 'Offensive' Shareholder Activism in the United States," in *Origins of Shareholder Advocacy*, ed. Jonathan G. S. Koppell (New York: Palgrave Macmillan, 2011), 253–76; Douglas V. Austin and Jay A. Fishman, *Corporations in Conflict—the Tender Offer* (Ann Arbor, MI: Masterco Press, 1970); Armour and Cheffins, "The Origins of the Market for Corporate Control," 1835–66.
44. Karr, *Fight for Control*, 3.
45. "Avery Asks Senate Inquiry to Find Out Who Wolfson's Backers Are in Ward Fight," *Wall Street Journal*, March 2, 1955.
46. See Securities and Exchange Commission, *Securities and Exchange Act Release Number 5166* (May 5, 1955); Securities and Exchange Commission, *Securities and Exchange Act Release Number 5299* (April 17, 1956).
47. For a discussion of the rules by the incoming SEC chairman, see J. Sinclair Armstrong, "Regulation of Proxy Contests by the SEC," *Virginia Law Review* 42, no. 8 (1956): 1075–85.
48. Adlai Stevenson, *The New America*, ed. Seymour E. Harris, John Bartlow Martin, and Arthur Schlesinger, Jr. (London: Rupert Hart-Davis, 1957), 8.
49. Robert M. Collins, "Growth Liberalism in the Sixties: Great Societies at Home and Grand Designs Abroad," in *The Sixties: From Memory to History*, ed. David Farber (Chapel Hill: University of North Carolina Press, 1994), 11–44.
50. Charles L. Fontenay, *Estes Kefauver: A Biography* (Knoxville: University of Tennessee Press, 1991), 23–24.
51. Russell Baker, *The Good Times* (New York: Penguin Group, 1992), 304.
52. Donald I. Rogers, "Estes Kefauver on Prod Again," *Arizona Daily Star*, March 13, 1957.
53. Fontenay, *Estes Kefauver*, 360–62.
54. John M. Blair, *Seeds of Destruction: A Study in the Functional Weaknesses of Capitalism* (New York: Covici, Friede, 1938), 91.

55. "Opening Campaign Speech of Senator Estes Kefauver," Murfreesboro, TN, June 11, 1960, Box 1339 of 1716, Estes Kefauver Papers, Betsey B. Creekmore Special Collections and University Archives, University of Tennessee, Knoxville Repository.
56. See, e.g., *Congressional Record*, December 12, 1950, 16450.
57. Estes Kefauver, *In a Few Hands: Monopoly Power in America* (New York: Pantheon, 1965).
58. US Congress, Senate, Subcommittee on Antitrust and Monopoly of the Committee on the Judiciary, *Administered Prices, Part 1: Opening Phase—Economists' Views: Hearings Before the Subcommittee on Antitrust and Monopoly of the Committee on the Judiciary*, 85th Cong., 1st Sess., 1957, 2.
59. Kefauver, *In a Few Hands*, 3.
60. These findings are discussed at length in Kefauver, *In a Few Hands.*
61. Associated Press, "Kefauver Warns Big Business Is Enterprise Threat," *Sacramento Bee*, December 8, 1962.
62. US Congress, Senate, Subcommittee on Antitrust and Monopoly of the Committee on the Judiciary, *Administered Prices, Part 11: Price Notification Legislation: Hearings Before the Subcommittee on Antitrust and Monopoly of the Committee on the Judiciary*, 85th Cong., 1st Sess., 1959, 5511–31.
63. US Congress, Senate, Subcommittee, *Administered Prices, Part 11*, 5528.
64. "Meet Wall Street's Carrie Nation," *New York Times Herald*, June 23, 1949.
65. "CBS Promise: A Big Cleanup," *New York Daily News*, April 21, 1960.
66. "Assistant Gadfly Leaves Queen," *New York Times*, May 5, 1966.
67. "Pressure Group," *New Yorker*, June 25, 1949.
68. "New Concept of Stockholders," Letter to the Editor by Wilma Soss, *New York Times*, August 20, 1949.
69. "Lewis Gilbert, 86, Advocate of Shareholder Rights," *New York Times*, December 8, 1993.
70. These and other demands were included in the "Annual Report of Stockholders Activities at Annual Meetings" as early as the 1950s.
71. "The Crusading Minority Stockholder," *St. Louis Post-Dispatch*, October 15, 1953; Brookings Report of 1952, quoted in Janice M. Traflet, *A Nation of Small Shareholders: Marketing Wall Street After World War II* (Baltimore: Johns Hopkins University Press, 2013), 75–76.
72. Lewis D. Gilbert, *Dividends and Democracy*, (Larchmont, NY: American Research Council, 1956), 19–20.
73. Gilbert, *Dividends and Democracy*, 21.
74. Gilbert, *Dividends and Democracy*, 39.
75. "Bethlehem's Chairman Refuses to Cut His $200,000 Salary," Associated Press, April 13, 1938.
76. Gilbert, *Dividends and Democracy*, 35.
77. Fred S. McChesney, "General Introduction," in *The Collected Works of Henry G. Manne*, ed. Henry N. Butler, vol. 1 (Indianapolis, IN: Liberty Fund, 2009), viii.

78. Henry Manne, oral history interview by James Stocker, August 6, 2012, Securities and Exchange Commission Historical Society, Washington, DC, 1–2.
79. McChesney, "General Introduction," vii–viii.
80. Manne, oral history interview by Stocker, 10. Partly this was a reunion of a group that had been forged at the University of Chicago when Stigler, Friedman, Director, and Wallis were in graduate school. Angus Burgin, *The Great Persuasion: Reinventing Free Markets Since the Depression* (Cambridge, MA: Harvard University Press, 2012), 157.
81. The William Volker Fund played an important role in supporting Hayek and in popularizing *The Road to Serfdom*. See Kim Phillips-Fein, *Invisible Hands: The Businessmen's Crusade Against the New Deal* (New York: Norton, 2009), 41–45. See also the earlier and substantive Elizabeth A. Fones-Wolf, *Selling Free Enterprise: The Business Assault on Labor and Liberalism, 1945–60* (Urbana: University of Illinois Press, 1994).
82. R. H. Coase, "Law and Economics at Chicago," *Journal of Law & Economics* 36, no. 1 (1993): 245–46; Edmund W. Kitch, "The Fire of Truth: A Remembrance of Law and Economics at Chicago, 1932–1970," *Journal of Law & Economics* 26, no. 1 (1983): 180–81.
83. Directories, 1949–1950, Box 80, Folder 23, Friedrich A. von Hayek Papers, Hoover Institution Archives.
84. Director appeared with W. Allen Wallis and Friedman at a meeting of the Citizens Board for a program entitled, "A Positive Program for Conservatives," March 29, 1950, Box 216, Folder 4, Milton Friedman Collection, Hoover Institution Archives.
85. Manne, oral history interview by Stocker, 7. "Director and Posner made a perfect pair as a teacher and student," Posner's biographer, William Domnarski, has written. "One colleague, whose office was next door to Posner's, said the two spent hours discussing law and economics, Director lecturing and Posner, the intellectual sponge, taking it all in. Director would come to Posner's office at least weekly, often daily, and the two would talk for hours at a time." See William Domnarski, *Richard Posner* (New York: Oxford University Press, 2016), 55, 54–58.
86. Domnarski, *Richard Posner*, 184; Kitch, "The Fire of Truth," 184, 190.
87. Aaron Director, "Review of *Unions and Capitalism* by Charles E. Lindblom," *University of Chicago Law Review* 18, no. 1 (September 1, 1950): 166; Philip Mirowski and Dieter Plehwe, *The Road from Mont Pèlerin: The Making of the Neoliberal Thought Collective, With a New Preface* (Cambridge, MA: Harvard University Press, 2015), 217–18. See also Matt Stoller, *Goliath: The 100-Year War Between Monopoly Power and Democracy* (New York: Simon & Schuster, 2020), 224–56.
88. Quoted in Steven M. Teles, *The Rise of the Conservative Legal Movement: The Battle for Control of the Law* (Princeton, NJ: Princeton University Press, 2008), 104.

89. See generally Henry G. Manne, "An Intellectual History of the George Mason University School of Law," Antonin Scalia Law School, George Mason University, accessed May 5, 2023, https://www.law.gmu.edu/about/history.
90. Manne remembered with deep affection the legacy of Louis Wolfson after Wolfson's death: Henry G. Manne, "The Original Corporate Raider," *Wall Street Journal*, January 18, 2008, Opinion.
91. Ludwig von Mises, *Human Action, The Scholar's Edition* (1949; repr., Auburn, AL: Ludwig von Mises Institute, 1966), 42.
92. von Mises, *Human Action*, 164. Contrast this view with the classic treatise: John Dewey, *Individualism, Old and New* (New York: Minton, Balch & Company, 1930).
93. F. A. Hayek, "The Use of Knowledge in Society," *American Economic Review* 35, no. 4 (1945): 526.
94. Hayek, "The Use of Knowledge in Society," 527.
95. Henry G. Manne, review of *Review of Corporation Giving in a Free Society*, by Richard Eells, *University of Chicago Law Review* 24, no. 1 (1956): 199.
96. Such themes were also reprised in *The Hudsucker Proxy*, a 1994 dark comedy directed by Joel and Ethan Coen in which a naïve mailroom boy (played by Tim Robbins) is made president of a company as a part of a stock scam orchestrated by a company director (played by Paul Newman). It's truly one of the best films made about American business.

Chapter Three: Building the City of God

1. Fortune 500 list, 1957.
2. Harold Brayman, "Formula for Reform," *Vital Speeches of the Day* 18, no. 4 (December 15, 1951): 119–20.
3. Thomas J. Watson, Jr., *A Business and Its Beliefs: The Ideas That Helped Build IBM* (New York: McGraw-Hill, 1963), 80.
4. James W. Corada, *IBM: The Rise and Fall and Reinvention of a Global Icon* (Cambridge, MA: MIT Press, 2019), 202.
5. Jordan A. Schwarz, *Liberal: Adolf A. Berle and the Vision of an American Era* (New York: Free Press, 1987), 365.
6. 1939: US Bureau of the Census, *Sixteenth Census of the United States: 1940. Census of Manufactures, 1939*, vol. 1, 230. 1947–1967: *1967 Census of Manufactures* (1971), vol. 1, 3–4. 1972–1992: *Census of Manufactures, 1992*, General Summary (1996), MC92-S-1; Table 3–7 in *Historical Statistics of the United States*, Millennium Edition Online, ed. Susan B. Carter et al. (Cambridge: Cambridge University Press, 2006).
7. Daniel Bell, *The End of Ideology: On the Exhaustion of Political Ideas in the Fifties* (New York: Free Press, 1960); John Kenneth Galbraith, *American Capitalism: The Concept of Countervailing Power* (New York: Houghton Mifflin,

1952); John Kenneth Galbraith, *The Affluent Society* (New York: Houghton Mifflin, 1958); C. Wright Mills, *The Power Elite* (Oxford: Oxford University Press, 1956).

8. M. A. Adelman, "The Measurement of Industrial Concentration," *Review of Economics and Statistics* 33, no. 4 (1951), 278, 270. See also M. A. Adelman, "Is Big Business Getting Bigger?" *Fortune*, January 1952.
9. Federal Trade Commission, *Present Trend of Corporate Mergers and Acquisitions* (Washington, DC: Government Printing Office, 1947), 11.
10. "Northrop Aircraft Acquires Control of Salsbury Motors," *Wall Street Journal*, December 21, 1945.
11. "Big Coal Merger Goes Into Effect: Pittsburgh Consolidation Is Formally Set Up as Largest Bituminous Producer. Subsidiaries Organized," *New York Times*, November 27, 1945.
12. Federal Trade Commission, "Present Trend of Corporate Mergers and Acquisitions," 6.
13. Federal Trade Commission, *The Merger Movement: A Summary Report* (Washington, DC: Government Printing Office, 1948), 28.
14. With apologies to DBH.
15. Earl Newsom Speech, March 13, 1948, Box 17, Folder 30, Earl Newsom Papers, Wisconsin Historical Society.
16. Gardiner C. Means, "Industrial Prices and Their Relative Inflexibility," US Senate Document no. 13, 74th Cong., 1st Sess. (Washington, DC: Government Printing Office, 1935). See also Gardiner C. Means, "Big Business, Administered Prices, and the Problem of Full Employment," *Journal of Marketing* 4, no. 4 (1940): 370–78.
17. Gardiner C. Means, "Industrial Prices and Their Relative Inflexibility," US Senate Document no. 13, 74th Cong., 1st Sess. (Washington, DC: Government Printing Office, 1935), 1
18. Senator Estes Kefauver convened hearings in 1957 to investigate administered prices. The 1960 Democratic Party platform called for the restraint of administered prices.
19. See Naomi Lamoreaux, Table Ch510–524—Corporate Assets, Liabilities, Receipts, Dividends, and Income Tax: 1926–1997, in *Historical Statistics of the United States*, Millennium Edition Online, ed. Susan B. Carter et al. (Cambridge: Cambridge University Press, 2006).
20. US Congress, Joint Committee on the Economic Report, *Corporate Profits: Hearings Before the Joint Committee of the Economic Report, Congress of the United States*, 80th Cong., 2nd Sess., 1948, 116.
21. "B. F. Goodrich Says It Plans $200 Million, Five-Year Expansion," *Wall Street Journal*, April 18, 1956.
22. Adolf A. Berle, *The 20th Century Capitalist Revolution* (New York: Harcourt, Brace, 1954), 40.
23. Berle, *The 20th Century Capitalist Revolution*, 164.

24. Berle, *The 20th Century Capitalist Revolution*, 39.
25. No one better traces the rise of the professional managerial class in the late nineteenth and early twentieth centuries than Alfred D. Chandler, Jr., in *The Visible Hand: The Managerial Revolution in American Business* (Cambridge, MA: The Belknap Press of Harvard University Press, 1977).
26. Ralph J. Cordiner, *New Frontiers for Professional Managers* (New York: McGraw-Hill, 1956), 1.
27. Gardiner C. Means, "Collective Capitalism and Economic Theory," *Science* 126, no. 3268 (1957): 287, 293.
28. Galbraith, *American Capitalism*, 113.
29. Galbraith, *American Capitalism*, 112.
30. Galbraith, *American Capitalism*, 55.
31. Francis Xavier Sutton et al., *The American Business Creed* (Cambridge, MA: Harvard University Press, 1956).
32. Sutton et al., *The American Business Creed*, 9.
33. Sutton et al., *The American Business Creed*, 36.
34. Robert L. Heilbroner, "The View from the Top: Reflections on a Changing Business Ideology," in *The Business Establishment*, ed. Earl F. Cheit (New York: Wiley, 1964), 6.
35. Editors of *Fortune* and Russell W. Davenport, *U.S.A.: The Permanent Revolution* (New York: Prentice-Hall, 1951), 67.
36. Editors of *Fortune* and Davenport, *U.S.A.: The Permanent Revolution*, 79–80.
37. Theodore Levitt, *The Twilight of the Profit Motive* (Washington, DC: Public Affairs Press, 1955), 15.
38. Table Ch1–18—Active Proprietorships, Partnerships, and Corporations–Entities, Receipts, and Profit: 1916–1998 [All industries], in *Historical Statistics of the United States*, Millennium Edition Online, ed. Susan B. Carter et al. (Cambridge: Cambridge University Press, 2006).
39. United States Congress Joint Economic Committee, and United States Congress Joint Committee on the Economic Report Subcommittee on Profits, *Corporate Profits: Hearings Before the Joint Committee on the Economic Report, Congress of the United States, Eightieth Congress, Second Session, Pursuant to Sec. 5 (A) of Public Law 304, 79th Congress* (Washington, DC: US Government Printing Office, 1949), 1.
40. Calculated from John Joseph Wallis, Table Ea731–739—Federal Income Tax Returns-Corporate: 1909–1991, in *Historical Statistics of the United States*, Millennium Edition Online, ed. Susan B. Carter et al. (Cambridge: Cambridge University Press, 2006).
41. Lawrence B. Glickman, *Free Enterprise: An American History* (New Haven, CT: Yale University Press, 2019), 84; Kim Phillips-Fein, *Invisible Hands: The Businessmen's Crusade Against the New Deal* (New York: Norton, 2009).
42. Statement of M. E. Coyle, Hearings on Corporate Profits, 511.
43. Statement of Robert G. Dunlop, Hearings on Corporate Profits, 262.
44. Hearings on Corporate Profits, 475.

45. Hearings on Corporate Profits, 472.
46. US Congress, Senate, Committee on Armed Services, *Nominations: Hearings Before the Committee on Armed Services*, 83rd Cong., 1st Sess., 1953, 26.
47. Fortune 500 list; General Motors Corporation, *1955 Annual Report*; Organization for Economic Co-operation and Development, "Civilian Labor Force: All Persons in the United States" (DISCONTINUED) [USALFTOTQDSMEI], FRED, Federal Reserve Bank of St. Louis, accessed June 11, 2022, https://fred.stlouisfed.org/series/USALFTOTQDSMEI.
48. Jennifer Delton, "The Triumph of Social Responsibility in the National Association of Manufacturers in the 1950s," in *Capital Gains: Business and Politics in Twentieth-Century America*, ed. Richard R. John and Kim Phillips-Fein (Philadelphia: University of Pennsylvania Press, 2016); Jennifer A. Delton, *Rethinking the 1950s: How Anticommunism and the Cold War Made America Liberal* (New York: Cambridge University Press, 2013).
49. For an excellent discussion of the midcentury philanthropic scene in the United States, see Olivier Zunz, *Philanthropy in America: A History* (Princeton, NJ: Princeton University Press, 2012), 169–200.
50. Jerome L. Himmelstein, *Looking Good and Doing Good: Corporate Philanthropy and Corporate Power* (Bloomington: Indiana University Press, 1997), 18–22.
51. F. Emerson Andrews, "New Giant in Giving: Big Business; American Corporations Are Now Contributing Millions for Causes That Once Were Financed Almost Entirely by Private Citizens.," *New York Times*, December 2, 1951.
52. Beardsley Ruml and Theodore Geiger, *The Five Percent* (Washington, DC: National Planning Association, 1951), 5.
53. Ruml and Geiger, *The Five Percent*, 10.
54. "Participation in Political Affairs by General Electric Employees: A Policy Study," Box 1, Folder: Politics and the Corporation, 1956–1959, Richard Eells Papers, Columbia University Special Collections.
55. "Corporate Giving. Revised Edition, December 1958. Part 1: Corporate Giving Programs of 16 Leading Companies," Box 1, Folder: Corporate Giving, 1954–1958, Richard Eells Papers, Columbia University Special Collections.
56. "Hi, Neighbor! Many Companies Find a Sociable Approach Pays Off in Business," *Wall Street Journal*, June 5, 1956.
57. "More Companies Prod Employees to Donate to Political Parties," *Wall Street Journal*, October 13, 1964.
58. Theodor V. Houser, *Big Business and Human Values* (New York: McGraw-Hill, 1957), 49–50.
59. "Area Hospital Gets $30,000 from Kodak," *Democrat and Chronicle* (Rochester, NY), September 27, 1959.
60. "Hi, Neighbor!" *Wall Street Journal*.
61. A survey conducted in 1951 was representative of the general trends of the decade. See Public Relations News, "Corporate Giving: A Survey," *Management Review; Saranac Lake, N.Y., Etc.* 40, no. 5 (May 1, 1951): 262. See also Richard Eells, "Corporate Giving: A Study for General Electric Edu-

cational Relations and Support Services," Internal Report, 1958, Richard Eells Papers, 1954–1958, Columbia University Rare Book & Manuscript Library Collections.

62. Peter F. Drucker, "The Responsibilities of Management," *Harper's Magazine*, November 1954.
63. Richard Eells, *Corporation Giving in a Free Society* (New York: Harper & Brothers, 1956), ix.
64. Eells, *Corporation Giving in a Free Society*, 2.
65. On the influence of the Cold War on the development of civil rights, see especially Jennifer Delton's important work, *Rethinking the 1950s*; see also Mary L. Dudziak, *Cold War Civil Rights: Race and the Image of American Democracy* (Princeton, NJ: Princeton University Press, 2000).
66. Eells, *Corporation Giving in a Free Society*, 87.
67. Editors of *Fortune* and Davenport, *U.S.A.: The Permanent Revolution*, 79.
68. See generally Rakesh Khurana, *From Higher Aims to Hired Hands: The Social Transformation of American Business Schools and the Unfulfilled Promise of Management as a Profession* (Princeton, NJ: Princeton University Press, 2010), 195–231.
69. Frank W. Abrams, "Management's Responsibilities in a Complex World," *Harvard Business Review* 29, no. 3 (May 1951), 30.
70. Morris Sayre, President of Corn Products Refining Company, speech in 1948, quoted in Howard Bowen, *Social Responsibilities of the Businessman* (New York: Harper & Brothers, 1953), 52n9.
71. Houser, *Big Business and Human Values*, 31.
72. Thomas Reeves, *Freedom and the Foundation: The Fund for the Republic in the Era of McCarthyism* (New York: Knopf, 1969), 22–23.
73. "Draft: Freedom and Justice in Modern America: An Inquiry," June 18, 1957; "Consulting Cases: Fund for the Republic—Corporations Seminar Papers, 1957–1958," Box 59, Gardiner Means Papers, FDR Presidential Library.
74. James Arthur Ward, *Ferrytale: The Career of W.H. "Ping" Ferry* (Stanford, CA: Stanford University Press, 2001), 61–62.
75. Memo from Scott Buchanan to Seminar on Corporations, December 18, 1957, Box 152, Folder 15, Fund for the Republic Archives, Mudd Library, Princeton University.
76. W. H. Ferry, "Report on the Project on the Corporation," July 1, 1958, Box 153, Folder 12, Fund for the Republic Archives, Mudd Library, Princeton University.
77. The transcripts of most of these early seminars were distributed to participants and are held in multiple archives. These transcripts have given me a helpful window into the ambitions and intellectual depth of the project.
78. On the role of private foundations generally, see Ellen Lagemann, *The Politics of Knowledge: The Carnegie Corporation, Philanthropy, and Public Policy* (Chicago: University of Chicago Press, 1992).

79. Letter from Frank K. Kelly to Robert M. Hutchins, August 6, 1957, Box 161, Folder 6, Fund for the Republic Archives, Mudd Library, Princeton University.
80. Ward, *Ferrytale*, 9–11.
81. Ward, *Ferrytale*, 41.
82. Victor S. Navasky, "The Happy Heretic," *Atlantic Monthly*, July 1966; "'Ping' Ferry," *The Nation*, October 23, 1995.
83. Summary of Discussion at Williamstown Meeting, August 28–29, 1957, Box 161, Folder 6, Fund for the Republic Archives, Mudd Library, Princeton University.
84. W. H. Ferry, "Notes for a Discussion of the Corporation and Economy," March 5, 1959, Box 153, Folder 12, Fund for the Republic Archives, Mudd Library, Princeton University.
85. "Report and Recommendation to the Board," May 7, 1959, Box 164, Folder 3, Fund for the Republic Archives, Mudd Library, Princeton University.
86. "Meeting of Ad Hoc Advisers to the Study of the Corporation," November 19, 1959, Box 161, Folder 2, Fund for the Republic Archives, Mudd Library, Princeton University.
87. W. H. Ferry, Memo to Members of the Committee of Advisors, Study of the Corporation, May 18, 1960, Box 164, Folder 15, Fund for the Republic Archives, Mudd Library, Princeton University.
88. W. H. Ferry, "Notes for a Discussion of the Corporation and Economy."
89. Bayless Manning, "The Shareholder's Appraisal Remedy: An Essay for Frank Coker," *Yale Law Journal* 72, no. 2 (1962): 245n37.
90. "Meeting of Ad Hoc Advisers to the Study of the Corporation," November 19, 1959, Fund for the Republic Archives.
91. "Economic Power and the Free Society: A Preliminary Discussion of the Corporation. A.A. Berle, Jr. and Others," Box 59, Folder: Consulting Cases: Fund for the Republic-Papers (1), Gardiner Means Papers, FDR Presidential Library.
92. Eugene V. Rostow, "To Whom and for What Ends Is Corporate Management Responsible?" in *The Corporation in Modern Society*, ed. Edward S. Mason (Cambridge, MA: Harvard University Press, 1959), 63.
93. Rostow, "To Whom and for What Ends Is Corporate Management Responsible?" 55–56.
94. Edward S. Mason, "The Apologetics of 'Managerialism,'" *Journal of Business* 31, no. 1 (1958): 4–5.
95. Galbraith, *American Capitalism*, 60.
96. Heilbroner, "The View from the Top," 35.
97. "Economic Power and the Free Society: A Preliminary Discussion of the Corporation. A.A. Berle, Jr. and Others," Gardiner Means Papers, FDR Presidential Library.
98. Berle, *The 20th Century Capitalist Revolution*, 187–88.

Chapter Four: Fighting for Jobs

1. S. Prakash Sethi, *Business Corporations and the Black Man: An Analysis of Social Conflict: The Kodak-FIGHT Controversy* (Scranton, PA: Chandler, 1970), 17.
2. Laura Warren Hill, "'Strike the Hammer While the Iron Is Hot': The Black Freedom Struggle in Rochester, NY, 1940–1970" (Binghamton: Binghamton University–State University of New York, 2010), 102–3; R. D. G. Wadhwani, "Kodak, Fight and the Definition of Civil Rights in Rochester, New York 1966–1967," *Historian* 60, no. 1 (September 1997): 59–60; P. David Finks, "Crisis in Smugtown: A Study of Conflict, Churches, and Citizen Organizations in Rochester, New York, 1964–1969" (PhD diss., Union Graduate School, July 1975), 21; Michael W. Flamm, *In the Heat of the Summer: The New York Riots of 1964 and the War on Crime* (Philadelphia: University of Pennsylvania Press, 2016), 209–10; "The Spark and How It Flared," *Democrat and Chronicle* (Rochester, NY), July 26, 1964; "Governor Pledges Full Use of Powers to Curb Violence," *New York Times*, July 26, 1964.
3. Isabel Wilkerson, *The Warmth of Other Suns: The Epic Story of America's Great Migration* (New York: Vintage, 2011); Hill, "'Strike the Hammer While the Iron Is Hot,'": The Black Freedom Struggle in Rochester, NY, 1940–1970" (Binghamton University - State University of New York, 2010), 105–9. This social data comes from Wadhwani, "Kodak, Fight and the Definition of Civil Rights in Rochester," 60–61.
4. Malcolm McLaughlin, *The Long, Hot Summer of 1967: Urban Rebellion in America* (New York: Palgrave Macmillan, 2014), 7, vii.
5. Thomas J. Sugrue, *The Origins of the Urban Crisis: Race and Inequality in Postwar Detroit* (Princeton, NJ: Princeton University Press, 1996), 23.
6. Table Ad782–791—Unemployment Rate, by Sex, Race, and Nativity: 1940–1997, in *Historical Statistics of the United States, Millennium Edition* (New York: Cambridge University Press, 2006).
7. Nick Bryant, *The Bystander: John F. Kennedy and the Struggle for Black Equality* (New York: Basic Books, 2007), 228.
8. Quoted in Judson MacLaury, "President Kennedy's E.O. 10925: Seedbed of Affirmative Action," *Federal History* 2 (January 1, 2010): 48.
9. Quoted in Bryant, *The Bystander*, 229.
10. Frank Dobbin, *Inventing Equal Opportunity* (Princeton, NJ: Princeton University Press, 2009), 4.
11. "Civil Rights Maverick," *New York Times*, June 23, 1962.
12. "Civil Rights Maverick," *New York Times*.
13. Bryant, *The Bystander*, 307.
14. Hobart Taylor, Jr., oral history interview, January 11, 1967, JFK Library, 17.
15. David Hamilton Golland, *Constructing Affirmative Action: The Struggle for Equal Employment Opportunity* (Lexington, KY: University Press of Kentucky, 2011), 45. On the political and intellectual history of Plans for Progress, see the indispensable David L. Chappell, *Inside Agitators: White*

Southerners in the Civil Rights Movement (Baltimore: Johns Hopkins University Press, 1994), 184–211.

16. Robert Troutman to John F. Kennedy, August 22, 1962, Kenan Research Center at the Atlanta History Center.
17. Golland, *Constructing Affirmative Action*, 44.
18. Dobbin, *Inventing Equal Opportunity*, 34.
19. Dobbin, *Inventing Equal Opportunity*, 39.
20. Jennifer Delton, *Racial Integration in Corporate America, 1940–1990* (New York: Cambridge University Press, 2009), 38.
21. Delton, *Racial Integration in Corporate America*, 38.
22. Chappell, *Inside Agitators*, xxii.
23. Chappell, *Inside Agitators*, 208–9.
24. Lyndon B. Johnson, Remarks at a Meeting of the National Alliance of Businessmen, March 16, 1968, in Gerhard Peters and John T. Woolley, The American Presidency Project, accessed May 10, 2023, https://www.presidency.ucsb.edu/node/237313.
25. For a discussion of this policy ideal in the recent Democratic Party, see Lily Geismer, *Left Behind: The Democrats' Failed Attempt to Solve Inequality* (New York: PublicAffairs, 2022).
26. Allen R. Janger and Ruth G. Shaeffer, *Managing Programs to Employ the Disadvantaged* (New York: National Industrial Conference Board, 1970), 64.
27. Information taken from "Managing Programs to Employ the Disadvantaged," National Conference Board, 63–74.
28. M. Leon Lopez, "A New Start for Dropouts," *The Harvester World* 57, no 4 (1966).
29. "How to Turn Dropouts Into Steady Workers," *BusinessWeek*, August 31, 1968, 64–68.
30. "Managing Problems to Employ the Disadvantaged," *1970 Annual Report*, National Conference Board, 73; "I-H 'Buddy' Erases Job Fears," *Indianapolis News*, August 12, 1968.
31. National Advisory Commission on Civil Disorders, *The Kerner Report: The 1968 Report of the National Advisory Commission on Civil Disorders* (Washington, DC: Government Printing Office, 1968), 231–32.
32. National Advisory Commission on Civil Disorders, *The Kerner Report*, 232.
33. National Advisory Commission on Civil Disorders, *The Kerner Report*, 233–35.
34. Sanford D. Horwitt, *Let Them Call Me Rebel: Saul Alinsky, His Life and Legacy* (New York: Vintage, 1992); Marvin Chandler, "Rochester Black Freedom Struggle," interview by Lauren Warren Hill, May 13, 2009, Rochester Black Freedom Struggle Oral History Project, University of Rochester Rare Books and Special Collections, Rochester, NY; Finks, "Crisis in Smugtown," 34, 37–38.
35. Horace Becker, "Rochester Black Freedom Struggle," interview by Lauren Warren Hill, August, 8, 2008, Rochester Black Freedom Struggle Oral His-

tory Project, University of Rochester Rare Books and Special Collections, Rochester, NY; "FIGHT Plans to Expose 'Slumlords,' Absent Owners," *Democrat and Chronicle* (Rochester, NY), April 21, 1965; "Xerox 'Step Up' Provides an Ally," *Democrat and Chronicle* (Rochester, NY), November 16, 1965.

36. "FIGHT Presses Kodak for Job Opportunities," *Democrat and Chronicle* (Rochester, NY), September 3, 1966. Much of this section is dependent on Wadhwani, "Kodak, Fight and the Definition of Civil Rights in Rochester"; Finks, "Crisis in Smugtown"; Sethi, *Business Corporations and the Black Man*; and Laura Warren Hill, "FIGHTing for the Soul of Black Capitalism: Struggles for Black Economic Development in Postrebellion Rochester," in *The Business of Black Power: Community Development, Capitalism, and Corporate Responsibility in Postwar America*, ed. Laura Warren Hill and Julia Rabig (Rochester, NY: University of Rochester Press, 2012).
37. Sethi, *Business Corporations and the Black Man*, 26–27; Wadhwani, "Kodak, Fight and the Definition of Civil Rights in Rochester," 64; "Picture's Fuzzy as Kodak Fights FIGHT," *Washington Post*, January 9, 1967.
38. Sethi, *Business Corporations and the Black Man*, 16–17; Finks, "Crisis in Smugtown," 118–19; "Critics Assailed by Head of Kodak," *New York Times*, January 7, 1967; Letter from FIGHT to Kodak, September 14, 1966, reproduced in Finks, "Crisis in Smugtown," 325–28.
39. Chandler, "Rochester Black Freedom Struggle."
40. Finks, "Crisis in Smugtown," 124.
41. Sethi, *Business Corporations and the Black Man*, 31; Wadhwani, "Kodak, Fight and the Definition of Civil Rights in Rochester," 66; Finks, "Crisis in Smugtown," 125–27.
42. "Kodak, FIGHT Agree on New Job Program," *Democrat and Chronicle* (Rochester, NY), December 21, 1966; "'Rochester's Agony' . . . As an Outsider Sees It," *Democrat and Chronicle* (Rochester, NY), April 23, 1967; Horwitt, *Let Them Call Me Rebel*, 491–493; Wadhwani, "Kodak, Fight and the Definition of Civil Rights in Rochester," 59–75; Sethi, *Business Corporations and the Black Man*, 32–33.
43. Florence quoted in Sethi, *Business Corporations and the Black Man*, 33; Finks, "Crisis in Smugtown," 129–30; Chandler, "Rochester Black Freedom Struggle"; Horwitt, *Let Them Call Me Rebel*, 491.
44. Quoted in Horwitt, *Let Them Call Me Rebel*, 490; Sethi, *Business Corporations and the Black Man*, 29; Finks, "Crisis in Smugtown," 122; Wadhwani, "Kodak, Fight and the Definition of Civil Rights in Rochester," 65–67; "Black Power Passing Phase," *Democrat and Chronicle* (Rochester, NY), October 24, 1966; "Kodak, FIGHT Agree on New Job Program," *Democrat and Chronicle*; "Kodak Tags Accord with FIGHT 'Unauthorized,'" *Democrat and Chronicle* (Rochester, NY), December 23, 1966.
45. James Ridgeway, "Attack on Kodak," *New Republic*, January 21, 1967; "Pic-

ture's Fuzzy as Kodak Fights FIGHT," *Washington Post*; Finks, "Crisis in Smugtown," 146.

46. Finks, "Crisis in Smugtown," 150; Wadhwani, "Kodak, Fight and the Definition of Civil Rights in Rochester," 65–66; "Black Power Passing Phase," *Democrat and Chronicle* (Rochester, NY), October 24, 1966.
47. "Troopers Mobilizing for Protests Expected at Kodak Co. Meeting," *The Courier-News* (Bridgewater, NJ), April 24, 1967; "Alinsky in Flemington," *Democratic and Chronicle* (Rochester, NY), April 25, 1967.
48. Finks, "Crisis in Smugtown," 155; "Kodak Holds Its Meeting Amid Racial Protests," *New York Times*, April 26, 1967; "Black Power Protests Mark Kodak Meeting," *Los Angeles Times*, April 26, 1967; Wadhwani, "Kodak, Fight and the Definition of Civil Rights in Rochester," 71–72; "FIGHT and Kodak Spar at Stockholders Meeting," *The Courier-News* (Bridgewater, NJ), April 26, 1967.
49. Finks, "Crisis in Smugtown," 157–58; "Stockholders Back Kodak," *Democrat and Chronicle* (Rochester, NY), April 26, 1967.
50. Horwitt, *Let Them Call Me Rebel*, 495–96.
51. "FIGHT Plan Rapped," *Democrat and* Chronicle (Rochester, NY), May 12, 1967; Wadhwani, "Kodak, Fight and the Definition of Civil Rights in Rochester," 72–74. As the historian Lauren Warren Hill has argued, the strategy of cutting FIGHT out of decision making and precluding black-owned and -operated institutions was used by Kodak officials to "define Black capitalism in a way that actually precluded Black power." Hill, "FIGHTing for the Soul of Black Capitalism," 57. The Fight-KODAK dispute ought to be understood through the lens of debates within the Black Power movement over the role that business should play in the black community. E. Franklin Frazier, an African American sociologist, articulated a popular viewpoint in his 1955 book, *The Black Bourgeoisie*, that black entrepreneurship was a mistaken substitute for a more thoroughgoing attack on modern capitalism. But beginning in the late 1960s, a new generation of Black Power activists built and operated businesses such as bookstores and record shops that sought to create an alternative entrepreneurial and consumer culture for the Black Power movement. This turn toward economic power was based on the radical idea of community control, says historian Joshua Clark Davis, the notion that "black-controlled spaces and organizations were integral to African American self-determination and Black Power." See Joshua C. Davis, *From Head Shops to Whole Foods: The Rise and Fall of Activist Entrepreneurs* (New York: Columbia University Press, 2017), 46, 44–47.
52. Franklin Florence, "The Meaning of Black Power," in Arthur L. Smith, *Rhetoric of Black Revolution* (Boston: Allyn and Bacon, 1969), 162–63; Ed Chambers quoted in Sethi, *Business Corporations and the Black Man*, 21.
53. Victor Lasky, *Never Complain, Never Explain: The Story of Henry Ford II* (New York: Penguin Group, 1983), 132.

54. Delton, *Racial Integration in Corporate America*, 229.
55. "New Job Drive Turns to Old Twist," *BusinessWeek*, March 2, 1968.
56. Hubert McDonald, "A Study of the National Alliance of Businessmen in Columbus, Ohio (Spring–Summer, 1968)" (Chicago: Loyola University Chicago, 1970), 16–18.
57. Lawrence A. Johnson, *Employing the Hard-Core Unemployed* (New York: American Management Association, 1969), 11.
58. National Alliance of Businessmen, *Jobs '70, Revised November 1971* (Washington, DC: US Department of Labor Manpower Administration, 1971).
59. Examples culled from Johnson, *Employing the Hard-Core Unemployed*, 57–65.
60. Quoted in Johnson, *Employing the Hard-Core Unemployed*, 200.
61. Joseph R. Goeke and Caroline S. Weymar, "Barriers to Hiring the Blacks," *Harvard Business Review* 47, no. 5 (October 9, 1969): 146.
62. "Setback for Minority Business," *New York Times*, November 30, 1981.
63. Blaine J. Yarrington, "Corporate Social Responsibility: Ritual or Reality," address to the International Assembly of Better Business Bureaus, Chicago, IL, May 27, 1972, quoted in Phillip T. Drotning, "Organizing the Company for Social Action," in *The Unstable Ground: Corporate Social Policy in a Dynamic Society*, ed. S. Prakash Sethi (Los Angeles: Melville Publishing, 1974), 264–65.
64. One study found that 60 percent of 232 major corporations that appeared on *Fortune*'s lists of the largest industrial and nonindustrial firms had an executive-level officer or committee in charge of corporate social responsibility (CSR) programs. Seventy percent had established policies on the nature and extent of company involvement in social responsibility areas; see Vernon M. Buehler and Y. K. Shetty, "Managing Corporate Social Responsibility," *Management Review* 64, no. 8 (August 1975): 4–17. On the changing relationship between business and the state in the 1960s and 1970s, see Joshua Zeitz, *Building the Great Society: Inside Lyndon Johnson's White House* (New York: Viking, 2018); Richard Flacks and Nelson Lichtenstein, eds., *The Port Huron Statement: Sources and Legacies of the New Left's Founding Manifesto* (Philadelphia: University of Pennsylvania Press, 2015), 272; Chandler, "Rochester Black Freedom Struggle."
65. Robert A. Dahl, *After the Revolution?: Authority in a Good Society* (New Haven, CT: Yale University Press, 1990), 100, 102; David Vogel, *Lobbying the Corporation: Citizen Challenges to Business Authority* (New York: Basic Books, 1978), 6; Chandler, "Rochester Black Freedom Struggle."

Chapter Five: "A Bundle of Assets"

1. Quoted in Stanley H. Brown, *Ling: The Rise, Fall, and Return of a Texas Titan* (Washington, DC: Beard Books, 1999).
2. Robert Sobel, *The Rise and Fall of the Conglomerate Kings* (Washington, DC: Beard Books, 1999), 81.

3. Brown, *Ling*, 62–65.
4. Sobel, *Rise and Fall of the Conglomerate Kings*, 83.
5. Brown, *Ling*, 65–67.
6. Sobel, *Rise and Fall of the Conglomerate Kings*, 83.
7. John F. Winslow, *Conglomerates Unlimited: The Failure of Regulation* (Bloomington: Indiana University Press, 1973), viii.
8. Timothy Hurley, "The Urge to Merge: Contemporary Theories on the Rise of Conglomerate Mergers in the 1960s," *Journal of Business & Technology Law* 1, no. 1 (January 1, 2006): 186.
9. Winslow, *Conglomerates Unlimited*, 65.
10. Andrew L. Turner and Eric J. Weigel, "Daily Stock Market Volatility: 1928–1989," *Management Science* 38, no. 11 (1992): 1586–609.
11. Jonathan Barron Baskin and Paul J. Miranti, Jr., *A History of Corporate Finance* (New York: Cambridge University Press, 1997), 232.
12. Sobel, *Rise and Fall of the Conglomerate Kings*, 165.
13. Sobel, *Rise and Fall of the Conglomerate Kings*, 86–87.
14. Winslow, *Conglomerates Unlimited*, 64.
15. James J. Ling, "A Dialogue on Conglomerate Mergers: An Insider Looks at Conglomerates," *Kentucky Law Journal* 57, no. 3 (1969): 392.
16. Memo included in US Congress, House, Antitrust Subcommittee of the Committee on the Judiciary, *Investigation of Conglomerate Corporations, Part 6: Hearings Before the Antitrust Subcommittee of the Committee on the Judiciary*, 91st Cong., 2nd Sess., 1970, 416.
17. Winslow, *Conglomerates Unlimited*, 65.
18. Ling, "A Dialogue on Conglomerate Mergers," 393.
19. Moody's Seasoned Aaa Corporate Bond Yield [AAA], FRED, Federal Reserve Bank of St. Louis, accessed January 4, 2021, https://fred.stlouisfed.org/series/AAA.
20. "U.S. Seeks Curb on Conglomerate in Antitrust Test," *New York Times*, March 24, 1969.
21. "Ling-Temco-Vought Sets Layoffs of 40% of Staff," *New York Times*, May 19, 1970.
22. "Fuller Disclosure on Tender Offers Asked," *Los Angeles Times*, March 22, 1967.
23. Testimony of Manuel F. Cohen at US Congress, Senate, Subcommittee on Securities of the Committee on Banking and Currency, *Full Disclosure of Corporate Equity Ownership and in Corporate Takeover Bids: Hearings Before the Subcommittee on Securities of the Committee on Banking and Currency*, 90th Cong., 1st Sess., 1967.
24. Henry Manne, oral history interview by James Stocker, August 6, 2012, Securities and Exchange Commission Historical Society, Washington, DC, 48.
25. Henry G. Manne, "A Salute to 'Raiders,'" *Barron's*, October 23, 1967.
26. Edward Nik-Khah, "George Stigler, the Graduate School of Business,

and the Pillars of the Chicago School," in *Building Chicago Economics: New Perspectives on the History of America's Most Powerful Economics Program*, ed. Philip Mirowski, Robert Van Horn, and Thomas A. Stapleford, Historical Perspectives on Modern Economics (Cambridge: Cambridge University Press, 2011), 116–48.

27. George J. Stigler, "Public Regulation of the Securities Markets," *Journal of Business* 37, no. 2 (1964): 120.
28. Manne, "A Salute to 'Raiders.'"
29. Henry G. Manne, "Cash Tender Offers for Shares: A Reply to Chairman Cohen," in *The Collected Works of Henry G. Manne, Volume 1: The Economics of Corporations and Corporate Law*, ed. Henry N. Butler (Indianapolis, IN: Liberty Fund, 2009), 255. Originally published in *Duke Law Journal*, no. 2 (1967): 231–53.
30. John Kenneth Galbraith, "1929 and 1969: Financial Genius Is a Short Memory and a Rising Market," *Harper's Magazine*, November 1, 1969.
31. Israel Shenker, "Galbraith: '29 Repeats Itself Today," *New York Times*, May 3, 1970.
32. John McDonald, "Some Candid Answers from James J. Ling, Part II," *Fortune*, September 1969.
33. James J. Ling to William H. Osborn, Jr., October 28, 1965, quoted in US Congress, House, Antitrust Subcomittee of the Committee on the Judiciary, *Investigation of Conglomerate Corporations: Hearings Before the Antitrust Subcommittee of the Committee on the Judiciary*, 91st Cong., 2nd Sess., 1970, 413–14.
34. For an important history of the development of managerial theory and its contribution to a new form of business strategy, see Louis Hyman, *Temp: How American Work, American Business, and the American Dream Became Temporary* (New York: Penguin, 2018).
35. Hyman, *Temp*, 112n10.
36. Hyman, *Temp*, 113.
37. In contrast, for example, to what legal scholar K. Sabeel Rahman calls the "structuralist" view of regulation that "rests on a greater skepticism of both expertise and markets, but also on a greater willingness to contemplate a *moralized* judgment about the social value of finance." See K. Sabeel Rahman, *Democracy Against Domination* (New York: Oxford University Press, 2016), 21.
38. Henry G. Manne, "Some Theoretical Aspects of Share Voting: An Essay in Honor of Adolf A. Berle," *Columbia Law Review* 64, no. 8 (December 1964): 1442.
39. Henry G. Manne, *Insider Trading and the Stock Market* (New York: Free Press, 1966). Republished in *The Collected Works of Henry G. Manne, Volume 2: Insider Trading*, ed. Stephen Bainbridge (Indianapolis, IN: Liberty Fund, 2009), 11.
40. Manne, *Insider Trading and the Stock Market*, 148–49.
41. Manne, *Insider Trading and the Stock Market*, 168.

42. Manne, *Insider Trading and the Stock Market*, 59.
43. Henry Manne, "Economic Aspects of Required Disclosure Under Federal Securities Laws," in *Wall Street in Transition: The Emerging System and Its Impact on the Economy* (New York: New York University Press, 1974), 60.
44. Manne, "Economic Aspects of Required Disclosure Under Federal Securities Laws," 66.
45. Henry G. Manne, "How Law and Economics Was Marketed in a Hostile World: A Very Personal History," in *The Origins of Law and Economics: Essays by the Founding Fathers*, ed. Francesco Parisi and Charles Kershaw Rowley (Cheltenham, UK: Edward Elgar, 2005), 310–11.
46. Association with Hayek and Friedman had even more currency after they won Nobel Prizes in Economics in 1974 and 1976, respectively. Steven M. Teles, *The Rise of the Conservative Legal Movement: The Battle for Control of the Law* (Princeton, NJ: Princeton University Press, 2010), 102.
47. Manne, interview by Stocker, 33.

Chapter Six: The Rise of the Corporate Guerrilla Fighter

1. "Bombs Go Off at G.M. Building, Rockefeller Center, Chase Plaza," *New York Times*, November 11, 1969; Bryan Burrough, *Days of Rage: America's Radical Underground, the FBI, and the Forgotten Age of Revolutionary Violence* (New York: Penguin, 2016), 17–24; "Letter to Times on Bombings Here," *New York Times*, November 12, 1969.
2. For a narrative of the bombings and violence committed by radical underground insurgents from the late 1960s to the early 1980s, see Burrough, *Days of Rage*.
3. Numbers on public trust of business come from widely cited Yankelovich, Skelly & White and Louis Harris surveys; see *Washington Journalism Review* 2 (1980): 91.
4. "Power to Which People?" *New Republic*, February 20, 1971; "Protests Erupt at Honeywell," *Washington Post*, April 29, 1970; "I.T.T. Office Here Damaged by Bomb," *New York Times*, September 29, 1973; Robert L. Heilbroner, *In the Name of Profit: Profiles in Corporate Irresponsibility* (New York: Doubleday, 1972), 192; Herman Nickel, "The Corporation Haters," *Fortune*, June 16, 1980.
5. Samuel Melville, *Letters from Attica* (New York: Morrow, 1972); Staughton Lynd, "Attack War Contractors' Meetings," *The Guardian*, November 29, 1969.
6. Meg Jacobs, *Pocketbook Politics: Economic Citizenship in Twentieth-Century America* (Princeton, NJ: Princeton University Press, 2007); "Proxies for People—A Vehicle for Involvement," *Yale Review of Law and Social Action* 1 (Spring 1971): 69.
7. The corporate protests have been noted by historians of the postwar era; most notably, see chapter 7, "The Attack on the Free Enterprise System," in

Kim Phillips-Fein, *Invisible Hands: The Businessmen's Crusade Against the New Deal* (New York: Norton, 2009), 150–65; see also Benjamin C Waterhouse, "The Corporate Mobilization Against Liberal Reform: Big Business Day, 1980," in *What's Good for Business: Business and American Politics Since World War II*, ed. Kim Phillips-Fein and Julian E. Zelizer (New York: Oxford University Press, 2012); and Benjamin C. Waterhouse, *Lobbying America: The Politics of Business from Nixon to NAFTA* (Princeton, NJ: Princeton University Press, 2015). Historians have tended to treat this mobilization of corporate reform from the perspective of the CEOs and the emergence of a business lobby. Chapter 6 of *Taming the Octopus* seeks to recenter the activists as a part of a longer history of the politics of corporate power. "The Corporation Becomes a Target," *Time*, May 11, 1970; Phillip I. Blumberg, "The Politicization of the Corporation," *Business Lawyer* 26, no. 5 (1971): 426–27; The Conference Board, *Handling Protest at Annual Meetings* (New York: The Conference Board, 1971), ii–iii; "'Keep Your Cool,' Dow Advises Targets of Antiwar Protestors," *New York Times*, June 4, 1970; Donald E. Schwartz, "The Public-Interest Proxy Contest: Reflections on Campaign GM," *Michigan Law Review* 69, no. 3 (1971): 421; Jarol B. Manheim, *The Death of A Thousand Cuts: Corporate Campaigns and the Attack on the Corporation* (Mahwah, NJ: Lawrence Erlbaum, 2000), 2–10; Lynd, "Attack War Contractors' Meetings."

8. Robert M. Neer, *Napalm: An American Biography* (Cambridge, MA: Harvard University Press, 2013), 116–17; "Dow Chemical Office Picketed for Its Manufacture of Napalm," *New York Times*, May 29, 1966; "20 Are Seized Picketing Dow for Making Napalm," *New York Times*, August 10, 1966; "Ire Against Fire," *Time*, November 3, 1967.
9. Maurice Ford, "The Right to Recruit on College Campuses," *New Republic*, November 11, 1967; "An Open Letter to the Corporations of America," in "*Takin' It to the Streets: A Sixties Reader*, ed. Alexander Bloom and Wini Breines (New York: Oxford University Press, 1995), 251–52; "9 Dow Protesters Charged in Capital," *New York Times*, March 25, 1969; David Vogel, *Lobbying the Corporation: Citizen Challenges to Business Authority* (New York: Basic Books, 1978), 43–44.
10. "Why Dow Continues to Make Napalm," *BusinessWeek*, February 10, 1968.
11. John Dittmer, *The Good Doctors: The Medical Committee for Human Rights and the Struggle for Social Justice in Health Care* (New York: Bloomsbury, 2009), 18–37; Sarah C. Haan, "Civil Rights and Shareholder Activism: SEC v. Medical Committee for Human Rights," *Washington & Lee Law Review* 76, no. 3 (Summer 2019): 1174.
12. "Dr. Quentin D. Young, Public Health and Civil Rights Advocate, Dies at 92," *New York Times*, March 17, 2016.
13. "Quentin Young, Chicago Doctor and Social Activist, Dies at 92," *Washington Post*, March 8, 2016; SEC v. Med. Comm. for Human Rights, 404 US 403, 406 (1972): 662; "Clergy Urge Dow Stockholder Vote on Napalm," *New*

York Times, May 5, 1968; "Dow Defends Napalm as GI Saver," *Washington Post*, May 9, 1968; Davis D. Joyce, *Howard Zinn: A Radical American Vision* (Buffalo, NY: Prometheus Books, 2010), 207; Kenneth Lipartito and David B. Sicilia, eds., *Constructing Corporate America: History, Politics, Culture* (New York: Oxford University Press, 2004), 200.

14. SEC v. Med. Comm. for Human Rights, 404 US 403, 406 (1972): 679–80; Vogel, *Lobbying the Corporation*, 45–46.
15. "Dow Declares It Has Stopped Production of Napalm for U.S.," *New York Times*, November 15, 1969; Gerstacker quoted in Neer, *Napalm*, 144; "U.S. Court Widens Rights of Holders," *New York Times*, July 10, 1970; SEC v. Med. Comm. for Human Rights, 404 US 403, 406 (1972): 681; Introduction of the Corporate Participation Act, S. 4003, 91st Cong., 2nd Sess., *Congressional Record* 116 (June 3, 1970), 20928–29; Marc I. Steinberg, *The Federalization of Corporate Governance* (New York: Oxford University Press, 2018), 166–67.
16. On Lockheed's contracts, see "Ire Against Fire," *Time*; Vogel, *Lobbying the Corporation*, 45.
17. "What Did the GM Meeting Accomplish," *Evening Sun* (Baltimore, MD), July 7, 1971; "Napalm Assailed at Dow Meeting," *New York Times*, May 8, 1969.
18. Ralph Nader, "The American Automobile: Designed for Death?" *Harvard Law Record*, December 11, 1958.
19. Ralph Nader, *Unsafe at Any Speed: The Designed-In Dangers of the American Automobile* (New York: Grossman, 1965), ix, 59.
20. "Ribicoff Applauds Auto Safety Plans," *New York Times*, February 11, 1966; "G.M. Criticized on Auto Safety," *New York Times*, July 13, 1965; "Auto Safety Hearings Set Feb. 1," *Washington Post*, January 14, 1966; "Ribicoff Accuses Auto Makers of Arguing 'Safety Doesn't Sell,'" *New York Times*, July 15, 1965; US Congress, Senate, Subcommittee on Executive Reorganization of the Committee on Government Operations, Traffic Safety: *Examination and Review of Efficiency, Economy, and Coordination of Public and Private Agencies' Activities and the Role of the Federal Government*, pt. 3, 89th Cong., 2nd Sess., 1966, 1269–70; US Congress, Senate, Subcommittee on Public Roads of the Committee on Public Works, S. 3052, A Bill to Provide for a Coordinated National Highway Safety Program to Accelerate Highway Traffic Safety Programs, and for Other Purposes, 89th Cong., 2nd Sess., 1966; Morton Mintz, "Detective Admits GM Instructions to Muzzle Nader," *Washington Post*, February 5, 1967; Mark Green, *Bright, Infinite Future: A Generational Memoir on the Progressive Rise* (New York: St. Martin's Press, 2016), 47–51.
21. "'Investigators' Hound Auto Safety Witness," *Washington Post*, March 7, 1966; James Ridgeway, "The Dick," *New Republic*, March 12, 1966; "Ribicoff Summons G.M. on Its Inquiry of Critic," *New York Times*, March 10, 1966.
22. William Greider, "Law Students, FTC Tangle Over Apathy," *Washington Post*, November 13, 1968; "Nader's Raiders Is Their Name, and Whistle-

Blowing Is Their Game . . . ," *New York Times*, March 21, 1971; Green, *Bright, Infinite Future*, 50.

23. Jacobs, *Pocketbook Politics*, 259; Lizabeth Cohen, *A Consumer's Republic: The Politics of Mass Consumption in Postwar America* (New York: Vintage, 2004), 351–55; Christopher Lasch, "Can the Left Rise Again?" *New York Review of Books*, October 21, 1971.
24. Robert A. Dahl, "Governing the Giant Corporation," in *Corporate Power in America*, ed. Ralph Nader and Mark J. Green (New York: Grossman, 1973), 10–12.
25. US Congress, Senate, Subcommittee on Executive Reorganization of the Committee on Government Operations, Traffic Safety: *Examination and Review of Efficiency, Economy, and Coordination of Public and Private Agencies' Activities and the Role of the Federal Government*, pt. 4, 89th Cong., 2nd Sess., 1966, 1467.
26. Statement by Ralph Nader, 91st Cong., 2nd Sess., *Congressional Record* 116, pt. 4 (February 24, 1970), 4699–700; "The Fortune 500 Data Bank," *Fortune*, February 1970; Quoted in Vogel, *Lobbying the Corporation*, 72.
27. Statement by Ralph Nader, 91st Cong., 2nd Sess., *Congressional Record* 116, pt. 4 (February 24, 1970), 4701; Vogel, *Lobbying the Corporation*, 72; "The New Public Interest Lawyers," *Yale Law Journal* 79, no. 6 (1970): 1069–152; "For Former Supporters of McCarthy and Kennedy, New Politics Is a Many-Splintered Thing," *New York Times*, October 5, 1969; "Business and the Public Interest," *New York Times*, December 19, 1971.
28. Charles McCarry, *Citizen Nader* (New York: Saturday Review Press, 1972), 222–23; Vogel, *Lobbying the Corporation*, 71–73.
29. "Nader to Press for G.M. Reform," *New York Times*, February 8, 1970; Schwartz, "The Public-Interest Proxy Contest," 422. For a partial list of corporate responsibility groups, see "A Who's Who of Corporate Responsibility Action Groups," *Business and Society Review* 1 (Winter 1973): 81–86.
30. Statement by Ralph Nader, 91st Cong., 2nd Sess., *Congressional Record* 116, pt. 4 (February 24, 1970), 4699–702; Appendix B in Schwartz, "The Public-Interest Proxy Contest," 534–37.
31. "Nader Panel Rebuffed by GM on Plea to List Consumers' Demands," *Wall Street Journal*, March 6, 1970; Richard B. Smith, interview by Richard Rowe, June 9, 2002, Securities and Exchange Commission Historical Society, Washington, DC, 20–21.
32. "Campaign to Make GM Responsible: Proxy Statement," Advertisement, *Detroit Free Press*, May 3, 1970. The most comprehensive newspaper profile is here: "Campaign GM: The Leaders and Their Battle Plan," *Detroit Free Press*, May 17, 1970.
33. "The Greening of James Roche," *New York Magazine*, December 21, 1970; "'Campaign GM' Says It's Winning 'On All Fronts,'" *New York Times*, April 22, 1970; George E. Brown, Jr., "Support for Campaign to Make General

Motors Responsible," 91st Cong., 2nd Sess., *Congressional Record* 116, pt. 12 (May 19, 1970), 16397.

34. "Critics Dominate Meeting of G.M," *New York Times*, May 23, 1970.
35. "GM Airs Policies, Wins Votes," *Detroit Free Press*, May 23, 1970; "Audience Listens to Both Sides," *Detroit Free Press*, May 23, 1970; E. J. Kahn, Jr., "We Look Forward to Seeing You Next Year," *New Yorker*, June 20, 1970.
36. Kahn, Jr., "We Look Forward to Seeing You Next Year"; "GM Easily Turns Back the First Assault from Within by Liberal Reform Activists," *Wall Street Journal*, May 25, 1970.
37. "G.M. Names 5 Directors as Public-Issue Advisers," *New York Times*, September 1, 1970; "G.M. Elects First Negro as Member of Its Board," *New York Times*, January 4, 1971; Leon Howard Sullivan, *Moving Mountains: The Principles and Purposes of Leon Sullivan* (King of Prussia, PA: Judson Press, 1998), 2. See also Jessica Ann Levy, "Black Power in the Boardroom: Corporate America, the Sullivan Principles, and the Anti-Apartheid Struggle," *Enterprise & Society* 21, no. 1 (March 2020): 170–209.
38. "G.M. Will Face Its Critics at Its Annual Meeting Today," *New York Times*, May 21, 1971; "G.M. Names 5 Directors as Public-Issue Advisers," *New York Times*; McCarry, *Citizen Nader*, 224–25.
39. Vernon M. Buehler and Y. K. Shetty, "Managing Corporate Social Responsibility," *Management Review* 64, no. 8 (August 1975): 4–17.
40. Quoted in Vogel, *Lobbying the Corporation*, 75.
41. Milton Friedman, "A Friedman Doctrine—The Social Responsibility of Business Is to Increase Its Profits," *New York Times Magazine*, September 13, 1970.
42. Friedman, "A Friedman Doctrine."
43. See, for example, K. Praveen Parboteeah and John B. Cullen, *Business Ethics* (London: Routledge, 2013); William H. Shaw, *Business Ethics: A Textbook with Cases* (Boston: Cengage, 2016).
44. This application of game theory to the social order runs through conservative economic theory all the way to Frank Knight, though its principal expositor was James Buchanan. Nancy MacLean, *Democracy in Chains: The Deep History of the Radical Right's Stealth Plan for America* (New York: Viking, 2017), 97–98. "The whole game analogue for social order runs through Frank Knight's writing, but I know of no single place where he concentrates full attention on this. I have often wished he had put these ideas in one place." Letter from James Buchanan to Friedrich Hayek, September 2, 1975, Box 13, Folder 14, Hayek Papers, Hoover Institution Archives.
45. Milton Friedman, "Responsibility: Insights from Economics," Faculty Seminar I, Institute for Religious and Social Studies, March 8, 1965, Box 8, Folder 15, Milton Friedman Papers, Hoover Institution Archives.
46. James Weinstein, *The Corporate Ideal in the Liberal State, 1900–1918* (Boston: Beacon Press, 1968), xii. See also Gabriel Kolko, *The Triumph of Conservatism: A Reinterpretation of American History, 1900–1916* (New York: Free Press,

1963); Martin J. Sklar, "Woodrow Wilson and the Political-Economy of Modern United States Liberalism," *Studies on the Left* 1, no. 3 (Fall 1960); Martin J. Sklar, *The Corporate Reconstruction of American Capitalism, 1890–1916: The Market, the Law, and Politics* (Cambridge: Cambridge University Press, 1988). The classic anthology of these revisionists is Barton J. Berntein, ed., *Towards a New Past: Dissenting Essays in American History* (New York: Vintage, 1969); Howard Brick, *Transcending Capitalism: Visions of a New Society in Modern American Thought* (Ithaca, NY: Cornell University Press, 2015), 265–73.

47. "Nader to Press for G.M. Reform," *New York Times.*

Chapter Seven: Making Social Responsibility Corporate

1. Robert M. Neer, *Napalm: An American Biography* (Cambridge, MA: Harvard University Press, 2013), 144.
2. "Autos: A Question of Concern," *Time*, September 14, 1970.
3. Henry C. Egerton and Conference Board, *Handling Protest at Annual Meetings* (New York: The Conference Board, 1971), 40.
4. Egerton and Conference Board, *Handling Protest at Annual Meetings*, 41–42.
5. "Audience Listens to Both Sides," *Detroit Free Press*, May 23, 1970.
6. Committee for Economic Development, *Annual Report - Committee for Economic Development*, accessed May 11, 2023, https://catalog.hathitrust.org/Record/100713025.
7. Robert M. Collins, "Positive Business Responses to the New Deal: The Roots of the Committee for Economic Development, 1933–1942," *Business History Review* 52, no. 3 (1978): 369–91; Kim McQuaid, "Corporate Liberalism in the American Business Community, 1920–1940," *Business History Review* 52, no. 3 (1978): 342–68; Charlie Whitham, "The Committee for Economic Development, Foreign Trade and the Rise of American Corporate Liberalism, 1942–8," *Journal of Contemporary History* 48, no. 4 (October 1, 2013): 845–71.
8. Jennifer A. Delton, *Rethinking the 1950s: How Anticommunism and the Cold War Made America Liberal* (New York: Cambridge University Press, 2013), 58–59.
9. Research and Policy Committee of the Committee for Economic Development, *Social Responsibilities of Business Corporations* (New York: Committee for Economic Development, 1971) 33.
10. Adam Winkler, *We the Corporations: How American Businesses Won Their Civil Rights* (New York: Liveright, 2018), 281–89.
11. On the role of free enterprise ideas and the history of think-tanks in American political history, see Jason Stahl, *Right Moves: The Conservative Think Tank in American Political Culture Since 1945* (Chapel Hill: University of North Carolina Press, 2016); and Lawrence B. Glickman, *Free Enterprise: An American History* (New Haven, CT: Yale University Press, 2019).

12. See Michael Useem, *The Inner Circle: Large Corporations and the Rise of Business Political Activity in the U.S. and U.K.* (New York: Oxford University Press, 1984).
13. Keith Davis and Robert L. Blomstrom, *Business and Its Environment* (New York: McGraw-Hill, 1966), 174.
14. Davis and Blomstrom, *Business and Its Environment*, 171.
15. Keith Davis, "Can Business Afford to Ignore Social Responsibilities?" *California Management Review* 2, no. 3 (April 1, 1960): 71.
16. Howard Bowen, *Social Responsibilities of the Businessman* (New York: Harper & Brothers, 1953), 6.
17. For a good discussion of early corporate social responsibility (CSR) literature, see Archie B. Carroll et al., *Corporate Responsibility: The American Experience* (New York: Cambridge University Press, 2012), 230–63.
18. Clarence C. Walton, *Corporate Social Responsibilities: Problems in a Business Society* (Belmont, CA: Wadsworth, 1967), vii.
19. George Albert Steiner, *Business and Society* (New York: Random House, 1971), 164.
20. Description of the program in Walton, *Corporate Social Responsibilities*, 132–69. The list of service opportunities is on pp. 156–57.
21. "Case Study: IBM's Fund for Community Service," *Business & Society Review* (March 1, 1975): 92–93.
22. For example: IBM Advertisement, *Ebony*, February 1, 1974; IBM Advertisement, *Ebony*, December 1, 1978.
23. Human Resources Network, *The Handbook of Corporate Social Responsibility: Profiles of Involvement* (Radnor, PA: Chilton Book Co., 1975), 506.
24. Human Resources Network, *The Handbook of Corporate Social Responsibility*, 304.
25. Human Resources Network, *The Handbook of Corporate Social Responsibility*, 459.
26. Human Resources Network, *The Handbook of Corporate Social Responsibility*, 563–67.
27. Vernon M. Buehler and Y. K. Shetty, "Managerial Response to Social Responsibility Challenge," *Academy of Management Journal* 19, no. 1 (1976): 66–78. See also Sandra L. Holmes, "Structural Responses of Large Corporations to a Social Responsibility Ethic," *Academy of Management Proceedings*; Henry Eilbirt and I. Robert Parket, "The Practice of Business: The Current Status of Corporate Social Responsibility," *Business Horizons*, August 1973.
28. Theodore Cross, "Why Business and Society Review?" *Business & Society Review*, no. 1 (Spring 1972): 4.
29. R. Joseph Monsen, Jr., "The Social Attitudes of Management," in *Contemporary Management: Issues and Viewpoints*, ed. Joseph William McGuire (Englewood Cliffs, NJ: Prentice-Hall, 1974), 615–16.
30. John W. Collins and Chris G. Ganotis, "Is Corporate Responsibility Sabotaged by the Rank and File?" *Business & Society Review/Innovation*, no. 7 (September 1973): 82.

31. Phillip Drotning, "Why Nobody Takes Corporate Social Responsibility Seriously," *Management Review* 62, no. 3 (March 1973): 63.
32. "How Corporate Social Responsibility Became Institutionalized," *Business-Week*, June 30, 1973.
33. Thomas D. Boyd, "Whatever Happened to the National Alliance of Businessmen?" *Business & Society Review*, no. 12 (Winter 1974): 50.
34. Milton Moskowitz, "Emergence of the Corporate Conscience," *New York Times*, January 6, 1974.
35. Peter F. Drucker, *The Effective Executive* (New York: Harper & Row, 1966), 3.
36. Drucker, *The Effective Executive*, 51.
37. US Bureau of Labor Statistics, All Employees, Manufacturing [MANEMP], FRED, Federal Reserve Bank of St. Louis, accessed August 9, 2022, https://fred.stlouisfed.org/series/MANEMP.
38. Barry T. Hirsch, David A. Macpherson, and Wayne G. Vroman, "Estimates of Union Density by State," *Monthly Labor Review* 124, no. 7 (July 2001): 51–55.
39. M. J. Heale, *Contemporary America: Power, Dependency, and Globalization since 1980* (Hoboken, NJ: Wiley, 2011), 5.
40. Daniel Bell, *The Coming of Post-Industrial Society; a Venture in Social Forecasting* (New York: Basic Books, 1973), 14.
41. Bell, *The Coming of Post-Industrial Society*, 272.
42. Alvin Toffler, *Future Shock* (New York: Bantam, 1970), 99.
43. Toffler, *Future Shock*, 116.
44. US Bureau of Economic Analysis, Gross Domestic Product [GDP], FRED, Federal Reserve Bank of St. Louis, accessed August 9, 2022, https://fred.stlouisfed.org/series/GDP.
45. Robert Brenner, *The Boom and the Bubble: The US in the World Economy* (New York: Verso, 2003), 40–41.
46. US Bureau of Economic Analysis, Gross Domestic Product [GDP], FRED, Federal Reserve Bank of St. Louis, accessed August 9, 2022, https://fred.stlouisfed.org/series/GDP; US Bureau of Labor Statistics, Unemployment Rate [UNRATE], FRED, Federal Reserve Bank of St. Louis, accessed August 9, 2022, https://fred.stlouisfed.org/series/UNRATE.
47. Unemployment and inflation stats come from Table Cb18–22, *Historical Statistics of the United States*, Millennium Edition Online, ed. Susan B. Carter et al. (Cambridge: Cambridge University Press, 2006); Kim Phillips-Fein, *Invisible Hands: The Businessmen's Crusade Against the New Deal* (New York: Norton, 2009), 153.
48. See Jackson Lears, "Technocratic Vistas: The Long Con of Neoliberalism," *Hedgehog Review* 19, no. 3 (Fall 2017).
49. See Daniel T. Rodgers, *Age of Fracture* (Cambridge, MA: The Belknap Press of Harvard University Press, 2012).
50. Irving Kristol, "The Credibility of Corporations," *Wall Street Journal*, January 17, 1974.

Chapter Eight: "There Is No Such Thing as a Corporate Responsibility"

1. "Meet Ralph Nader's Most Outspoken Critic," *BusinessWeek*, July 24, 1971; Henry Manne, oral history interview by James Stocker, August 6, 2012, Securities and Exchange Commission Historical Society, Washington, DC, 33.
2. "Hard Times," *Indianapolis News*, May 21, 1971.
3. "Business/People," *Democrat and Chronicle* (Rochester, NY), September 29, 1971; Donald E. Schwartz, "Towards New Corporate Goals: Co-Existence with Society," *Georgetown Law Journal* 60 (1971–1972), 788n10.
4. Henry G. Manne, "The Paradox of Corporate Responsibility," in *White House Conference on the Industrial World Ahead: A Look at Business in 1990* (Washington, DC: US Government Printing Office, 1972), 95–98.
5. Henry G. Manne, "Who's Responsible: What the Anti-Corporate Zealots Are Pushing Is Coercion," *Barron's National Business and Financial Weekly*, May 17, 1971.
6. "Meet Ralph Nader's Most Outspoken Critic," *BusinessWeek*.
7. "GM Chief Attacks Fly-by-Night Critics," *Detroit Free Press*, March 26, 1971.
8. "GM Chief Attacks Fly-by-Night Critics," *Detroit Free Press*.
9. "Meet Ralph Nader's Most Outspoken Critic," *BusinessWeek*.
10. See David Ciepley's work on the "neoliberal corporation": David Ciepley, "The Neoliberal Corporation," in *The Oxford Handbook of the Corporation*, ed. Thomas Clarke, Justin O'Brien, and Charles R. T. O'Kelley (Oxford University Press, 2019), 274–96. See, too, William Lazonick and Mary O'Sullivan, "Maximizing Shareholder Value: A New Ideology for Corporate Governance," *Economy and Society* 29, no. 1 (January 1, 2000): 13–35.
11. Quoted in Alfred Rappaport, *Creating Shareholder Value: The New Standard for Business Performance* (New York: Free Press, 1986), 13.
12. Oliver E. Williamson, "Revisiting Legal Realism: The Law, Economics, and Organization Perspective," in *Coasean Economics Law and Economics and the New Institutional Economics*, ed. Steven G. Medema, Recent Economic Thought Series (Dordrecht: Springer Netherlands, 1998), 119–59.
13. See, for example, Nicholas Mercuro, "The Jurisprudential Niche Occupied by Law and Economics," *Journal of Jurisprudence* 2 (2009): 61–110.
14. Steven M. Teles, *The Rise of the Conservative Legal Movement: The Battle for Control of the Law* (Princeton, NJ: Princeton University Press, 2010), 96–97.
15. Richard A. Posner, *Economic Analysis of Law* (Boston: Little, Brown, 1973).
16. This way of understanding the relationship between markets and state power that sees markets not simply as forces "disembedded" from institutional structures but rather deployed and defined by institutional structures has been developed in a sophisticated way by Quinn Slobodian in terms of the "encasement of the market." See Quinn Slobodian, *Globalists: The End of Empire and the Birth of Neoliberalism* (Cambridge, MA: Harvard University Press, 2018), 5–7.

17. Armen A. Alchian and Harold Demsetz, "Production, Information Costs, and Economic Organization," *American Economic Review* 65, no. 5 (1972): 777.
18. Alchian and Demsetz, "Production, Information Costs, and Economic Organization," 777.
19. Alchian and Demsetz, "Production, Information Costs, and Economic Organization," 794n18.
20. Alchian and Demsetz, "Production, Information Costs, and Economic Organization," 789n14.
21. Michael C. Jensen and William H. Meckling, "Theory of the Firm: Managerial Behavior, Agency Costs and Ownership Structure," *Journal of Financial Economics* 3, no. 4 (October 1976): 311.
22. Gerald F. Davis, *Managed by the Markets: How Finance Re-Shaped America* (New York: Oxford University Press, 2009), 83.
23. Henry G. Manne, "The 'Higher Criticism' of the Modern Corporation," *Columbia Law Review* 62, no. 3 (1962): 429n95.
24. Ronald Cass, "One Among the Manne: Changing Our Course," *Case Western Reserve Law Review* 50, no. 2 (January 1, 1999): 206.
25. Letter from Henry Manne to President W. Allen Wallis, "Report on Law Schools," January 1968, 3–4. Quoted in Teles, *The Rise of the Conservative Legal Movement*, 103.
26. Quoted in Teles, *The Rise of the Conservative Legal Movement*, 104.
27. Teles, *The Rise of the Conservative Legal Movement*, 104–5.
28. Quoted in Teles, *The Rise of the Conservative Legal Movement*, 104.
29. Charles R. Halpern and John M. Cunningham, "Reflections on the New Public Interest Law: Theory and Practice at the Center for Law and Social Policy," *Georgetown Law Journal* 59 (1970–1971), 1096–97.
30. Teles, *The Rise of the Conservative Legal Movement*, 22–57.
31. Letter from Henry Manne to Pierre Goodrich, December 15, 1972. Quoted in Teles, *The Rise of the Conservative Legal Movement*, 105.
32. Manne, interview by Stocker, 42.
33. Henry G. Manne, "How Law and Economics Was Marketed in a Hostile World: A Very Personal History," in *The Origins of Law and Economics: Essays by the Founding Fathers*, ed. Francesco Parisi and Charles Kershaw Rowley (Cheltenham, UK: Edward Elgar, 2005), 313.
34. J. Kelley, *Bringing the Market Back in: The Political Revitalization of Market Liberalism* (London: Springer, 1997), 68–69.
35. Arthur Allen Leff, "Economic Analysis of Law: Some Realism About Nominalism," *Virginia Law Review* 60, no. 3 (1974): 452.
36. Manne, "How Law and Economics Was Marketed in a Hostile World," 315.
37. Manne, "How Law and Economics Was Marketed in a Hostile World," 315.
38. Manne, "How Law and Economics Was Marketed in a Hostile World," 315–16; Teles, *The Rise of the Conservative Legal Movement*, 106.
39. Teles, *The Rise of the Conservative Legal Movement*, 106–7.
40. Quoted in Teles, *The Rise of the Conservative Legal Movement*, 107.

41. Henry G. Manne, "An Intellectual History of the George Mason University School of Law," Antonin Scalia Law School, George Mason University, accessed May 5, 2023, https://www.law.gmu.edu/about/history.
42. Manne, "An Intellectual History."
43. "You're five years too late for me to give a damn," Manne told Yale. Manne, interview by Stocker, 39.
44. Confidential Memorandum from Henry G. Manne on The Center for Studies in Law and Economics at the University of Miami Law School, April 16, 1974. Quoted in Teles, *The Rise of the Conservative Legal Movement*, 109.
45. Teles, *The Rise of the Conservative Legal Movement*, 109.
46. "Big Corporations Bankroll Seminars for U.S. Judges," *Washington Post*, January 20, 1980.
47. "Big Corporations Bankroll Seminars for U.S. Judges," *Washington Post.*
48. "Paid Course May Pass Judges' Group," *Washington Post*, August 23, 1980.
49. Calculation comes from the list in "Appendix B: Cumulative List of Participating Federal Judges," in Henry N. Butler, "The Manne Programs in Economics for Federal Judges Symposium: The Legacy of Henry G. Manne—Pioneer in Law & Economics and Innovator in Legal Education May 21–22, 1999," *Case Western Reserve Law Review* 50 (1999–2000): 376–87.
50. Quoted in Henry N. Butler, "The Manne Programs in Economics for Federal Judges Symposium: The Legacy of Henry G. Manne—Pioneer in Law & Economics and Innovator in Legal Education May 21–22, 1999," *Case Western Reserve Law Review* 50 (1999–2000): 358.
51. Butler, "The Manne Programs in Economics for Federal Judges Symposium," 358.
52. Quoted in Butler, "The Manne Programs in Economics for Federal Judges Symposium," 358n19.
53. Cass, "One Among the Manne," 207.
54. Manne excelled at fund-raising. Perhaps this was because, as Ronald Cass said, businesses and foundations that funded the LEC were "confident that it was improving the quality of judges' analysis of issues with obvious economic dimensions"; see Cass, "One Among the Manne," 209.
55. George L. Priest, "Henry Manne and the Market Measure of Intellectual Influence," *Case Western Reserve Law Review* 50, no. 2 (1999): 330.
56. "Paid Course May Pass Judges' Group," *Washington Post*, August 23, 1980.
57. Teles, *The Rise of the Conservative Legal Movement*, 124–32.
58. Letter from Milton Friedman to Henry Manne, June 12, 1984, Box 165, Folder 1, Milton Friedman Collection, Hoover Institution Archives.
59. Letter from Henry Manne to Milton Friedman, May 31, 1984, Box 165, Folder 1, Milton Friedman Collection, Hoover Institution Archives.
60. Teles, *The Rise of the Conservative Legal Movement*, 124–32.
61. Manne, interview by Stocker, 44.
62. John J. Miller, "A Law School with a Twist," *National Review*, March 27, 2006.

63. Durkin's public interest politics played an important role in his 1974 campaign for Senate. "Durkin Optimistic for New Congress," *Portsmouth Herald*, February 13, 1974; US Congress, Senate, Committee on Commerce, *Corporate Rights and Responsibilities: Hearings Before the Committee on Commerce*, 94th Cong., 2nd Sess., 1976, 1–2.
64. Committee on Commerce, *Corporate Rights and Responsibilities*, iii–iv.
65. "Nader Calls for Federal Charter of Business," *Washington Post*, January 25, 1976.
66. Ralph Nader, Mark J. Green, and Joel Seligman, *Taming the Giant Corporation* (New York: Norton, 1976).
67. Harris represented an insurgent Democratic populism that positioned itself in opposition to corporate power. See, for example, Fred R. Harris, *The New Populism* (New York: Saturday Review Press, 1973).
68. Committee on Commerce, *Corporate Rights and Responsibilities*, 199.
69. Committee on Commerce, *Corporate Rights and Responsibilities*, 225.
70. Henry G. Manne, "Federal Chartering: The New Attack on Corporations," *Reason*, May 1977.
71. Committee on Commerce, *Corporate Rights and Responsibilities*, 226.
72. Committee on Commerce, *Corporate Rights and Responsibilities*, 226.
73. Committee on Commerce, *Corporate Rights and Responsibilities*, 227.

Chapter Nine: Nothing to Ask Permission For

1. "Alice Tepper Marlin: Pushing Big Business to Tend to Social Concerns," *Miami News*, April 28, 1982.
2. "Probing Industry's Conscience," *New York Times*, November 25, 1979; "Alice Tepper Marlin," *Miami News*.
3. "For Alice Tepper Marlin, Being 'The Conscience of Business' Requires Balance," *People*, June 9, 1980; James Ledbetter, *Unwarranted Influence: Dwight D. Eisenhower and the Military-Industrial Complex* (New Haven, CT: Yale University Press, 2011), 174.
4. The Council on Economic Priorities, *Efficiency in Death: The Manufacturers of Anti-Personnel Weapons* (New York: Harper & Row, 1970); Ledbetter, *Unwarranted Influence*, 175.
5. Ledbetter, *Unwarranted Influence*, 175.
6. Rodney Alexander and Elisabeth Sapery of the Council on Economic Priorities, *The Shortchanged: Women and Minorities in Banking* (New York: Dunellen Publishing, 1973); Joe Zalkind of the Council on Economic Priorities, *Guide to Corporations: A Social Perspective*, ed. Stephen Moody and Lee Stephenson (Chicago: Swallow Press, 1974).
7. Alice Tepper Marlin, *Shopping for a Better World: A Quick and Easy Guide to Socially Responsible Supermarket Shopping*, Ecology (New York: Ballantine, 1992).
8. "American Notebook: Anti-Bomb Lady," *New York Times*, Sepember 27, 1970.

9. Peter Drucker, *The Unseen Revolution: How Pension Fund Socialism Came to America* (New York: Harper & Row, 1976).
10. Associated Press, "Object to War Profits? Peace Stocks Proposed," *Tucson Daily Citizen*, August 13, 1969.
11. Derrick B. Jelliffe, "Breast-Milk and the World Protein Gap," *Clinical Pediatrics* 7, no. 2 (February 1, 1968): 96; Tehila Sasson, "Milking the Third World? Humanitarianism, Capitalism, and the Moral Economy of the Nestlé Boycott," *American Historical Review* 121, no. 4 (October 2016): 1203; Lisa H. Newton, "Truth Is the Daughter of Time: The Real Story of the Nestle Case," *Business and Society Review* 104, no. 4 (December 17, 2002): 368–69; D. B. Jelliffe, "Commerciogenic Malnutrition?" *Nutrition Reviews* 30, no. 9 (September 1, 1972): 201; Robert L. Heilbroner, *In the Name of Profit: Profiles in Corporate Irresponsibility* (New York: Doubleday, 1972).
12. Hugh Geach, "The Baby Food Tragedy," *New Internationalist*, August 1973; Mike Muller, *The Baby Killer: A War on Want Investigation Into the Promotion and Sale of Powdered Baby Milks in the Third World* (London: War on Want, 1974), 1.
13. "Shrivelled Children, Swollen Profits," *The Guardian*, March 12, 1974; "13 Swiss Convicted in Nestle Libel Case," *Washington Post*, June 25, 1976; Sasson, "Milking the Third World?" 1210; George A. Garland, "An Examination of the Nestle Controversy" (unpublished manuscript, October 18, 1982), 46; INFACT Records, ca. 1977–1993, Box 3, State Historical Society of Wisconsin Archives Division (hereafter INFACT Records).
14. "Formula for Malnutrition," *Corporate Examiner*, April 1975; "The Ralph Naders of the Church," *Chicago Tribune*, January 18, 1975.
15. Herman Nickel, "The Corporation Haters," *Fortune*, June 16, 1980; Bryan Knapp, "'The Biggest Business in the World': The Nestlé Boycott and the Global Development of Infants, Nations and Economies, 1968–1988," (PhD diss., Brown University, 2015), 119; "Drop in Breast Feeding Causes Health Problems in Poor Countries," *New York Times*, April 16, 1975; Sisters of the Precious Blood, Inc. v. Bristol-Myers Co., 431 F. Supp. 385 (SDNY 1977); "Nuns Storming the Boardroom to Save Babies' Lives," *Chicago Tribune*, April 8, 1978.
16. "Group Pickets Nestle Co.," *Minneapolis Star*, June 30, 1977; "Marchers Protest Formula Maker," *Star Tribune*, July 5, 1977; Sasson, "Milking the Third World?," 1216; "Nestle in the USA—Giant in Disguise?" Part 6, Box 1, Folder 8, Nestle as a Corporation, INFACT Records, 1971–1993.
17. "Chronology," Part 1, Box 8, Folder 5–6, INFACT Records, 1971–1990; "Has Nestle Really Changed?" *INFACT Newsletter*, Winter 1978; *INFACT Newsletter*, 1979–1981; "Nestle and Critics Meet," *INFACT Newsletter*, March 1978; "Role of Infant-Formula Makers in Developing Nations Hit," *Washington Post*, May 24, 1978; Subcommittee on Health and Scientific Research, Committee on Human Resources, *Marketing and Promotion of Infant Formula in the Developing Nations: Hearings Before the Subcommittee on Health*

and Scientific Research, Committee on Human Resources (Washington, DC: US Government Printing Office, 1978), 1–2, 127–28.

18. "Boycott over Infant Formula," *BusinessWeek*, April 23, 1979; "New Recipe at Nestle That Mixes in Planning," *BusinessWeek*, February 2, 1981. The company's earnings decline was only reported a year later: "Nestle's Net Up in 1981," *New York Times*, April 14, 1981; Memo from E. W. Saunders to A. Furer, August 2/4, 1980, Box 2, Folder 2, Part 1, INFACT Records; "Infant-Formula Maker Battles Boycotters by Painting Them Red," *Washington Post*, January 4, 1981.
19. Rafael D. Pagan, Jr., "Carrying the Fight to the Critics of Multinational Capitalism: Think and Act Politically," *Vital Speeches of the Day*, July 15, 1982; Rafael D. Pagan, Jr., "The Future of Public Relations and the Need for Creative Understanding of the World Around Us," 35th Public Relations Society of America National Conference, San Francisco, CA, November 8, 1982; "Baby-Food Industry Agrees to a Curb on the Promotion of Infant Formulas," *New York Times*, October 13, 1979; World Health Organization and United Nations Children's Fund (UNICEF), "Joint WHO/UNICEF Meeting on Infant and Young Child Feeding, Geneva, 9–12 October 1979: Statement, Recommendations, List of Participants" (Geneva: World Health Organization, 1981), 29; World Health Organization, "International Code of Marketing of Breast-milk Substitutes" (Geneva: World Health Organization, 1981).
20. "Two AID Officials Dispute Reagan Decision to Oppose Code for Infant Formula," *Washington Post*, May 17, 1981; Sasson, "Milking the Third World?," 1222; Frank Falkner, *Infant Feeding: Anatomy of a Controversy 1973–1984*, ed. John Dobbing (London: Springer-Verlag, 1988), 123.
21. "Foundations Shy at Plan for G.M.," *New York Times*, May 3, 1970.
22. Donald E. Schwartz, "The Public-Interest Proxy Contest: Reflections on Campaign GM," *Michigan Law Review* 69, no. 3 (1971): 506.
23. The statement is quoted in full in Thomas J. McNichols, *Policy Making and Executive Action: Cases on Business Policy*, 4th ed. (New York: McGraw-Hill, 1972), 786–87.
24. Olivier Zunz, *Philanthropy in America: A History* (Princeton, NJ: Princeton University Press, 2012), 218–19.
25. Roger Kennedy, Foreword to *Corporate Social Responsibility and the Institutional Investor: A Report to the Ford Foundation* (New York: Praeger, 1973), vi.
26. Martin A. Larson, *Praise the Lord for Tax Exemption: How the Churches Grow Rich—While the Cities and You Grow Poor* (New York: Robert B. Luce, 1969), 46.
27. "Progress Report on Corporate Responsibility, November 15, 1971," Rockefeller Foundation Internal Report, Earl Newsom Papers, Box 38 (M96–002), State Historical Society of Wisconsin Archives Division, 6.
28. "Black Militant Halts Service at Riverside Church," *New York Times*, May 5, 1969.

29. "Episcopal Church Urges G.M. to Close Plants in South Africa," *New York Times*, February 2, 1971.
30. Quoted in "Progress Report on Corporate Responsibility, November 15, 1971," Rockefeller Foundation Internal Report, 8.
31. See *Report of the Ad Hoc Committee on Princeton's Investments in Companies Operating in Southern Africa*, CPUC Resources Committee, https://cpucresources.princeton.edu/sites/g/files/toruqf1341/files/past/Report-of-the-Ad-Hoc-Committee-on-Princetons-Investments-in-Companies-Operating-in-Southern-Africa.-January-1969.pdf.
32. "Students, Faculty Butt Heads over Reports on Investments," *Daily Princetonian*, January 10, 1969.
33. "Progress Report on Corporate Responsibility, November 15, 1971," Rockefeller Foundation Internal Report, 10.
34. Quoted in Peter Landau, "Do Institutional Investors Have a Social Responsibility," *Institutional Investor*, July 1970, 28.
35. Table Cj1054—1080 Flow-of-Funds Balance Sheet – Personal Sector: 1945–1997, in *Historical Statistics of the United States*, Millennium Edition Online, ed. Susan B. Carter et al. (Cambridge: Cambridge University Press, 2006).
36. Drucker, *The Unseen Revolution*, 1.
37. See Landau, "Do Institutional Investors Have a Social Responsibility."
38. Hillel Gray, *New Directions in the Investment and Control of Pension Funds* (Washington, DC: Investor Responsibility Research Center, 1983), 7.
39. "Unions Map Investment Guidelines," *Washington Post*, March 9, 1980.
40. Geoffrey Jones, *Profits and Sustainability: A History of Green Entrepreneurship* (New York: Oxford University Press, 2017), 281.
41. John C. Harrington, *Investing with Your Conscience : How to Achieve High Returns Using Socially Responsible Investing* (New York: Wiley, 1992), 7–8.
42. "Progress Report on Corporate Responsibility, November 15, 1971," Rockefeller Foundation Internal Report.
43. For a discerning look at the social audit from a contemporary observer, see Phillip I. Blumberg, "The Public's 'Right to Know': Disclosure in the Major American Corporation," *Business Lawyer* 28, no. 4 (1973): 1025–61.
44. Theodore J. Kreps, "Measurement of the Social Performance of Business," Investigation of Concentration of Economic Power: Monograph no. 7 (Washington, DC: US Government Printing Office, 1940); Howard Bowen, *Social Responsibilities of the Businessman* (New York: Harper & Brothers, 1953). For a short history of the origins of this term, see Archie B. Carroll and George W. Beiler, "Landmarks in the Evolution of the Social Audit," *Academy of Management Journal* 18, no. 3 (1975): 589–99.
45. Blumberg, "The Public's 'Right to Know,'" 1025.
46. "Market Place: How to Press Fight," *New York Times*, May 9, 1972.
47. Alvin Toffler, *The Third Wave* (New York: William Morrow, 1980), 258.
48. David F. Linowes, "Let's Get on with the Social Audit: A Specific Proposal," *Business & Society Review/Innovation*, no. 4 (Winter 1972): 40.

49. Linowes, "Let's Get on with the Social Audit," 40–41.
50. An evocative term coined by Eli Cook in *The Pricing of Progress: Economic Indicators and the Capitalization of American Life* (Cambridge, MA: Harvard University Press, 2017), 2.
51. David F. Linowes, "Socio-Economic Accounting," *Journal of Accountancy* 126, no. 5 (November 1968): 40–41.
52. Raymond A. Bauer and Dan H. Fenn, *The Corporate Social Audit* (New York: Russell Sage Foundation, 1972), 19.
53. Bauer and Fenn, *The Corporate Social Audit*, 36.
54. Bauer and Fenn, *The Corporate Social Audit*, 40-41.
55. General Motors Corp., *1972 Report on Progress in Areas of Public Concern*, February 10, 1972.
56. Ernst & Ernst, *Social Responsibility Disclosure: 1978 Survey* (Cleveland, OH: Ernst & Ernst, 1978.)
57. "Corporate Status Index Planned," *New York Times*, October 20, 1977.
58. "Firms' Social Performance Index Begins to Take Shape," *Commerce America*, December 19, 1977.
59. "Social Auditing in the U.S. Gets a Slow Start," *BusinessWeek*, November 6, 1978.
60. US Congress, House, Subcommittee of the Committee on Appropriations, *Departments of State, Justice, and Commerce, the Judiciary, and Related Agencies Appropriations for 1978: Hearings Before the Subcommittee of the Committee on Appropriations*, 95th Cong., 2nd Sess., 1978, 35.
61. "Social Performance Index Idea Not Welcomed," Associated Press, January 14, 1978.
62. Juanita Kreps, oral history interview, January 17, 1986, Interview C–0011, Southern Oral History Program Collection (#4007), Wilson Library, University of North Carolina at Chapel Hill.
63. "Critics Proclaim Big Business Day to Condemn 'Crime in the Suites,'" *Los Angeles Times*, April 17, 1980; "Critics and Proponents Mark Role of Business: 'No-Growth Nightmare,'" *New York Times*, April 17, 1980; "Coalition Attacks Big Business," *Washington Post*, April 18, 1980; "Nader Proposes Cuts on Big Business Power," *Hartford Courant*, April 18, 1980.
64. "Big Business Day; The Voice of the "Stakeholder" Is Rising," *Washington Post*, April 14, 1980; Mark Green, "The Case for Corporate Democracy," *Regulation*, May/June 1980.
65. "Kick-a-Businessman Day," *BusinessWeek*, April 21, 1980; Herbert Stein, "Let's Hold a 'No Business Day," *Wall Street Journal*, January 7, 1980.
66. For a discussion of this business mobilization, see Benjamin Waterhouse, "The Corporate Mobilization Against Liberal Reform: Big Business Day, 1980," in *What's Good for Business: Business and American Politics Since World War II*, ed. Kim Phillips-Fein and Julian Zelizer (New York: Oxford University Press, 2012), 233–48; "Nader Proposes Cuts on Big Business Power,"

Hartford Courant; "Critics and Proponents Mark Role of Business," *New York Times*, April 17, 1980.

67. US Congress, Senate, Subcommittee on Securities of the Committee on Banking, Housing, and Urban Affairs, *Protection of Shareholders' Rights Act of 1980: Hearing Before the Subcommittee on Securities of the Committee on Banking, Housing, and Urban Affairs*, 96th Cong., 2nd Sess., 1980, 4.
68. "Big Business Day," *Washington Post*.
69. See, for example, Robert D. Haas, "The Corporation Without Boundaries," in *New Paradigm in Business: Emerging Strategies for Leadership and Organizational Change*, ed. Michael Ray (New York: Tarcher, 1993).
70. Gerald F. Davis, Kristina A. Diekmann, and Catherine H. Tinsley, "The Decline and Fall of the Conglomerate Firm in the 1980s: The Deinstitutionalization of an Organizational Form," *American Sociological Review* 59, no. 4 (1994): 566.
71. Louis Hyman, "Rethinking the Postwar Corporation: Management, Monopolies, and Markets," in *What's Good for Business: Business and American Politics since World War II*, ed. Kim Phillips-Fein and Julian E. Zelizer (New York: Oxford University Press, 2012), 202–4; Andrei Shleifer and Robert W. Vishny, "The Takeover Wave of the 1980s," *Science* 249, no. 4970 (1990): 745–49.
72. James Weinstein, *The Corporate Ideal in the Liberal State, 1900–1918* (Boston: Beacon Press, 1968).
73. A lot of my understanding of this period is dependent on Jonathan Levy. For his understanding of the federal government's tools of economic management suddenly becoming obsolete, see Jonathan Levy, *Ages of American Capitalism: A History of the United States* (New York: Random House, 2021), 572–83.
74. Levy, *Ages of American Capitalism*, 593.
75. Forgetting perhaps that markets are constituted by corporate structures already; see Gerald F. Davis, *The Vanishing American Corporation: Navigating the Hazards of a New Economy* (Oakland, CA: Berrett-Koehler, 2016). For a more sophisticated treatment of the relationship between conglomerates and financial markets in the postwar era, see Gerald F. Davis, *Managed by the Markets: How Finance Re-Shaped America* (New York: Oxford University Press, 2009).
76. Davis, Diekmann, and Tinsley, "The Decline and Fall of the Conglomerate Firm in the 1980s," 547–70.
77. Coca-Cola Company, *1984 Annual Report*.
78. James P. Walsh and Rita D. Kosnik, "Corporate Raiders and Their Disciplinary Role in the Market for Corporate Control," *Academy of Management Journal* 36, no. 4 (1993): 671–700.
79. Bryan Burrough and John Helyar, *Barbarians at the Gate: The Fall of RJR Nabisco* (New York: Harper & Row, 1990).
80. "Icahn on Icahn," *Fortune*, February 29, 1988.

81. Shleifer and Vishny, "The Takeover Wave of the 1980s," 745.
82. "U.S. Must Update Its Merger Laws," *Atlanta Journal-Constitution*, March 10, 1985. Manne would advocate for even greater deregulation to spur hostile takeovers as a cure for business scandal exemplified by Enron. Henry G. Manne, "Bring Back the Hostile Takeover," *Wall Street Journal*, June 26, 2002.
83. Henry G. Manne, "Mergers and the Market for Corporate Control," *Journal of Political Economy* 73, no. 2 (1965): 110–20.
84. Douglas M. Eichar, *The Rise and Fall of Corporate Social Responsibility* (New York: Routledge, 2017), 3–4; Carol Hymowitz and Matt Murray, "Raises and Praise or Out the Door: How GE's Chief Rates and Spurs His Employees," *Wall Street Journal*, June 21, 1999.
85. Noel Tichy and Ram Charan, "Speed, Simplicity, Self-Confidence: An Interview with Jack Welch," *Harvard Business Review*, September 1, 1989.
86. Megan Carpenter, "When General Electric Jobs Left Schenectady So Did a Way of Life," *The Guardian*, November 6, 2016.
87. Chris Churchill, "For GE Workers, 'Nothing Good' About Welch," *Albany Times Union*, March 5, 2020.
88. David Gelles, *The Man Who Broke Capitalism: How Jack Welch Gutted the Heartland and Crushed the Soul of Corporate America—and How to Undo His Legacy* (New York: Simon & Schuster, 2022), 44.
89. Quoted in Gelles, *The Man Who Broke Capitalism*, 92.
90. Churchill, "For GE Workers."
91. Jay R. Ritter and Richard S. Warr, "The Decline of Inflation and the Bull Market of 1982–1999," *Journal of Financial and Quantitative Analysis* 37, no. 1 (March 2002): 29.
92. Joseph E. Stiglitz, *The Roaring Nineties: A New History of the World's Most Prosperous Decade* (New York: Norton, 2004), 4.
93. For an overview of this history, see Archie B. Carroll et al., *Corporate Responsibility: The American Experience* (New York: Cambridge University Press, 2012), 288–91.
94. Richard T. De George and Joseph A. Pichler, *Ethics, Free Enterprise & Public Policy: Original Essays on Moral Issues in Business* (New York: Oxford University Press, 1978).
95. Norman E. Bowie, "Business Ethics," in *New Directions in Ethics: The Challenge of Applied Ethics*, ed. Joseph P. DeMarco and Richard M. Fox (New York: Routledge, 1986), 158.
96. Richard De George, "The Accountable Corporation," presented at the Third Biennial Global Business Ethics Conference, Markkula Center for Applied Ethics, February 19, 2005; Norman E. Bowie, "Business Ethics," in *New Directions in Ethics: The Challenge of Applied Ethics*, ed. Joseph P. DeMarco and Richard M. Fox (New York: Routledge, 1986), 166; Norman E. Bowie, "Business Ethics," in *New Directions in Ethics: The Challenge of Applied Ethics*, ed. Joseph P. DeMarco and Richard M. Fox (New York: Routledge, 1986), 166.

97. De George, "The Accountable Corporation."
98. "Money Was the Only Way," *Time*, December 1, 1986.
99. For a bracing journalistic account of this episode, see Connie Bruck, *The Predators' Ball: The Inside Story of Drexel Burnham and the Rise of the Junk Bond Raiders* (New York: Penguin, 1988).
100. US Congress, Senate, Subcommittee on Securities of the Committee on Banking, Housing, and Urban Affairs, *Oversight of the Securities and Exchange Commission and the Securities Industry: Hearing Before the Subcommittee on Securities of the Committee on Banking, Housing, and Urban Affairs*, 100th Cong., 1st Sess., 5.
101. Steve Coll, "Shad to Endow Ethics Program at Harvard," *Washington Post*, March 31, 1987.
102. Philip Knight, "Nike in the Global Economy," C-SPAN, May 12, 1998, https://www.c-span.org/video/?105477-1/nike-global-economy.
103. Davis, *Managed by the Markets*, 240.
104. Davis, *Managed by the Markets*, 21.
105. For example, "Activist Finds Abuses at Vietnam Nike Plants," *Washington Post*, March 28, 1997.
106. "Nike Shoe Plant in Vietnam Is Called Unsafe for Workers," *New York Times*, November 8, 1997.
107. "The Story of a Shoe," *World Watch*, March/April 1998.
108. Michael Moore, *The Big One* (Miramax Films, 1998).
109. Matthew Kish, "The Moment It All Changed," *Portland Business Journal*, May 23, 2014.
110. "Nike to Increase Minimum Age in Asia for New Hirings, Improve Air Quality," *New York Times*, May 13, 1998.
111. David Vogel, *The Market for Virtue: The Potential and Limits of Corporate Social Responsibility* (Washington, DC: Brookings Institution Press, 2005).
112. Knight, "Nike in the Global Economy."
113. "Groups Reach Agreement for Curtailing Sweatshops," *New York Times*, November 5, 1998; Ruth Pearson, Gill Seyfang, and Rhys Jenkins, *Corporate Responsibility and Labour Rights: Codes of Conduct in the Global Economy* (Oxfordshire, UK: Taylor & Francis, 2013), 23–24.
114. Kofi Annan, "Address to World Economic Forum," Davos, Switzerland, January 31, 1999, https://www.un.org/sg/en/content/sg/speeches/1999-02-01/kofi-annans-address-world-economic-forum-davos.
115. Steve Hilton and Giles Gibbons, quoted in Jeremy Moon, *Corporate Social Responsibility: A Very Short Introduction* (New York: Oxford University Press, 2014), 20.
116. Maria Hengeveld, "Nike Boasts of Empowering Women Around the World," *Slate*, August 26, 2016, http://www.slate.com/articles/business/the_grind/2016/08/nike_s_supply_chain_doesn_t_live_up_to_the_ideals_of_its_girl_effect_campaign.html.
117. Benedict XVI, *Caritas in veritate*, encyclical letter, Vatican website, June

29, 2009, https://www.vatican.va/content/benedict-xvi/en/encyclicals/documents/hf_ben-xvi_enc_20090629_caritas-in-veritate.html.

118. "Special Report: Corporate Social Responsibility," *The Economist*, December 14, 2002.
119. Griff Witte, "CEOs Move to Improve Ethics Training," *Washington Post*, January 15, 2004.
120. R. F. Stewart, J. K. Allen, and J. M Cavender, "The Strategic Plan," LRPS Report no. 168, Long Range Planning Service, Stanford Research Institute, Menlo Park, CA.
121. Quoted in R. Edward Freeman, *Strategic Management: A Stakeholder Approach* (Boston: Pitman, 1984), 31.
122. Ram Charan and R. Edward Freeman, "Stakeholder Negotiations: Building Bridges with Corporate Constituents," *Management Review* (November 1979): 8.
123. This is a phrase that Freeman uses frequently, and the meaning of it is laid out here, in contrast to what he and his coauthors call the "new story of business": R. Edward Freeman, Bidhan L. Parmar, and Kirsten Martin, *The Power of And: Responsible Business Without Trade-Offs* (New York: Columbia Business School Publishing, 2020), 1–28.
124. R. Edward Freeman and Daniel R. Gilbert, *Corporate Strategy and the Search for Ethics* (Englewood Cliffs, NJ: Prentice-Hall, 1988), xiii.
125. R. Edward Freeman, Jeffrey S. Harrison, and Andrew C. Wicks, *Managing for Stakeholders: Survival, Reputation, and Success*, Series in Ethics and Leadership (New Haven, CT: Yale University Press, 2007), 3.
126. The sociologist Andrew Lynn has developed important critiques of the ethical coherence of stakeholder theory, and I am indebted to them (and if you are interested, you should read these and whatever else he writes): Andrew Lynn, "Why 'Doing Well by Doing Good' Went Wrong: Getting Beyond 'Good Ethics Pays' Claims in Managerial Thinking," *Academy of Management Review* 46, no. 3 (July 2021): 512–33; Andrew Lynn, "Ethics, Economics, and the Specter of Naturalism: The Enduring Relevance of the Harmony Doctrine School of Economics," *Journal of Business Ethics* 178, no. 3 (July 1, 2022): 661–73. Matthew Caulfield and Andrew Paul Lynn, "Federated Corporate Social Responsibility: Constraining the Responsible Corporation," *Academy of Management Review*, July 11, 2022.
127. See, for example, Robert A. G. Monks, *Corpocracy: How CEOs and the Business Roundtable Hijacked the World's Greatest Wealth Machine—And How to Get It Back* (Hoboken, NJ: Wiley, 2008).
128. David Gelles and David Yaffe-Bellany, "Shareholder Value Is No Longer Everything, Top C.E.O.s Say," *New York Times*, August 19, 2019.
129. "Stakeholder Theory with R. Edward Freeman," Business Roundtable Institute for Corporate Ethics, Business Ethics Video Series, May 13, 2009, https://www.youtube.com/watch?v=_sNKIEzYM7M.

Conclusion: Larry Fink, President of the World

1. Milton R. Moskowitz, "Choosing Socially Responsible Stocks," *Business & Society Review*, no. 1 (Spring 1972): 71.
2. Stanley G. Vance, "Are Socially Responsible Corporations Good Investment Risks?" *Management Review* 64, no. 8 (August 1975): 18.
3. Kenneth E. Aupperle, Archie B. Carroll, and John D. Hatfield, "An Empirical Examination of the Relationship Between Corporate Social Responsibility and Profitability," *Academy of Management Journal* 28, no. 2 (June 1985): 446–63.
4. Moses L. Pava and Joshua Krausz, "The Association Between Corporate Social-Responsibility and Financial Performance: The Paradox of Social Cost," *Journal of Business Ethics* 15, no. 3 (March 1996): 321–57. The last word on this question was likely Joshua D. Margolis and James P. Walsh, "Misery Loves Companies: Rethinking Social Initiatives by Business," *Administrative Science Quarterly* 48, no. 2 (June 1, 2003): 268–305.
5. *Who Cares Wins: Connecting Financial Markets to a Changing World*, Global Compact, accessed May 15, 2023, https://www.unepfi.org/fileadmin/events/2004/stocks/who_cares_wins_global_compact_2004.pdf.
6. "Who Cares Wins," Global Compact, 9.
7. Suzanna Andrews, "Larry Fink's $12 Trillion Shadow," *Vanity Fair*, April 2010.
8. Joseph Checkler and Jenny Strasburg, "BlackRock to Buy R3," *Wall Street Journal*, April 18, 2009; David Ricketts and Mark Cobley, "Inside BlackRock's 'Once in a Lifetime Deal' with Barclays, 10 Years Later," *Barron's*, June 11, 2019.
9. Christine Williamson, "BlackRock's BGI Acquisition 10 Years Ago Fuels Rapid Growth," *Pensions & Investments*, June 11, 2019.
10. Williamson, "BlackRock's BGI Acquisition 10 Years Ago Fuels Rapid Growth."
11. Christine Williamson, "BlackRock AUM Recedes from $10 Trillion High," *Pensions & Investments*, April 13, 2022; Palash Ghosh, "No End in Sight to BlackRock's Growth as It Approaches $10 Trillion," *Pensions & Investments*, November 19, 2021; "State Street Reports First-Quarter 2022 Financial Results," State Street Corporation, accessed October 4, 2022, https://newsroom.statestreet.com/press-releases/press-release-details/2022/State-Street-Reports-First-Quarter-2022-Financial-Results/default.aspx.
12. Lucian Bebchuk and Scott Hirst, "The Specter of the Giant Three," *Boston University Law Review* 99, no. 3 (May 1, 2019): 721–42.
13. "Larry Fink's 2012 Letter to CEOs," BlackRock, accessed October 4, 2022, https://www.blackrock.com/corporate/investor-relations/2012-larry-fink-ceo-letter.
14. "Larry Fink's 2022 Letter to CEOs," BlackRock, accessed October 4, 2022.

15. Andrea Pawliczek, A. Nicole Skinner, and Laura A. Wellman, "A New Take on Voice: The Influence of BlackRock's 'Dear CEO' Letters," *Review of Accounting Studies* 26, no. 3 (September 1, 2021): 1088–136.
16. Matt Levine, "The Companies Are in Charge Now," Bloomberg.com, January 17, 2019, https://www.bloomberg.com/opinion/articles/2019-01-17/the-companies-are-in-charge-now.
17. Emilio Marti and Jean-Pascal Gond, "How Do Theories Become Self-Fulfilling? Clarifying the Process of Barnesian Performativity," *Academy of Management Review* 44, no. 3 (July 2019): 686–94. There are limits, however, to these distortive effects. See Samuel M. Hartzmark and Abigail B. Sussman, "Do Investors Value Sustainability? A Natural Experiment Examining Ranking and Fund Flows," *Journal of Finance* 74, no. 6 (2019): 2789–837.
18. "2023 Statehouse Anti-ESG Report," Pleiades Strategy, accessed August 28, 2023, https://www.pleiadesstrategy.com/state-house-report-bill-tracker-republican-anti-esg-attacks-on-freedom-to-invest-responsibly-earns-business-labor-and-environmental-opposition.
19. Pratima Bansal and Diane-Laure Arjaliès, "ESG Backlash in the US: What Implications for Corporations and Investors?," *Financial Times*, June 11, 2023.
20. Isla Binnie, "BlackRock's Fink Says He's Stopped Using 'Weaponised' Term ESG," *Reuters*, June 26, 2023.
21. Maxine Joselow, "'Greenhushing': Why Some Companies Quietly Hide Their Climate Pledges," *Washington Post*, July 13, 2023.
22. Eleanor Hawkins, "Corporate America Is Rebranding ESG," *Axios*, August 10, 2023.
23. "Wall Street Titans Confront ESG Backlash as New Financial Risk," *Financial Times*, March 1, 2023.
24. David Ciepley has helped me rethink this and many other things. See David Ciepley, "Beyond Public and Private: Toward a Political Theory of the Corporation," *American Political Science Review* 107, no. 1 (February 2013): 139–58.
25. I am also deeply reliant on the work of Adolf Berle and Gardiner Means and their thesis of the separation of ownership and control. See Adolf A. Berle and Gardiner C. Means, *The Modern Corporation and Private Property* (New York: Harcourt, Brace & World, 1932), 1–9, 71–72, 333–44.
26. "No-man rule," as Hannah Arendt called some advanced bureaucracies, could be applied to many Fortune 500 companies; see Hannah Arendt, *The Human Condition*, 2nd ed. (Chicago: University of Chicago Press, 1998), 40.

INDEX

Page numbers in *italics* refer to illustrations. Endnotes are indicated by *n* after the page number.